Predatory Priests, Silenced Victims

The Sexual Abuse Crisis and The Catholic Church

Predatory Priests, Silenced Victims

The Sexual Abuse Crisis and The Catholic Church

Edited by

Mary Gail Frawley-O'Dea

Virginia Goldner

 THE ANALYTIC PRESS

2007   Mahwah, New Jersey   London

Cover design by Tomai Maridou.

Lawrence Erlbaum Associates
Taylor & Francis Group
270 Madison Avenue
New York, NY 10016

Lawrence Erlbaum Associates
Taylor & Francis Group
2 Park Square
Milton Park, Abingdon
Oxon OX14 4RN

© 2007 by Taylor & Francis Group, LLC
Lawrence Erlbaum Associates is an imprint of Taylor & Francis Group, an Informa business

Printed in the United States of America on acid-free paper
10 9 8 7 6 5 4 3 2 1

International Standard Book Number-13: 978-0-88163-424-2 (Hardcover)

Visit the Taylor & Francis Web site at
http://www.taylorandfrancis.com

and the LEA Web site at
http://www.erlbaum.com

To Phred Frawley III,
who welcomed me back.

Contents

Preface
From the Bayou to Boston:
History of a Scandal*

Mary Gail Frawley-O'Dea

Most reporters agree that the Catholic Church's contemporary sexual abuse scandal began in Henry, Louisiana, when molestation allegations were made against Fr. Gilbert Gauthe in 1983 (Berry, 1992, 2000; Bruni & Burkett, 1993, 2002; Investigative Staff of *The Boston Globe*, 2002; Jenkins, 1996; Wills, 2000). The Gauthe case contained all the elements that eventually would become associated with the Church crisis. In fact, a review of the relevant literature, including more than 100 newspapers articles, suggests a deadeningly repetitive paradigm of perpetration and cover-up, first revealed in the Gauthe case and lived out for decades across the United States.

---

*Portions of this chapter appear in Frawley-O'Dea, Mary Gail. *Perversion of Power: Sexual Abuse in the Catholic Church*. Vanderbilt University Press, 2007.

Typically, a priest arrived in a parish or other Church setting sometime between 1960–1990. Often energetic and charismatic, he focused his ministry on youth activities. Gradually, he developed friendships with young people, frequently boys between 11 and 15 years old, some of them from troubled homes and in need of attention; others, from stable and loving families. All had been taught from birth to respect and trust priests as Christ's representatives on earth. Eventually, Father introduced sex into his relationship with a young person.

Somewhere along the way, a fellow priest, a parishioner, a victim's parent, or a victim complained about Father to the pastor, diocesan representative, or the bishop, either when the abuse was occurring or later. When an accusation was made, there were a couple of likely outcomes. Years ago, the complainant may have been scolded for trying to "bring scandal to the Church," an overused phrase connoting an offense considered by too many clerics to be far graver than anything Father may have done (Cozzens, 2002; Kennedy, 2001; Sipe, 1995; Wills, 2000). In this case, the chastened individual was sent home and, as rumors of the accusations surfaced in the gossip mill of the parish, he or she might end up shunned by both priests and fellow faithful (Bruni & Burkett, 1993, 2002; Briggs, 2002).

Back at the rectory, Father was confronted and, in a remarkable number of cases, acknowledged the accuracy of the allegations. Having confessed, he promised not to sin again. As the decades passed, it became increasingly likely that Father would be sent off for psychological evaluation and/or treatment; earlier on, his resolve to change was taken at face value. In either case, Father sooner or later left the parish or school and, either with no treatment or after being treated, turned up in another setting at which no one was informed about his prior alleged or acknowledged problems. Too many times he abused again and the sequence was repeated.

As years passed and the bishops came under public pressure to do more about sexual abuse, another scenario played out when a priest was accused of past or present abuse. At last, the complainant was taken seriously. He or she was assured that Father would be removed from any ministry involved with children. The Church offered to pay for the victim's counseling. As accusers became more aggressive in their demands for redress, sometimes engaging attorneys to help them, secret settlement agreements were reached in which money was given to plaintiffs. Although the Church has been lambasted for negotiating secret legal settlements, it was very often victims who wanted their abuse and the payouts to remain confidential.

By now, Father almost always was sent for psychological evaluation and treatment. Sometimes he was returned to ministry with access to children; sometimes he was placed in a hospital or nursing home ministry ostensibly removed from young people; sometimes he was laicized; sometimes he resigned. Treatment programs and discharge plans varied widely in their effectiveness and credibility. Recommendations about fitness for ministry did not always represent the priest's psychosexual organization well or his propensity to reoffend. When priests were reassigned, the receiving clergy and community typically were not informed about the priest's background.

Although the paradigm presented here varied widely, this was more or less the characteristic pattern of sexual abuse and response to it enacted by the Catholic Church for decades, perhaps for centuries.

Emblematic not only of the perpetration and cover-up of sexual abuse within the Church, the Gauthe case also shattered previously sacred relationships protecting the Catholic Church from scandals associated with sexually predatory priests. Lay people who at one time would have done what they were told by priests and bishops stood up to the clergy and demanded accountability for the crimes of a priest and the complicity of his ecclesiastical superiors. Newspaper publishers and editors, once deferential to the Church, stayed on the story and made it national news. Police, prosecutors, defense attorneys, and judges who years before might have colluded with secrecy and silence went forward with the Gauthe case even when it pained them deeply to battle their Church. Mental-health professionals who may once have known little about the impact of sexual trauma on young children testified about the terrible damage inflicted on Gauthe's young victims.

Between 1983 and 1987, an average of one case per week of past or present sexual abuse by a priest was reported nationwide (Sipe, 1990). Beginning in 1987, the hierarchy of the Catholic Church in America began to address more formally the burgeoning sexual abuse crisis. At one end of the spectrum of response, the Church attempted to protect itself from its "enemies," still defined by too many clergy as any entity external to the Church. Many members of the clergy blamed the media, anti-Catholicism, and/or money-hungry victims for their troubles.

While some bishops defensively postured, others, led by Joseph Cardinal Bernadin of Chicago, were ready to acknowledge the destructive reality of sexual abuse by priests and to respond as pastors rather than as corporate executives. Aware of both pastoral and corporate responsibilities and authority in his Archdiocese, Bernadin privileged the former, thus modeling a stance towards victims, the laity, and his priests that too few bishops chose to follow over the next decade. His actions in Chicago, however, did begin to change the way bishops approached sexual abuse within their own dioceses.

In 1992, the United States Conference of Catholic Bishops developed what came to be known as the Five Principles (United States Conference of Catholic Bishops, 1996). Based on Bernadin's work in Chicago, the principles urged greater openness about abuse allegations, prompt response to allegations, removal of accused offenders from ministry for referral for evaluation and treatment, compliance with civil law, and reaching out to victims and their families.

After 1992, many bishops indeed took steps to strengthen their response to new cases of alleged sexual abuse, including establishing advisory panels with lay representation to help them evaluate sexual abuse reports. The major drawback to the principles was that their execution by a given bishop rested on his determination that there was sufficient evidence to support an allegation. Unfortunately, by then many bishops themselves had left a trail of sufficient evidence to support the conclusion that they were either unable or unwilling to discern the credibility of an accusation against one of their priests. In addition, the principles did not address well enough the way in which bishops were to respond to many alleged adult survivors of priest abuse coming forward to accuse older priests of incidents occurring years ago and for which the statue of limitations had long expired.

In the early 1990s, networks for victims/survivors of priest abuse were founded. For over a decade, they persistently confronted the Church hierarchy as a group and individual dioceses about perceived mishandling of sexual abuse cases and they empowered many victims to feel safe enough to come forward to speak of their victimizations perhaps for the first time.

Now much more fully aware that too many priests sexually abused too many minors much too often, the United States Conference of Catholic Bishops formed an Ad Hoc Committee on Sexual Abuse in 1993. The committee was mandated to develop suggested diocesan guidelines for responding to accused and/or guilty clergy—as well as to victims and their families—and to help bishops better screen candidates for the seminary. Eventually, the committee proposed a standardized diocesan approach to sexual abuse allegations that was adopted effectively in many dioceses nationwide (Bishops' Ad Hoc Committee on Sexual Abuse, unpublished, 1996). For the rest of the 90s, many bishops responded more pastorally to complaints about their priests, especially new complaints. Things got much better, but they did not improve sufficiently in enough dioceses to stave off the coming widening scandal.

In 2002, the dam broke for sexual abuse scandals involving the Catholic Church. After Fr. John Geoghan's serial abuse of children in the 1960s, 1970s, and 1980s, and the Boston Archdiocese's concomitant cover-up became front-page news in January, new developments were measured in days rather than years. The year witnessed the resignations of several bishops because of their sexual histories with adults or children (Heinen and Zahn, 2002; Johnson, 2002; Slowik, 2002). Bishops were hauled into attorneys' offices and courts to provide depositions and trial testimony (Investigative Staff of *The Boston Globe*, 2002; Kurkjian and Carroll, 2002) and judges demanded public submission of diocesan documents that heretofore would have remained secreted within chancery vaults (Investigative Staff of *The Boston Globe*, 2002; Burge 2002). In April, the American cardinals were called to Rome to discuss with the Pope the ongoing "American problem" (Investigative Staff of *The Boston Globe*, 2002). Both the United States Conference of Catholic Bishops (USCCB) and the Conference of Major Superiors of Men (CMSM), the analog to the USCCB for religious orders, used their summer meetings to apologize profusely to victims and to pass finally the strongest measures yet to keep abusing priests—past, present and future—away from children (USCCB, 2002; CMSM, 2002).

Back in the dioceses, priests whose abusive incidents went back decades were relieved of their ministerial duties and/or resigned themselves (Blaney, 2002; Gembrowski and Dolbee, 2002; Dillon, 2002; Thorsen and Ruixdeluzuriaga, 2002; Tunkieicz and Heinen, 2002). Dioceses struggled for cash as their stock portfolios followed the market into bear territory and contributions lagged due to the scandals (Investigative Staff of *The Boston Globe*, 2002; Marchocki, 2002; Scheid, 2002). The Voice of the Faithful in Boston and other groups of laypeople, aware of the power of their purses, organized to exert financial and pastoral power within their dioceses (Cebula, 2002; Convey, 2002; O'Donnell, 2002). At the other end of the spectrum, conservative Catholics also organized to defend their Church, forming groups with names like Faithful Voice. By the end of the summer, accused priests began to countersue their alleged victims for slander (Breckenridge, 2002; Dillon, 2002; Smith & Fallik, 2002). Rank-and-file priests, feeling as abandoned by their hierarchy as victims always had felt, also organized to support each other and to take on a voice in the controversy.

The Vatican, long suspicious of what too many within it want to view as a peculiarly American problem, seriously questioned many of the steps taken by the bishops and their counterparts in the religious orders over the summer of 2002. In October, Rome rejected some portions of the *Charter for the Protection of Children and Young People* passed by the bishops in June. Specifically, Vatican officials wanted a tighter definition of sexual abuse, a determinate statute of limitations on potential allegations, due process for accused priests that conformed to canon law, and a limited delegation of authority to lay councils appointed to oversee sexual abuse cases. Some Vatican priests disagreed that allegations of sexual abuse should be reported to civil authorities and also were appalled at the costly settlements made to victims. In November 2002, the United States Conference of Catholic Bishops revised the Dallas norms to conform to Vatican demands. Although the bishops insisted that the spirit of the Dallas reforms remained intact, the process for removing a priest from ministry became once again more cumbersome and, perhaps more important, more secret.

The Church's own *annus horribile* ended with the resignation of Cardinal Law of Boston from his position as archbishop. After the court-ordered release of thousands of pages of Boston church documents revealed decades of sexual misconduct by priests, some of it horrendously ugly and lurid, coupled with the repeated failure of many bishops to confront the incidents effectively, both the priests and the laypeople of Boston demanded Law's expulsion. In mid-December, Pope John II accepted the resignation of the heretofore most powerful American prelate.

While the denouement of the Catholic Church's sexual abuse scandal is yet to be written, the consequences of it for victims are clearer. For thousands of men and women across the country, the Catholic sexual abuse crisis is not a newspaper story but rather a central thematic strand of their own lives. The sexual violation of a child or adolescent by a priest, in fact, is incest. It is a sexual and relational betrayal perpetrated by *the* father of the child's extended family, a man in whom the child is—or was—taught from birth onward to trust above everyone else in his life, to trust second only to God. The aftermath of clergy sexual abuse, therefore, is devastating and long-lasting. The traumatogenic sequelae of sexual abuse by a priest were exacerbated for many victims by the dishonesty of Church officials and by their willingness to endlessly cover up the criminal behaviors of their priests.

REFERENCES

Berry, J. (1992), *Lead Us Not into Temptation*. Urbana: University of Illinois Press, 2000.

Blaney, B. (2002), Amarillo diocese hit hard by sex abuse. Associated Press in *Washingtonpost.com, Washington Post On-Line*, September 25.

Breckenridge, T. (2002), Group pushes for top U.S. bishop to stop priests form suing accusers. *Cleveland.com, The Plain Dealer On-Line*, August 31.

Briggs, D. (2002), Accused priest's parish defends him fiercely. *Cleveland.com, The Plain Dealer On-Line*, September 3, 2003.

Bruni, F. & Burkett, E. (1993, 2002), *A Gospel of Shame*. New York: Perennial.

Burge, K. (2002), Records depict Mahan as high-risk sex abuser. *Boston.com, Boston Globe On-Line*, August 23.

Cebula, J. (2002), Catholics shaken by clergy scandal confer on reform group. *Indystar.com, The Indianapolis Star On-Line*, August 8.

Conference of Major Superiors of Men (CMSM) (2002), Improving pastoral care and accountability in response to the tragedy of sexual abuse. *Cmsm.org/Assembly2002/care.html#care*.

Convey, E. (2002), Grassroots groups square off on scandal. *Bostonherald.com, Boston Herald On-Line,* August 26.

Cozzens, D. (2002), *Sacred Silence.* Collegeville, MN: The Liturgical Press.

Dillon, S. (2002), Accused priests charge slander. *NYTimes.com, The New York Times On-Line,* August 25.

Gembrowski, S. & Dolbee, S. (2002), Abuse allegations true, priest admits. *Signonsandiego.com, Union-Tribune On-Line,* August 10.

Investigative Staff of *The Boston Globe* (2002), *Betrayal: The Crisis in the Catholic Church.* Boston, MA: Little, Brown.

Heinen, T. & Zahn, M. (2002), Weakland begs for forgiveness. *Jsonline.com, Milwaukee Journal Sentinel On-Line,* June 1.

Jenkins, P. (1996), *Pedophiles and Priests.* New York: Oxford University Press.

Johnson, M. (2002), With embattled priest moving on, parish learns dark secret of beloved predecessor. *Jsonline.com, Milwaukee Journal Sentinel On-Line,* June 20.

Kennedy, E. (2001), *The Unhealed Wound.* New York: St. Martin's Griffin.

Kurkjian, S. & Carroll, M. (2002). Archdiocese eyes more legal rights for accused priests. *Boston.com, The Boston Globe On-Line,* September 25.

Marchocki, K. (2002), Bishop: Catholics reducing gifts to church charities. *Theunionleader.com, The Union Leader On-Line,* September 24.

O'Donnell, N. (2002), Catholic group's event attracts thousands. *The Journal News,* September 21.

Scheid, B. (2002), Diocese slashes budgets. *Norwichbulletin.com, Norwich Bulletin On-Line,* September 4.

Sipe, A. W. R. (1990), *A Secret World: Sexuality and the Search for Celibacy.* New York: Brunner/Mazel.

——— (1995), *Sex, Priests, and Power.* New York: Brunner/Mazel.

Slowik, T. (2002), Ex-bishop suspends ministry. *Suburbanchicagonews.com, The Herald News On-Line,* September 5.

Smith, B. & Fallik, D. (2002), Priests accused of sexual abuse are fighting back in court. *Stltoday.com, St. Louis Post Dispatch On-Line,* August 25.

Thorsen, L. & Ruizdeluzuriaga, T. (2002), Zero-tolerance forces priest out. *Jsonline.com, Milwaukee Sentinel On-Line,* August 17.

Tunkieicz, J. & Heinen, T. (2002), At Blessed Sacrament's masses, suspicions about sexual conduct confirmed. *Jsonline.com, Milwaukee Journal Sentinel On-line,* August 25.

United States Conference of Catholic Bishops (USCCB) (1996), *Restoring Trust, Volume III.* Bishop's Ad Hoc Committee on Sexual Abuse.

———. (2002). Charter for the protection of children and young people. *Usccb.org/bishops/charter.htm,* June 27.

Wills, G. (2000), *Papal Sin.* New York: Doubleday.

——— (2002). The bishops at bay. *The New York Review of Books,* August 25.

1

Introduction
The Catholic Sexual Abuse Crisis:
Gender, Sex, Power, and Discourse*

Virginia Goldner

The Reverend Ann Richards, who spent six years coordinating sexual misconduct cases involving Episcopal clergy, describes the priesthood as "a strenuous way of life." A priest, she writes in her chapter for this volume, is "a numinous figure, representing God and all the energies associated with God in the religious tradition." Such a role, she explains, "requires emotional strength, maturity, self-knowledge, tolerance of great ambiguity, and most important for the present topic ... the ability to ... hold boundaries.... [When] undertaken consciously, it can be very fulfilling and freeing. Blundered into, it can lead to great grief and emotional hurt to others, because the emotional strains of the job are usually great enough to threaten the maintenance of appropriate boundaries, at least occasionally."

*Some of the chapters in this book (chaps. 5, 6, 9, 12, 16, and 16) are adapted from papers that appeared in the journal Studies in Gender and Sexuality (2004), as part of its special double issue devoted to the clergy sexual abuse scandal.

Richards's explication of the moral and psychic demands of the priestly role, and of its potential perversion, takes us into the heart and soul of this volume. Our focus here is on the Catholic scandal, although we include some Protestant voices as an important reminder that Catholic clergy are not alone in transgressing sexual boundaries. We know, in fact, that sexual abuse is also alleged against Jewish rabbis (Rosenblatt, 2004; Schwab, 2002; Wiener, 2001); Islamic clerics (Associated Press, 2005; Freund, 2005); Buddhist monks (BBC News, 2005; Senanayake; 2005); and Hare Krishna officials (Das, 2003).

It is the Catholic sexual abuse scandal, however, that has assumed center stage in the public theater because, as biblical scholar and clinician Gillian Walker says in her paper for this collection,

> the sexual transgressions of Catholic clergy are not necessarily worse than those in other religious or secular institutions, but they fascinate the laity and non-Catholic observers (since) they are in violation of (both) the Catholic clergy's public commitment to celibacy and (the Church's) promulgation of a restrictive sexual moral code.

The moral outrage that has brought so much attention to the Catholic case is probably fueled by this prurient curiosity, but it is the steady stream of revelations documenting the systematic cover-up of clergy sexual misconduct that has kept the pressure on. As is now well-known, the spread of sexual abuse throughout Church lands was aided and abetted by religious authorities who not only evaded the claims of victims and their families, but actually prepared the ground for new victims by sending known predatory priests to unsuspecting parishes, where they would inevitably reabuse another generation of idealistic boys and girls of faith. This astoundingly cynical pattern of indifference toward the flock, with its catastrophic dereliction of pastoral duty, laid bare a clerical infrastructure riddled with pathology, insularity, and arrogance—one that has privileged the abuser over the victim, the clergy over the laity, the Institutional Church over the pastoral church.

In taking the measure of this devastating betrayal of a community of believers by the institution of their Church, it is important to eschew one-size-fits-all theories that focus on single "causes" like mandatory celibacy, homosexuality, the sexual repressiveness of the church, the sexual permissiveness of the culture, and so on. As the chapters in this volume demonstrate, the root causes of the Catholic sexual abuse crisis are embedded in an intricate matrix of power relationships, traditions, and teachings that, in their aggregate, created a socioreligious context that produced emotionally and sexually immature priests, misrecognized pedophile and ephebophile priests, and tolerated clergy abuse of minors and of clerical subordinates (seminarians and junior priests).

Some of the contributing factors to this debacle are straightforward and uncontested, such as the shortage of priests, the improper screening of candidates, and the poor "formation" or training of seminarians. (See especially the chapters by Martin and Richards). There is much debate about others, especially the hot-button issues of mandatory celibacy and homosexuality, both of which are taken up in complex and multifaceted ways throughout this volume. (See especially chapters by Doyle, Frawley-O'Dea and Goldner, Jordan, and Walker). Other "institutional, theological, and dogmatic aspects of Catholicism" (Carroll, 2002, p. 12, cited in Walker's chapter) are implicated in the Church's defensive, morally corrupt response to victims and truth seekers, and are discussed throughout, but especially in the section of this volume titled "The Institutional Church vs. The Pastoral Church."

THE SEXUAL ABUSE TRIANGLE

In organizing the work of our contributors, we have found it helpful to highlight the multidimensionality of clergy sexual misconduct by invoking a triangular configuration of experiential perspectives at work in sexual abuse. Davies and Frawley (1994), in their landmark text on the treatment of adult survivors of childhood sexual abuse, distinguish three subjective positions that are paradigmatically in play when sexual victimization of a minor occurs. They are the victim/survivor, the abuser/perpetrator (who may have been an earlier victim of another perpetrator), and the silent bystander who knows or senses something is wrong but who remains silent. In clergy sexual abuse cases, bystanders include family, other clergy, lay church members, mental health and other professionals, and the surrounding secular community.

The victim/survivor stories hinge on trust and betrayal, honesty and mendacity, memory and fantasy, trauma and recovery, blame and forgiveness. The bystander/community story hinges on the question of institutional complicity (abandoning/blaming the victim and protecting/identifying with the abuser), and also on the "unthought known" (Bollas, 1987) as well as Mary Gail Frawley-O'Dea's point that "whenever a minor is sexually violated, someone's eyes are closed." To understand the third group, the abuser/perpetrator, requires an appreciation of their individual psychodynamics, but also of the relational and systemic context in which such abuse takes place. Both topics are taken up by authors later in this volume.

Victims/Survivors

"It was always said that [my father and I]... had a 'special relationship' ... [and] to add to my confusion, I knew in some ways that we did," writes survivor Kathleen Dwyer. Her heroic and heartbreaking memoir of familial and clergy sexual violation illustrates how perpetrators typically (mis)appropriate theology and doctrine to mystify their victims. (See also chapters by Frawley-O'Dea, Gartner, and Kochansky and Cohen).

"I grew up in a white, very religious, poor, working class, Irish Catholic family, where Church was family and family was church," Dwyer explains. To justify his incestuous abuse of his daughter, Dwyer's father instructed her that "what 'we' did was what 'God' wanted 'us' to do, reminding her of the requirement to, "Honor thy father and mother."

"I was taught that God was father [and] that the priest/father was next to God.... I was to do anything and everything he might tell me to do. So when my father ... took me by the hand and brought me to the church at a time when it was not Mass, not Brownies, not choir, not First Friday, [and] not the paper drive, the [subsequent] ritual, sexual, and spiritual abuse by my church family [a priest and other church leaders] formed a seamless continuum."

Frawley-O'Dea distills the essence of Dwyer's account into one stark concept. "The sexual violation of a child or adolescent by a priest ... is incest. It is a sexual and relational betrayal perpetrated by *the* father of the child's extended family whom he or she was taught to trust second only to God." Sadly, but not surprisingly, those most easily preyed upon "are young people for whom something or someone is missing," writes Frawley-O'Dea. They are often, as Richard Garter explains, the "altar boys or choir boys ... [deeply) engaged in their religious lives ... (with) idealized views of their spiritual mentor." The sexual predator is exquisitely attuned to the victims' "yearning for an adult who ... understands them, makes time for them, and enjoys their company ... ingratiating himself into their lives ... evoking respect, trust, and dependency long before the first touch takes place" (Frawley-O'Dea).

This was precisely the case with Fr. M, one of our contributors, who was sexually abused by an uncle in childhood and, later, by two priests during his adolescence. After becoming a priest himself, he engaged in a consensual sexual relationship with a junior priest who eventually disclosed it to the bishop, resulting in our author's abrupt dismissal from his parish.

I grew up Catholic and was proud to be an altar boy. The summer I turned 12, my favorite priest left the parish. During his last Mass, I began to cry ... and the new priest came to comfort me ... [Over the summer], he became my best friend ... but seeds of confusion were sewn into the fabric of the relationship ... Watching television with my family, Fr. Larry and I would sit behind everyone and hold hands. This eventually led to more intimate touching.... [Eventually, we began engaging in more extensive sex.... My most dreadful memories are of us having sex and then immediately going downstairs to join my family for dinner. Father Larry would offer the blessing while I prayed silently that my family wouldn't know what had just happened upstairs.

"Can you imagine?" asks Frawley-O'Dea at the start of her chapter on the psychic consequences of such sinister seductions. As she explains, the psychological shock of overwhelming overstimulation and of absolute personal betrayal requires the activation of the severe defenses of splitting and dissociation, which produce their own devastating consequences. The adult survivor is trapped in the inner world of the abused child, a place of

terror, impotent but seething rage, and grief for which there are literally no words.... For victims of priest abuse, a Roman collar, the scent of incense, light streaming through stained glass at a certain time of day, organ music, or most certainly, interacting with priests and bishops can reevoke the frightening dissociated self-states of the (child) victim.

These extreme symptoms are further complicated by the impact of gender. Since victimization of any kind culturally codes as feminine, boys and men with a sexual abuse history also struggle with gender shame and the fear of homosexuality. (See Gartner for an extensive discussion of this issue; see also Celenza, who reports the treatment of a sexually abusive priest whose seduction of women was driven, in part, by the need to reassure himself that he was not gay.)

Those abusive priests who were sexually victimized in their youth by other priests also have to contend with the psychic perversion of sacred ritual in their spiritual lives. In Celenza's case of Father J, for example, a priest who engaged in sexual misconduct with adult women parishioners, he had been abused as an altar boy by a parish priest who got him to perform fellatio every week after Mass. During his treatment, this priest came to see that the weekly ritual contributed to his conviction that he was evil. He then "got caught up in a vicious cycle of cleansing, sinning, and needing to be cleansed again … via this quasi-purifying baptismal rite—the ejaculate representing staining–cleansing, holy–evil water."

The common thread across the victim/survivor accounts in this volume is betrayal, loss, and a yearning for what can never be restored. The writer Tom Lewis, for example, tells us that "in an atmosphere of total trust," an Episcopal acolyte seduced him to "… obtain a pleasure or satisfy a need at my expense, and without my consent.… My life was altered against my will. I lost my trust … in the adult world … [and was left with] a great deal of confusion and pain over … most of my life."

In a similar vein, Richard Gartner quotes one of his patients discussing this loss in spiritual terms. Describing himself as a "religious man without a church," the patient explains,

I went to seminary because Catholicism means something to me. But now I can't go into a church without feeling I will vomit. My wife says, "Let's go to an Episcopalian Church—it's almost the same!" But it's not the same. I'm not an Episcopalian. I'm a *Catholic*. And there's nowhere I can go to be one.

Predatory Priests

The Catholic sexual abuse crisis has publicly displayed the worst of the Church's priesthood and culture. But it is important to remember that not all, not even a large minority of priests, abused their positions of trust. Many have lived out a personally meaningful celibacy much of the time, or have engaged seriously in long-term therapy after one or a few transgressions that took place many years ago. Nonetheless, Leslie Lothstein (2004), clinical director of a treatment program for impaired clergy, has made the case that "the data overwhelmingly imply that the sexual abuse of minors by Catholic clergy ... may represent a public health crisis" (p. 168). Religion professor Mark Jordan, also writing in these pages, points out that sexual abuse of minors also has a long history. "The long chronicle that runs down from the Middle Ages shows that priests and monks have always been accused of abusing the minors entrusted to them."

Of the 45,000 Catholic priests serving in the United States between 1950 and 2004, approximately 4.75% (5,214) have been identified as having molested minors, a number that Frawley-O'Dea & Goldner believe is "probably low," but which Fr. Martin believes is still "slightly higher than in other professions." The total number of victims violated by these priests and others not yet identified for the 54-year period studied has been estimated at 11,000, but Frawley-O'Dea and Goldner make the case that a more accurate estimate is between 40,000–60,000 minors.

Although priests who have sexually molested minors have done so across both genders and a relatively wide age range, there is general agreement among researchers that their victims were predominantly pubescent or postpubescent males between 11 and 17 years of age. There is an unsavory politics that surrounds the finding that the prime victims of clergy abuse are older teenage males. This has allowed some Vatican officials, bishops, and conservative pundits to blame the sexual abuse crisis on the increase of homosexual priests in the Church. Experts on sexual abuse have debunked this position, making the case that the sexual abuse of minors has nothing to do with homosexuality per se, since most homosexual men and women, like psychosexually mature heterosexuals of both genders, choose age peers as romantic and sexual partners. Indeed in earlier times, as Jordan explains, priests have been shown to abuse not only parishioners and seminarians, but also prostitutes, servants, penitents, and even patients in their care. While some had not yet entered puberty, most were "pubescent teenagers ... the young and vulnerable, not only boys, but girls."

In Lothstein's (2004) view, while homosexuality may be a risk factor for some priests abusing adolescent males, it is not the cause of that abuse. Indeed, if there is an explosive finding emerging from all the studies, and from the historical record, it is that most minors, both boys and girls, are abused by heterosexual priests. This should not seem entirely far-fetched since the sexual abuse of minors is a crime of opportunity, and the selection of boys by abusive priests may be due, in part, to their ready availability in contrast to girls, who are in the Catholic context even more "off-limits." (See especially Walker; see also Kohchansky & Cohen, Frawley-O'Dea and Goldner.)

While it would be reductionistic to construct a single psychic template of "the" sexually abusive priest, a psychodynamic profile has emerged and is discussed in illuminating detail by Kochansky and Cohen, who argue that directly and indirectly "the structure of the church as an institution, along with its teachings and ritual, unintentionally supported" pathological personality structures in its clergy.

Until very recently, when changes were introduced as a result of the scandals, seminaries typically produced many priests who were developmentally, socially, and sexually immature. This should not be surprising, since many clerical abusers of the past five decades "entered seminaries in their teens and were ordained with no education or counseling about sexuality, celibacy, or the maintenance of boundaries" (Martin). Priests in this cohort, who have been described as "the best educated 14-year-olds in our society, young teenagers on the bodies of men" (Cozzens, cited by Doyle), also exhibit psychosexual disturbances including sexual orientation confusion, deficits in sexual knowledge, and fear of hetero- and homosexual desire. These conflicts are a reflection, in part, of the fact that many candidates sought the refuge of the seminary as a way of repressing conflictual homosexual feelings during the period when seminary admissions policies "encouraged a lack of sexual experience as a predictor and safeguard of celibacy, based on the theory that 'what they didn't know couldn't tempt them'" (Jordan, cited in Walker's chapter).

Beyond issues of arrested psychosexual development, narcissistic disturbances are commonly noted in the psychological profiles of abusive priests, who often present with severe narcissistic vulnerability and compensatory grandiosity. Kochansky and Cohen connect priestly narcissism to the self-selection of men who were "drawn to the priesthood to...neutralize feelings of inadequacy, impotence and inferiority through a social role that allowed them ... to feel superior, special, admired, and powerful."

Andrea Celenza in her chapter links Catholic theology and culture with the unconscious narcissistic conflicts of priests who ultimately abuse. She writes,

> Sexual misconduct occurs at the intersection of spirituality, sexuality, and unchallenged omnipotence.... The teachings of Christianity, the hierarchy of the Catholic church organization, and the demand for celibacy can offer pathological solutions for problems with sexuality, power, and narcissistic vulnerability.

Echoing Celenza, Rev. Thomas Doyle asserts that sexual misconduct is made easier by the Catholic culture of clericalism, which "supports the [development] and enactment of narcissistic personality features [in] priests." Doyle maintains that many of the common symptoms of narcissism "... are syntonic [with] an organizational culture infected with clericalism."

The mix of idealization/idolatry and isolation/abandonment that is structured into the role of the Catholic priest is especially challenging for priests who struggle with narcissistic needs and defenses. "The pedestal on which the Roman church puts its priests is a pedestal for public viewing only," writes Richards. While priests may be construed as

> idealized figures ... 'above' the realm of ordinary folk (Richards), they are also, as Lothstein (2004) explains, "overworked, overburdened, lonely, isolated, and socially stigmatized ... factors that may lead to

sexually inappropriate behaviors stemming from unexpressed depression, loneliness, hunger, and anger. [p. 168]

Shifting from a diagnostic and organizational perspective to a relational one, clinical researchers have also noted that ephebophile abusers (those erotically drawn to adolescents as opposed to children) unconsciously identify with their victims whom they experience as psychosexual peers. Intuiting or projecting a common yearning for a psychically absent father, the erotic activity into which they induct their victims is bathed in a "benevolent" paternalism. ("I am [he is] giving you [me] the interest and caring which you [I] long for," and at a more erotic level, "I am identifying with your awe toward me, your dependency on me, and your need for my adoration," Kochansky and Cohen; see also Frawley-O'Dea and Goldner.)

This ubiquitous, and ominous, father hunger finds an outlet in the male culture of clerical life. One clergy patient of Kochansky's "stated flat out that men who seek the priesthood are often escaping from their father's [rejection] in the hopes of being embraced by more loving fathers in seminary and after ordination."

But consider also the fate of those hopes in Celenza's account of Fr. J, who understood that his life in the priesthood was a way to surround himself with brothers and fathers. Celenza quotes him as saying, "'everyone is called father, never dad. There is no intimacy. I spend a lot of psychic energy trying to please father figures from [a] distance.'" Similarly, Richards quotes a Roman Catholic priest who left the Church, "Not one of my superiors ever said thank you to me. Not one, ever."

Silent Bystanders

The bystanders to the sexual abuse of minors by Catholic priests over the decades include both the church hierarchy and the laity. The hierarchy not only remained silent about abusive priests in their midst, sealing their crimes in secret chancery vaults, but also retained them in ministry, moving them, quite literally, to new sexual playgrounds in new parishes. At the same time, too many Catholic parents, teachers, housekeepers, and rectory neighbors saw signs of sexual abuse, heard rumors of terrible acts, had uneasy feelings about certain priests and their adolescent "friends," but said nothing. Our authors tell us much about these two groups of bystanders.

> The rot at the heart of the institutional church, writes Walker, emanates from its rigidly hierarchical, misogynistic, sex-fearing culture.... As the embryonic church developed its rituals, structures of belief, and administration, it internalized both the sexual pessimism and the misogyny of late antique Greco-Roman philosophy along with the Empire's abusive love of power.

The contemporary Catholic Church is still a male medieval monarchy. Catholic bishops and cardinals answer only to the Pope, and are isolated from influences outside and below. They are not acculturated toward transparency in decision-making, public airing of problems within the diocese, or consultation with lay or non-Catholic "outsiders" who might have recommended a different organizational response to abuse allegations. Out of habit and doctrine, the bishops looked only to their own hierarchy for approbation, where, as Jesuit priest James Martin observes, "there has been historically a deep antipathy to 'scandal.'" Criticism of the Church, he explains, whether from within or without,

> has often been interpreted as tantamount to an attack on the faith itself.... [As a result], many bishops placed the interests of priests [and the Catholic church as an institution] above those of victims ... handling the crisis as if they were corporate chief executive officers rather than Christian pastors.

Exacerbating the secrecy embedded in a monarchical system, Thomas Doyle asserts that the Catholic idealization of priests, often at the expense the faithful, is a consequence of clericalism, "the belief that clerics form a special elite and, because of their powers as sacramental ministers, are superior to the laity." Catholic clericalism has been historically implicated in many of the Church's problems, including the current sexual abuse scandal. As Doyle explains, the idea that "priests ... have been singled out by God to take the place of Jesus Christ on earth [facilitated] the belief that erring clerics were somehow beyond most forms of accountability."

Clericalism, as a theological premise, has also weakened the laity, who, according to a 1993 study, are actually "more clericalized than the clergy" (Shaw, 1993, cited in Doyle). "Lay clericalism," Doyle writes, "is grounded in an immature dependency on clergy to mediate the believer's spirituality and relationship with God." Catholic doctrine inculcates that dependency since, "in Catholicism, priests control the faithful's access to sacraments. [As a result], threats to the clergy's hierarchical power cartel [become] threats to the laity's personal spiritual security." According to Doyle, the cover-up "would not have been possible without the acquiescence of the Catholic laity … [who] traded adult negotiation of spirituality for ongoing clerical patronage/patronization."

But consider the experience of the Reverend Laurie Ferguson, a fourth-generation Presbyterian pastor, whose denomination was "created in resistance … to the [hierarchy] of the Roman church…. Our [democratic] church government," she writes, "[did] not protect … us from the human dynamic of abuse of power and office [or the passive acquiescence of those who should object to it]."

Describing her experience of investigating sexual misconduct cases over a 22-year period, Ferguson reports that the reaction of the laity in every congregation to such charges was "total—complete—denial. This primitive defense," she explains, "was rigidly overused [and] led to splitting, scapegoating, selective amnesia, and repetitive retraumatization [of victims]…." It is a telling irony, Ferguson writes,

> [that] we Presbyterians often wished we had bishops and the hierarchy that comes with them, so that one person would have [had the authority] to pull an [offending] pastor out [of service]. Instead, we were dealing with endless layers of [congregant] committees … which, in their "refusal to know," … often functioned much as the Roman Catholic hierarchy.

In language that echoes Doyle's description of the dynamics of clericalism in the Catholic laity, Ferguson concludes,

> In the congregation's unconscious the pastor was operating as the one who spoke for God, who held grace and forgiveness, knowledge and power, and who was the conduit for salvation…. In an unconscious bargain, the laity … lived out an immature faith, trading their internal and independent spiritual power for a dependent relationship on a pastor's faith and charisma.

Anne Richards (2004) reports the same experience in her dealings with Episcopal congregants.

> After a priest was accused of sexual misconduct, ... Without exception, and even in the most dramatic cases of prolonged, egregious misconduct, the parishioners refused to believe that their priest had transgressed; they reacted with great rage and steadfastly tried to find alibis or excuses for him. [p. 147]

Comparing the Catholic and Protestant traditions, "two different religious worlds," Ferguson concludes that they share

> two very similar dynamics: the powerful defense of denial, no matter what the cost, and the practice of idealization and projection. In the Roman Catholic tradition, the bishops idealize the church, which must be protected at all costs. In [Protestantism], it is idealization of a particular pastor. For both traditions, the idealization contains a projection the laity strives to maintain: that someone else will do our spiritual work for us; someone else holds our spiritual life in their hands.

The Priest as Transference Figure

The novelist Mary Gordon, writing in these pages, reflects on the iconic similarities between the role of the priest and that of the analyst:

> Both are anointed and set apart from the patient/practitioner: in the case of the analyst, the blankness allows for a greater range of transference; in the case of the priest, the empty biography makes space for the pure or unaccented word of God.

Richards expands on the connection between the spiritual, the erotic, and the transferential. "A priest," she writes, "attracts and generates sexual energy in a unique way.... The writings of the mystics in every religious tradition testify that spiritual energy and sexual energy are the same energy, and thus the priest is—by virtue of his or her vocation—a sexual icon."

This sexual mystique is confirmed by Gillian Walker, who describes childhood visits by priests and monks who were friends of the family: "It is hard to capture the air of eroticism suffusing those 'fatherly' visits, the eroticism inherent in the oedipal role of the father, with his privileged access to the Divine." As Mary Gordon explains, "The love [we] Catholics had for priests was something like the love we had for movie stars and something like the love we had for God. It only narrowly skirted idolatry."

In this erotically charged context, boundary violations by clergy are only a touch away. "When a priest is not equipped or willing to respect a lay person as 'off limits' for him personally," Reverend Richards writes,

> he no longer functions to represent God. He acts as God. He, and his victim, may never know the difference, which is why so many relationships resulting from boundary violations [can be experienced] as special, unique love relationships. They carry the scent of the divine, or a simulation thereof. Thus, there is a particular form of denial built right into sexual transgressions involving clergy.

SEXUALITY AND GENDER: CELIBACY AND MISOGYNY

Just as clergy homosexuality does not "cause" clergy sexual abuse, neither does mandatory celibacy. The simplistic notion that the inability to turn to women for sexual release causes clerics to prey on children and adolescents is simply wrong.

There are many powerful arguments against this erroneous premise, including the fact that celibacy was not officially mandated by the church until the 12th century, yet Vatican concerns about clergy sexual abuse go back far earlier. Moreover, the Church has strategically turned a blind eye to the fact that large numbers of priests in South American and African countries live in a state of concubinage. (See especially the chapters by Doyle and Walker; see also Richards and Jordan).

Celibacy per se, even mandatory celibacy, is not the risk factor that, in itself, can produce sexually abusive priests. Rather, it is the Catholic idealization of celibacy as a heroic sacrifice inoculating against sexuality, and in particular *hetero*sexuality, that has prepared the ground for sexual misconduct.

Indeed, Walker, in her chapter, cites the former priest, psychologist-researcher Richard Sipe, who reports that there were those in the church hierarchy who actually condoned homosexual activity as being less dangerous to celibacy than heterosexual experience. As one superior put it, "Once they get the taste of [that], it's tough to keep the discipline" (Sipe, 1990, p. 105, as cited in Walker).

Walker argues that the Catholic fear of heterosexual sexuality is a reflection of misogyny, a deeper phobic dread and hatred of women and of femininity. "Seminarians were inoculated against the allure of heterosexual sex by means of a curriculum replete with misogynist readings, and submitted to a discipline that isolated them from contact with any women other than their biological mothers and Mary, the Mother of Christ." These antisexual, misogynist doctrines were revered as spiritual/personal ideals when they should have been recognized as pathogenic pressures leading priests to hate and fear their sexuality, rather than to own and contain it.

The connection of sexual deprivation and shame to the deep structure of gender is further unpacked in the chapters by Mary Gordon and Mark Jordan who also address how the misogynistic, antisex lenses of Church doctrine legitimized the establishment of an all-male, celibate, monarchial priesthood that was, paradoxically, erotically obsessed with sexual purity. It also endowed that homosocial ruling class with a particular homoerotic charge of its own. (Note that celibate priests who are called, in St. Paul's phrase, "eunuchs for the kingdom of Heaven" are also described as "married" to the Church [Jesus]).

Mary Gordon considers the implications of this enthrallment with masculinity in terms of the gender pathology of what feminists call "phallic monism," a primitive unisex gender system defined solely in terms of the presence or absence of the penis/phallus. Access to sacramental power in the Catholic Church remains completely defined by its obsession with the penis. In this "have/have not" economy, women are refused entrance to the priesthood simply because of their genital (non)endowment. The doctrinal reason? "They do not look like men, and therefore do not reflect Jesus—a classic but weak theological argument to preserve an all-male priesthood" writes former priest, Eugene Cullen Kennedy (2002).

Gordon shows how this infatuation with the penis is complicated by its negation through mandatory celibacy. "For the potential priest," she writes, "maleness had to be legible [read 'genital'] … but his sexual identity had to remain symbolic, abstract, potential. There is the symbolic phallus and the literal penis between the literal legs. And these two are not, as priests have learned to their anguish, the same."

Clerical sexual abuse, Gordon speculates, takes root in this unique variant of maleness, one that is inextricably bound up with being a Catholic priest: "superhuman, semidivine, untouchable, and untouched."

BREAKING SILENCE/GIVING TESTIMONY/BEARING WITNESS

In reflecting on the powerful impact of this collection on us the editors, and on you, the reader, we want to close with some brief thoughts about the moral, political, and psychic action of this volume as a whole.

In this book, you will hear the voices of eight women, including the editors, and nine men. This gender parity is, of course, entirely absent from leadership discussions within the Catholic Church, and it is unusual even in the literature emerging on the crisis. In that spirit, we have also included the voices and experiences of both straight and gay authors, all of whom, individually and severally, speak eloquently to the question of who is human, who matters, and who should be recognized as an exemplification of the divine.

The mutative factor in any therapy includes the act of bearing witness to injustices large and small, so as to name and dignify the suffering that once had to be endured alone, in silence and without social recognition. We see this volume as another venue for giving testimony and bearing witness. Through the ordeal of working through this material, which insists on multiple sites of empathy and versions of truth, we have amassed an intimate documentary of the relational politics and human cost of clergy sexual abuse and victimization.

As we turn this volume over to you, the reader, we ask you to consider it not only for its intriguing and important content, but also to experience its transformational and redemptive potential.

REFERENCES

Associated Press (2005), Islamic schools under abuse scrutiny. *CNN.com,* September 18.

BBC News (2005), Child-abuser monk commits suicide. *News.bbc.co.uk,* May 17.

Bollas, C. (1987), *The Shadow of the Object: Psychoanalysis of the Unthought Known.* New York: Columbia University Press.

Das, S. (2003), Hardly Krishna. *The Age,* June 2.

Davies, J. M. & Frawley, M. G. (1994), *Treating the Adult Survivor of Childhood Sexual Abuse.* New York: Basic.

Freund, C. P. (2005), Madrassas molesters: Clerical abuse in the Islamic world. *Reason,* April.

Kennedy, E. C. (2002), Church's wound stays unhealed. *Boston Globe,* March 10.

Lothstein, L. (2004), Men of the flesh: The evaluation and treatment of sexually abused priests. *Psychoanalytic Dialogue,* May 2, 167–195.

Rosenblatt, G. (2004), A rabbi accused of sexual abuse seeks to reinvent himself. *The Jewish Journal,* October 1.

Schwab, C. R. (2002), *Sex, Lies and Rabbis: Breaking a Sacred Trust.* Bloomington, IN: First Books Library.

Senanayake, S. (2005), Buddhist Monk Convicted of Sexual Abuse. *The Buddhist Channel,* May 17.

Wiener, J. (2001), An end to denial. *The Jewish Journal of Greater Los Angeles,* September 7.

I

Predatory Priests

2

Abusive Priests:
Who They Were and Were Not*

Mary Gail Frawley-O'Dea
Virginia Goldner

INTRODUCTION

Adiscussion of abusive priests is burdened with the same hand-icap inherent in any discourse that attempts to generalize about sexual offenders. In truth, none of us knows very much about most sexual predators because the vast majority of them are never identified. What we do know is based on research with offenders who have come to the attention of either the mental health or the criminal justice systems. This is a biased sample because it is a group of individuals who may or may not represent the wider universe of the population being considered. In referring to information generated by these studies, therefore, we must be cautious in assuming that

*Portions of this chapter appear in Frawley-O'Dea, Mary Gail. *Perversion of Power: Sexual Abuse in the Catholic Church*. Vanderbilt University Press, 2007.

they validly inform us about sexually transgressive priests. Richard Sipe (personal communication, 2004), for example, feels that priests represent men who live in a culture far different than the general population and cannot be compared with sexual offenders from the general population. On the other hand, Karen Terry (personal communication, 2005), primary researcher of a study of abusive priests and an expert in the area of sexual offenders, feels that there is no reason to conclude that abusive priests differ significantly from other men who abuse. With this in mind, we turn to available data to generate hypotheses about abusive priests that, in turn, are left to future researchers to validate. Before doing so, however, it is important to address the potential correlation between homosexuality and sexual abuse, since there is a move within the Catholic Church to blame the scandal on homosexual priests.

HOMOSEXUALITY AND SEXUAL ABUSE

Roman Catholic priests reportedly abuse mostly males (John Jay College of Criminal Justice, 2004; United States Conference of Catholic Bishops, 2005). One study found that 64% of the accused priests abused males only; 22.6% abused females only; 3.6% abused both girls and boys, and in 10% of the cases the gender was unknown (John Jay College of Criminal Justice [John Jay], 2004). Other research indicated that 78% of allegations received in 2004 were from males while 22% were from females (United States Conference of Catholic Bishops [USCCB], 2005).

Not only were most reported victims of Catholic priests male, they also were pubescent. Almost 60% of male victims were first abused between the ages of 10-14 (USCCB, 2005). These are not, however, fully developed males.

Sherrel L. Hammer, M.D. (2002) of the University of Hawaii measured the onset of puberty by the nature of the boy's pubic hair and by testicular volume and length. She concludes that male puberty begins, on average, at 12.2 (pubic hair) or 11.2 (testicular growth) years and is not completed until 14 years of age. Similarly, Kirby Parker Jones, M.D. (1997) of the University of Utah cites 11.6 as the age of onset of male puberty and asserts that the pubertal process continues for two years. As Kohansky and Cohen discuss in this volume, sexual abuse of a pubertal boy may have signified sexual merger with a male perceived to be a psychosexual peer of the abuser. In addition, it may have been an unconscious act of hostility toward a boy who otherwise would not be available sexually to the priest. In other words, the abuser, who could have entered a minor seminary at age 14 or 15, may have unconsciously attacked his victim's sexuality at the same age he was when he entered the minor seminary, symbolically castrating the victim as he himself was symbolically castrated.

The gender and age of so many victims created space for Catholic commentators, including retired Vatican officials Jorge Arturo Cardinal Medina Estevez (Winfield, 2002) and Rev. Andrew Baker (Gibson, 2003; Winfield, 2002), conservative journalist Deal Hudson (Paulson, 2002a), and Fr. Charles Dahlby (Dahlby, 2003), to link the sexual abuse of young people with homosexual priests. In autumn 2005, it was reported that the Vatican would issue a ban on gays in the priesthood, declaring even celibate homosexual men inherently unfit for priesthood (Eisenberg, 2005).

The attack on gay priests by Vatican officials and others drew criticism from experts on sexual offenders. Robert Geffner, psychologist and editor of *The Journal of Child Sexual Abuse,* stated that research indicates that homosexuals are no more likely than heterosexuals to violate minors sexually (Elias, 2002). Leslie Lothstein, Director of Psychology at Hartford Hospital's Institute of Living, treated many sexually active priests, including some who abused minors. Lothstein insisted that the sexually active gay priests he treated had sex with age-appropriate men and that even priests who abused minor males were, in fact, mostly heterosexual (DiGiulio, 2002). David Finkelhor, Director of Crimes Against Children Research Center at the University of New Hampshire, views sexual attraction to minors as a separate sexual activity, an opinion also espoused by John Bancroft, physician and Director of the Kinsey Institute for Research in Sex, Gender, and Reproduction (Elias, 2002). Groth and Oliveri studied over 3,000 sexual offenders and did not find even one homosexual man who shifted from an attraction to adult men to a desire for minors (Gartner, 1999, pp. 98, 100). Conversely, they found that men who were nonexclusively fixated on children, or who regressed from an attraction to adults to an interest in children, all described themselves as heterosexual and, in addition, usually were homophobic (p. 99). Similarly, Dimock concluded that most minor boys are abused by heterosexual men, some of whom are indifferent to the gender of their victims, choosing either girls or boys based on the minor's availability and vulnerability (Gartner, 1999, p. 99). Finally, Hindman found that when three cohorts of sexual offenders were polygraphed, 47% of them acknowledged having molested boys while only 17% of the perpetrators self-reported that information (Hindman and Peters, 2001). Perhaps more sexual predators abuse boys than once was thought but are reluctant to say so and to be perceived as homosexuals.

Vatican officials, in their search to blame the sexual abuse scandal on someone or something external to institutional and doctrinal failings of the Church itself, conflated sexual orientation with psychosexual maturation, and with criminal behavior. Psychosexually mature, adult homosexual men have consensual sex with other adult men much as psychosexually mature, adult heterosexual men have consensual sex with adult women. Criminal heterosexuals sexually violate adult women and children of both genders; almost surely some criminal homosexuals sexually victimize adult men and some minors. These are crimes of power, ultimately having little to do with sex or the sexual orientation of the criminal. Both in and out of the priesthood, there also may be some number of psychosexually immature heterosexual or homosexual men who turn to minors of either gender because, in the subjective experience of the offender, the young people are experienced as psychosexual peers. Here, the problem is not the sexual orientation of the offender but rather his psychological immaturity and arrested development, a fact relentlessly presented to the Vatican (Associated Press, 2005) and just as relentlessly ignored.

To a large extent, victim gender selection by priests also reflected opportunity rather than sexual orientation. Consider, for example, prison sex in which heterosexual males with more power and authority within the inmate population select and rape other, less powerful men to achieve sexual release and to impose their power on another person. Boys were much more available to priests than were girls. Parents were thrilled to have a priest single their boy out for attention and encouraged their sons to spend time with Father, even allowing them to travel with the priest. Even years ago, parents would not have felt as comfortable having their girls spend too much time with the priest and he, in turn, would have known it would look suspicious to have girls tagging after him. Further, many priests were frightened of girls and women and misogynistic toward them; they would be put off from having sex with them. They might also be wary of impregnating pubescent or post-pubescent girls. Finally, some priests defined celibacy as refraining from sexual relationships with women and thus could convince themselves that sex with minor males did not jeopardize their celibate status.

While researchers and clinicians working with sexual offenders maintain that the vast majority of them are heterosexual, we must consider the possibility that some sexual abusers are homosexual men who deny their orientation, replacing recognition and acceptance with homophobia. Other priest abusers may have never consolidated any sexual orientation, claiming to be heterosexual in the breach of their confusion, conflict, or ignorance. The Vatican's proposed ban on gay priests will, of course, have no impact on these groups, other than implicitly directing them to remain psychosexually immature and thus potentially dangerous to adult parishioners and minors. Instead, the Vatican's policy will primarily persecute gay men who have accepted their homosexuality enough to speak about it.

Attempts by some Catholic lay commentators, priests, bishops, and Vatican officials to blame homosexual priests for the sexual abuse scandal is, in and of itself, another scandal. It is another morally corrupt strategy to deflect responsibility for the crisis onto the vulnerable and already marginalized. The Vatican's remarks on homosexual priests were so provocative and inconsistent with contemporary understandings of homosexuality, in fact, that the Episcopal bishops of Massachusetts went public with unusually open criticism of the Catholic Church. Bishops M. Thomas Shaw and Roy F. Cederholm warned that Vatican attempts to link homosexuality with the sexual abuse crisis were irresponsible, incorrect, and invited hate crimes against gays (Paulson, 2002b). It is difficult to imagine the pain suffered by devoted gay priests suddenly cast as potential perverts unsuitable for a spousal relationship with the Church or for "F/fatherhood."

EMPIRICAL DATA ON ABUSIVE PRIESTS

Since discussions about offending priests take place amidst murky scientific data, it is helpful to begin with the most solid empirical information available. We will use the findings of *The Nature and Scope of the Problem of Sexual Abuse of Minors by Catholic Priests and Deacons in the United States: A Research Study Conducted by the John Jay College of Criminal Justice* (John Jay College of Criminal Justice, 2004) (hereafter called the John Jay Study) commissioned by the United States Conference of Catholic Bishops and designed to capture descriptive data on the sexual abuse of children by Catholic priests between 1950 and 2002. Some of these findings are augmented by the *Report on the Implementation of the Charter for the Protection of Children and Young People* (United States Conference of Catholic Bishops, 2005) (hereafter called the 2004 Study), which included information about sexual abuse reported in the calendar year 2004. Because the John Jay Study encompasses data only through the end of 2002, and the 2004 Study covers only calendar year 2004, there are no data for calendar year 2003.

Number of Abusing Priests: John Jay researchers concluded that 4,392 priests, representing 4.3% of diocesan priests and 2.5% of religious priests, were credibly accused of sexual abuse of minors between 1950 and 2002 (John Jay, 2004). During 2004, another 411 priests were newly credibly accused of abuse (USCCB, 2005). If we hypothesize that a similar number of offenders were newly identified in 2003—the year for which there are no reported data—it suggests that between 1950 and 2004, at least 5,214 Roman Catholic priests were credibly accused of sexually abusing a minor. This accounts for approximately 4.75% of the priesthood.

These numbers are probably low for a variety of reasons. Two percent of diocesan priests and 20% of religious priests were not included in the John Jay Study. In the 2004 study, 7% of dioceses and eparchies (Eastern Orthodox rite equivalents of dioceses), and 29% of religious communities failed to provide 2004 data. Therefore, there is some undercounting of abusive priests in both studies. In addition, data collection in both studies depended on the willingness and ability of bishops and provincial superiors to self-report all pertinent information. Given the historical reluctance of bishops to face sexual abuse within their dioceses squarely, it is possible that some bishops withheld relevant information from the researchers. Further, some bishops over the years had successfully intimidated victims or their families from following through on sexual abuse complaints so no records exist in these cases. Moreover, record keeping was sloppy in some chanceries and provincial offices, raising the probability that some allegations were not available to be counted. Finally, it is almost certain that some number of victims have not yet, and may never, report their victimizations. The John Jay Study determined, in fact, that less than 13% of allegations were made in the years they occurred and over 25% were lodged more than 30 years after the reported abuse began.

In summary, then, we can conclude that in the course of 54 years, at least 4.75% of Roman Catholic priests in the United States sexually abused a minor.

Geographic Distribution of Abusers: Sexual abuse of minors by priests occurred at similar rates nationwide. According to the John Jay study, in all geographic regions, between 3% and 6% of priests were credibly accused of sexually violating minors. This suggests that sexual abuse was not confined to urban areas or to areas of the country considered to be particularly sexually liberal or especially sexually conservative.

In 2005, a controversy over the geographical distribution of clergy abuse erupted between conservative Pennsylvania Senator Rick Santorum and other politicians over remarks made by Santorum in 2002 that were resurrected in 2005. Santorum, a staunch Roman Catholic, suggested that the Archdiocese of Boston had a particularly egregious sexual abuse problem because of Boston's liberal culture. He was quoted as saying, "When the culture is sick, every element of it becomes infected. While it is no excuse for this scandal, it is no surprise that Boston, a seat of academic, political, and cultural liberalism in America, lies at the center of the storm" (Cooperman, 2005). Alan Cooperman (2005), reporter for the *Washington Post,* pointed out that although Boston was among the top 10 dioceses in terms of percentage of abusive priests, the Diocese of Covington, KY, had the highest percentage of abusers while in San Francisco—surely a city known for liberal attitudes towards sexuality—only 1.6% of the priesthood had been abusive between 1950 and 2002. The political rebukes and amount of press generated by Santorum's remarks highlighted the extent to which the sexual abuse scandal in the Church had infiltrated the national consciousness and public policy debates.

Perpetrators by Year of Ordination: The percentage of priests who allegedly abused minors varied by year of ordination. According to the John Jay Study, the percentage of all priests ordained in a given year that were credibly accused of abuse were:

Ordination Year	Approximate1 Percentage of Credibly Accused Priests
1960–1962	6.0
1963	8.0
1964	7.5
1965, 1966	8.0
1967	7.5
1968	8.0
1969	7.0
1970	8.0
1971, 1972	6.0
1973	9.0
1974	8.0
1975	9.0
1976, 1977, 1978, 1979	6.0
1980	7.0
1981	5.0
1982	6.0
1983	5.0
1984	3.0
1985, 1986	4.0
1987	3.0
1988, 1989	4.0
1990	3.0
1991	2.0
1992	1.0
1993	2.0
1994	1.0
1995, 1996	2.0
1997	1.0
1998	2.0
1999, 2000	1.0

[1]The John Jay study included a graph of ordination but exact percentages were not reported; approximates based on the graph are used here.

[2]Data were not available prior to 1960.

The percentages from 1984 to the present are likely to be understated given the age at which priests first begin to abuse, and considering the length of time it often takes for victims to come forward to report their abuse. In addition, seminaries began psychological evaluations of candidates in the 1980s, perhaps screening out at least some potential abusers (see Rev. James Martin, S.J., this volume). Finally, there are data on sexual abuse in the wider society suggesting that there has been some decline in the incidence of abuse since 1990, perhaps due to increased cultural awareness and thus vigilance about childhood sexual abuse, and the correlated early detection and incarceration of more offenders (John Jay, 2004).

It is startling to see that, from 1963 through 1980, the percentage of abusing priests per ordination class rarely fell below 6.0 and, in some years, rose to 9.0. Therefore, we would expect to see increases in the percentage of abusive priests in ordination classes after 1980, even if they do not reach previous heights.

Dates of Birth: In the John Jay Study, almost two-thirds of abusive priests were born before 1940; almost 90% before 1950. They grew up in a time of sexual repression in the wider society, especially in Catholic communities. In Catholic families and schools, children learned that sex was dangerous and sinful unless it occurred in marriage. Normal developmental sexual activities, like masturbation and sexual fantasy, were deemed very sinful and so the Catholic child and adolescent had no help processing and learning adaptive expressions of their emerging sexuality. In addition, the priests born prior to 1950 often entered minor seminaries at 14 or 15 years of age, preparing for a celibate life before they had moved through puberty and into a mature psychosexuality. These may also have been priests who were particularly vulnerable to being psychologically destabilized by the cultural changes, including liberalized attitudes towards sex, ushered in during the late 1960s and early 1970s. When some priests from these age cohorts acted out sexually, they may have chosen minors who were experienced as psychosexual equals.

Age of Priest at First Incidence of Offense: In the John Jay Study, the average age of a priest at his first reported incidence of sexual abuse was 39. That age rose from 38 in the 1950s to 48 in 2002. Prior to the study, conventional wisdom held that priests tended to abuse shortly after ordination when they left the protected environment of the seminary and were out in parishes running youth activities.

The John Jay results need further analysis but they suggest that priests may have begun to abuse only after a decade of ordained priesthood. Perhaps priests at that point in their careers more fully realized what they had sacrificed in choosing a celibate life. Many male relatives and parishioners of similar age would have established careers and family lives that stimulated the priest's envy and disillusionment with his own situation. Psychosexually immature and sexually inexperienced, some priests may have sexually appropriated young people in an enactment of rage, envy, and inadequacy as a man in society in order to achieve a subjective sense of empowerment. Sexual abuse of a male parishioner's child also represented an attack on that man's ability to protect his offspring, an aspect of fatherhood denied to the clerical Father.

History of Personal Victimization: Only 6.8% of accused priests in the John Jay Study reported histories of childhood abuse, with just over 4% claiming to have been sexually abused as a minor. Researchers note that these numbers reflect only what was available in diocesan or provincial files and may understate the number of priests with abusive backgrounds. Certainly, these statistics defy clinical lore that the majority of sexual offenders have been sexually violated earlier in life (Rossetti, 1997; Sipe, 1995). Sexual offender researcher Jan Hindman (2001), however, studied three cohorts of sexual perpetrators in Oregon and found that only 29%, 32%, and 30% respectively divulged sexual abuse histories under polygraph. During nonpolygraphed self-reports, approximately two-thirds of the men in each group reported having been sexually violated as children, numbers more in keeping with clinical reports.

While the John Jay numbers may understate the incidence of childhood sexual abuse among abusing priests, clinical reports may overstate that phenomenon. Many sexual predators are adept at eliciting sympathy from others and may realize that they will receive more consideration from law enforcement, juries, or mental health practitioners if they are viewed as sexual victims as well as victimizers.

Numbers of Victims Per Priest: According to the John Jay Study, 55.7% of credibly accused priests had only one victim; 26.9% had two to three; 13.9% had four to nine; and 3.5% had 10 or more. These are probably the least credible findings of the study. First, these statistics convey only the number of victims who came forward to accuse a priest and whose allegations were recorded and turned over to researchers. We know that many victims never disclose their abuse, or at least never report it to the Church, and we can be skeptical that all accusations indeed were recorded and submitted to John Jay. For example, one of Frawley-O'Dea's patients was abused by her grandfather beginning at age four. When she was eight years old, she told her parish pastor about the victimizations during a weekly confession. The priest suggested that they talk about it more extensively in his rectory office and he then sexually abused her weekly from ages eight to 12. This woman never reported the priest to anyone and spoke of her violations only in treatment.

In the 2004 study, half of the new allegations were lodged against priests who already had been accused of sexual abuse in prior years. Just those new results would change the John Jay data, increasing the number of victims for up to 350 priests included in the John Jay Study.

Next, sexual predators rarely are honest about their histories as offenders. Hindman and Peters (2001), for example, found in three studies that sexual victimizers self-reported 1.5, 2.5, and 2.9 victims each on average. Under polygraph, however, the same offenders disclosed an average of 9.0, 13.6, and 11.6 victims respectively, four to six times the number of victims self-reported by the perpetrators. The actual number of victims of priest abuse in the United States between 1950 and 2004 is probably more accurately 40,000 to 60,000 minors, not just over 11,000 as reported in the John Jay and 2004 studies.

Age of Victims: Both the John Jay Study and the 2004 Study found that the majority of victims were abused between the ages of 10 to 14. The John Jay Study, however, suggests that over the decades there was a shift toward male victims reporting having been abused for the first time between 15 to 17 years of age. The percentage of teens violated for the first time in that age group rose from 26% in the 1970s to 55% in the 1990s. Interestingly, however, because the average age of the priest when he began to abuse also increased over time, the average aggregate age difference between perpetrator and male victim seems to have remained fairly constant, at over 20 years. The age difference itself connotes intergenerational imposition of sex on a much younger male in relationship with an authority figure and/or the sexual immaturity of the perpetrator. Again, it is distinct from the sexual behaviors of mature homosexual men.

There are a number of other perspectives to take on the aging of victims at first incidence of abuse. First of all, it is possible that the age of victims appears to increase because older boys more quickly reach the developmental milestones that trigger recognition that something is wrong in their lives. In other words, the more recent the abuse, the more likely the victim to come forward first because he sees that his life is developing differently from, and not as well as, the lives of their agemates. In this case, we would expect to see the average age of first victimization to have decreased in the 1980s and 1990s as younger victims reach those same stages of life and come forward.

It is also possible that younger boys were not as available to priests in later years as fewer children attended Catholic elementary schools or were involved in Catholic youth activities than in earlier decades. In addition, by the 1980s, parents who had troubled children—the most vulnerable to abuse—were relying less on Catholic priests to counsel their children and more on guidance counselors and psychotherapists in and out of the public school systems. One family Frawley-O'Dea worked with in the mid-1980s, for example, said that, years ago, they would have taken their two boys to the priest to straighten them out, but now they were in psychotherapy.

Finally, as priests entered seminary later, their own psychosexual development may have moved toward late adolescence rather than puberty. When they crossed the line with a minor, they may have felt more comfortable with older boys who seemed like psychological peers. Our own hypothesis is that, as time goes on, the younger victims from the 1980s and 1990s will begin to come forward as they recognize problems in their lives, realigning the findings of the John Jay Study.

It is important to note that girls were abused most frequently at ages 11 to14, with almost 40% of female victims in that age group (John Jay, 2004; USCCB, 2005). As with male victims, the age of abuse onset appeared to increase over the years, probably also because younger female victims have not yet come forward.

Abusive Acts: In the John Jay study, most abusing priests committed acts more serious than "just" touching under a victim's clothes. About one-third of abusing priests sexually penetrated their victims or engaged them in oral sex, both representing very serious abuse. Only 2.9% of abusing priests solely engaged in sex talk or pornography use; just 9% only touched over the victim's clothes or had the victim's touch over the cleric's clothes; and only 15.8% stopped at touching under the clothing. In the majority of cases, therefore, the victimizing priest seriously sexually violated his victim.

In addition, few priests sexually assaulted their victims one time only. Over half of reporting victims claimed to have been abused by their violator "numerous times," while only 29% claim to have been abused just once (John Jay, 2004). This finding argues against construing sexual abuse by a priest as a momentary lapse of judgment but rather presses for viewing the perpetrator as dangerously likely to reabuse a young person many times.

Conventional wisdom has held that alcohol abuse by the perpetrator is often implicated in sexual victimization of a minor. In fact, the John Jay study concluded that the abusing priest used alcohol and/or drugs only 21.6% of the time. Again, this mitigates against an assumption that a priest will not abuse if he is clean and sober.

Position of Priest at Time of Abuse: John Jay results indicate that nearly 67% of abusive priests were pastors or associate pastors; another 10% were resident priests. Although all sexual abuse is terrible, sexual violation by a parish priest, über father/Father of the members of his congregation, is especially egregious. It is an abrogation of power that particularly enacts the metaphor of soul murder.

The descriptive data of the John Jay Study 2004 and the USCB 2005 Study on abusive priests give us an illuminating perspective on the aggregate characteristics of Catholic clergy who abused minors.

REFERENCES

Associated Press (2005), Researchers study gays in Catholic priesthood: Most molestation victims are older boys. *Thebostonchannel.com*, September 20.

Cooperman, A. (2005), Kennedy rebukes Santorum for comments: Republican repeats remark linking scandal to Boston "Liberalism." *Washingtonpost.com (Washington Post On-Line)*, July 14.

Dahlby, Fr. C. (2003), Scandal in the Roman Catholic Church: Behind the smoke and mirrors is a coverup of homosexual priests and bishops. *Catholiccitizens.org (Catholic Citizens of Illinois On-Line)*, October 28.

DiGiulio, K. (2002), Interview of Dr. Leslie Lothstein. *Natcath.org (National Catholic Reporter On-Line)*, August 16.

Eisenberg, C. (2005), Report: Pope bans gay seminarians. *Nynewsday.com (New York Newsday On-Line)*, September 20.

Elias, M. (2002), Is Homosexuality to blame for Church scandal? *Usatoday.com (USA Today On-Line)*, July 15.

Gartner, R. B. (1999), *Betrayed as Boys*. New York: Guilford Press.

Gibson, D. (2003), *The Coming Catholic Church*. San Francisco: Harper San Francisco.

Hammer, S. L. (2002), Chapter XX.I. Puberty. Case-based pediatrics for medical students and *residents, department of pediatrics, University of Hawaii John A. Burns School of Medicine. www2.Hawaii.edu/medicine/pediatrics/pedtexts/s20c01.html*, March.

Hindman, J. & Peters, J. M. (2001), Polygraph testing leads to better understanding of adult and juvenile sexual offenders. *Federal Probation, 65*: 8–14.

John Jay College of Criminal Justice (2004), The Nature and Scope of the Problem of Sexual Abuse of Minors by Catholic Priests and Deacons in the United States: A Research Study Conducted by the John Jay College of Criminal Justice. *Usccb.org* (United States Conference of Catholic Bishops website).

Jones, K. B. (1997), The Beginning and end of reproductive life: Pubertal and midlife changes. *Medstat.med.utah.edu/kw/human_reprod/lectures/pubertal_midlife/#2*.

Paulson, M. (2002a), Gay seminarian ban weighed: Vatican drafting a ruling expected in the next year. *Boston.com (The Boston Globe On-Line)*, November 6.

———— (2002b), Gay comments concern bishops. *Boston.com (The Boston Globe On-Line)*, December 10.

Rossetti, S. J. (1997), *A Tragic Grace: The Catholic Church and Sexual Abuse*. Collegeville, MN: The Liturgical Press.

Sipe, A. W. R. (1995), *Sex, Priests, and Power: Anatomy of A Crisis*. New York: Brunner/Mazel.

United States Conference of Catholic Bishops (2005), Report on the Implementation of the Charter for the Protection of Children and Young People. *Usccb.org* (United States Conference of Catholic Bishops website).

Winfield, N. (2002), Cardinal says gays shouldn't be priests. *Boston.com (The Boston Globe On-Line)*, December 6.

3

Priests Who Sexualize Minors: Psychodynamic, Characterological, and Clerical Cultural Considerations

Gerald E. Kochansky
Murray Cohen

In an earlier paper (Kochansky & Herrmann, 2004), a Jesuit priest and law professor examined the relationship between the long-standing tendency of the Roman Catholic hierarchy to avoid "scandal" and the church's failure to take appropriate legal and administrative actions against priests and other religious accused of the sexual molestation of minors.

That paper focused on the ways the construct of *narcissism* was relevant to the character traits of some, but certainly not all, priests, including higher church authorities; on certain church teachings and practices that may promote and reinforce such traits; and on sections of the code of canon law that places a high priority on the avoidance of scandal. All these factors may well have converged to foster self-protective tendencies that led to a failure on the part of the church both to guard adequately against future misconduct by those clergy who were in fact guilty and to respond compassionately to the emotional needs of their victims. The authors did not address factors contributing to the tendencies of some priests to eroticize minors and violate culturally accepted boundaries and legally proscribed standards of conduct designed to protect children; nonetheless, some of the authors' observations about the role of narcissism in the character organization of certain priests and in the church as an institution are relevant to the current inquiry about the psychodynamics and character organization of some priests who engage in sexually abusive behaviors.

This chapter combines clinical data and formulations derived from Kochansky's treatment of priests, seminarians, and other religious who have had a variety of emotional and psychological problems (although none had been charged with misconduct involving minors) with the observations of Cohen. A large majority of the perversions Cohen has seen in his research and practice have involved the sexualization of either prepubertal boys (pedophilia) or of postpubertal adolescent males (ephebophilia); within this latter group, the individuals in question included pediatricians, internists, child psychologists, high-school teachers, and school counselors—men who have made adolescent boys and girls a major part of their lives— as well as three men who were professionally involved with the Catholic church.

Our goal here is to apply the understandings that we have developed from our different areas of expertise to develop ideas about what might be *some* of the sources of, and *some* of the meanings of, the sexual behaviors of *some* priests who select children or adolescents as the objects of their sexual feelings. We emphasize "some" since it is simply not possible to construct one single template of development, dynamics, defenses, and/or conflicts that does justice to the complexity of the characterological factors involved in such behaviors. We believe that there are, however, some general statements that can be made based on our clinical and research experience.

Before summarizing our observations, we will briefly review some of the formulations and findings previously offered by other clinicians and researchers regarding priests who sexualize minors, and we will also describe some of the ways in which the structure of the church as an institution—and its teachings and rituals (formal and informal)—unintentionally support some of the psychodynamic features that characterize these priests.

GENDER AND AGE CHARACTERISTICS OF MINORS SEXUALIZED BY OFFENDING PRIESTS

Although priests who have sexually molested minors have done so across both genders and a relatively wide age range, there is general agreement that most of them have targeted male minors who are commonly classified as pubescent or postpubescent. Despite some debate about the average age at which puberty begins and ends biologically, and how this relates to frequently applied age criteria for defining puberty and postpuberty (discussed in another chapter of this book), the "Summary Report" of the descriptive study commissioned by the National Review Board for the Protection of Children and Young People of the United States Conference of Catholic Bishops and conducted by the John Jay College of Criminal Justice indicated that while the majority (54.2%) of young males sexually abused by priests were between 11 and 14 years of age, nearly an additional 30% were first abused between the ages of 15 and 17. Taken together, these data indicate that approximately 85% of male minors abused by priests were between the ages of 11 and 17 (Research Staff, 2004).

Whatever the contribution of "accessibility of victims" in this age group has been, the data indicate that the male minors whom priests have offended against were most often pubertal or postpubertal, as opposed to prepubertal; this is consistent with findings published by Leslie Lothstein (2004), who concluded that "[t]he majority of Catholic priests who act out with underage males do so with teenage boys." It is also consistent with a review of research relevant to the sexual abuse of male children and adolescents undertaken in the UK that reported "extra-familial abuse … [is] more common in boys, *especially older boys,* than girls." Although the age distribution in relation to the biological data regarding the onset of puberty may complicate the classification of priest abusers as pedophiles or ephebophiles (13 and below being the arbitrary cutoff for a pedophile diagnosis and 14 through 17 for ephebophilia), the data on the age of victims indicates that most of the offending priests have tended to sexualize older minors and therefore—the media's blanket use of the word "pedophile" notwithstanding—their psychodynamics and characterological features are more likely to be those of ephebophiles rather than pedophiles. This is an important distinction, since the psychodynamic and characterological features typically seen in ephebophiles are quite different from those of pedophiles.

There are some highly successful, relatively healthy men having mature heterosexual or homosexual attachments who, under a variety of life circumstances, will occasionally fondle a young child. However we might classify such behavior, it does not amount to pedophilia, which is characterized by an erotic *fixation* on prepubertal children, usually accompanied by rather severe emotional, psychological dysfunction together with asocial or antisocial values and attitudes, an obsessional character structure, and a major deficit in self-esteem. The child targeted by a pedophile may be a relative, a neighbor, or someone who is picked off the street. Unless the child is a relative (in which case the dynamics are of course more complicated), the intention is exploitative with an absence of any emotionally meaningful relationship or attachment. There is frequently a manifest aggressive, assaultive component to a pedophile's behavior, as the child is more often forced than seduced into a sexual involvement. And, finally, the obsessional features of the pedophile's sexual fixation seriously interfere with the formation of any intellectual, occupational, or social adaptation.

By contrast, men with erotic attachments to pubertal and postpubertal boys have quite different mental structures and dynamics; and since most priests who sexually abuse minors appear to reside in this group, we will focus upon their characteristics below.

AN OVERVIEW OF CLINICAL
AND RESEARCH FINDINGS

The major contributions to the literature on the psychological characteristics of priests who sexually abuse minors have been generated by clinicians who have devoted much of their professional lives to the treatment of clergy (usually in specialty residential units) referred to them for a history of such behavior. Stephen Rossetti, a diocesan priest and psychologist affiliated with Saint Luke Institute in Maryland, and Leslie Lothstein, a clinical psychologist at the Institute of Living in Connecticut, have communicated many valuable observations and formulations about this subgroup of priests in multiple journal articles and books (Rossetti, 1994, 1996; Lothstein, 1994, 2004), but this overview will include the findings of other clinicians and researchers as well.

Rossetti (1996) has emphasized the degree to which both priest and nonpriest sex offenders "are largely indistinguishable" from comparable individuals who are not offenders, "at least on the surface," including in many general clinical interviews and on objective personality/psychopathology tests such as the Minnesota Multiphasic Personality Inventory-2 (MMPI-2). By contrast, he has concluded that *projective* tests, especially the Rorschach scored by the Exner Comprehensive Scoring System (Exner, 1993), can counter defensiveness—especially the tendency of those who sexualize children to deny, when asked directly, that they have ever sexually abused a minor or have wishes or desires to do so currently—and reveal some of the "cognitive and emotional" impairments that characterize some individuals with such tendencies. Other findings (Celenza & Hilsenroth, 1997; Celenza, 1998, discussed more fully below) support Rossetti's with regard to the Rorschach.[1]

While Rossetti (1996) warns that there is no single "clinical profile" that characterizes adults who sexually abuse children, citing the variety of sexually abuse patterns ("fixated" versus "regressed," "aggressive" versus "more passive or nonviolent," etc.), he has proposed that an intensive psychosocial history "often reveal[s] similar patterns of psychosexual problems" among offenders. He identified six psychological indicators which he believes are commonly seen in clergy across many denominations who are at risk for sexually molesting children or who may have done so in the past. Referring to them as "red flags," he lists them as: confusion about sexual orientation, childish interests and behavior, lack of peer relationships, ex-

---

[1]On the other hand, the results of a study involving the detection of minimization of psychopathology on the Rorschach in clerics and nonclerics alleged sex offenders led one group of researchers, Wasyliw et al. (1998), to the conclusion that the standard Exner indicators of defensiveness on the Rorschach were not sufficiently sensitive and that therefore the Rorschach should not be used as such unless used in conjunction with other instruments.

tremes in developmental sexual experiences, personal history of sexual abuse or deviant sexual experiences, and an excessively passive, dependent, and conforming personality.

Lothstein (1994) has emphasized that individuals who sexualize children represent a population *heterogeneous* in the presence of additional paraphilias, parallel psychiatric, or neurological diagnoses, and the relative contributions of other relevant variables. He also reviewed a number of psychological theories about men who molest minors. While his summary of psychoanalytic formulations was lacking in complexity, he did, in referring to those men with childhood histories of having been sexually or physically abused, emphasize the role of Freud's critical concept of the *repetition compulsion* (Freud, 1921; Fenichel, 1945) and Anna Freud's (1937) concept of *identification with the aggressor* in association with discussing such childhood traumas as etiological factors. (A history of having been abused as a minor has been identified as frequently reported by both cleric and noncleric child molesters; see, for example, Haywood et al., 1996.) Our clinical experience certainly confirms the importance of these mechanisms in men with histories of ephebophilia and other perversions.

The importance of differentiating between *fixated* pedophiles, who are exclusively sexually attracted to and aroused by children or adolescents instead of adults, and *regressed* pedophiles, whose sexual relationships with minors are reactive to stress and stand in contrast to their more characteristic higher levels of psychosexual organization and functioning, was also emphasized by Lothstein. This still widely used classification in the evaluation and treatment of individuals convicted of illegal sexual behavior was developed by Cohen and his colleagues at the Treatment Center for Sexually Dangerous Persons at Bridgewater, Massachusetts (Prentky et al., 1997; Seghorn et al., 1984; Cohen et al., 1969, 1971, 1987). Working within their formulations, Lothstein proposed that fixated pedophiles are often developmentally immature, passive, heterosexually inhibited, and deficient in sexual knowledge as well as social skills. By contrast, the ephebophile's interest in older children usually "reflects a higher level of social and psychosexual development." On the other hand, Curtis Bryant (2002), a Jesuit priest, psychologist, and the previous director of inpatient services at Saint Luke Institute, has offered clinical observations to support his opinion that ephebophile priests, who have sex with adolescent males, are similar to pedophile priests in that they too are often socially immature, identify with the minor whom they sexualize, and lack opportunities to be intimate with women.

Lothstein additionally emphasized that aggression is *always* a critical component of the sexual interactions between either pedophiles *or* ephebophiles and minors. This conclusion is consistent with the findings of Gacano, Meloy, and Bridges (2000), who used the Rorschach to compare psychopaths, sexual homicide perpetrators, and nonviolent pedophiles. They found that "pedophiles show significantly more anger, which may stem from their general inadequacy, cognitive rigidness, less alloplastic (acting-out) style, and their introversive inability to gratify their needs." However, when given the opportunity to disavow hostility and psychopathology on objective testing (the Buss-Durkee Hostility Inventory and MMPI), individuals who are undergoing evaluation for alleged child sexual molestation and who deny the allegations also deny hostility and psychopathology (Wasyliw, Grossman, and Haywood, 1994). In a related finding, Haywood et al. (1996) reported that admitted noncleric child molesters "demonstrated more sociopathy and mental disorder in general while cleric offenders indicated more sexual conflictedness."

In a later work, Lothstein (2004) focusing on the evaluation and treatment of sexually abusing priests, described findings relevant to the question of personality organization, findings apparently based upon a variety of clinical data, including those derived from the administration of the Millon Multiaxial Clinical Inventory-III (MMCI-III)—an objective psychological test focusing on the assessment of personality traits and disorders. He reported that the individuals in his sample of abuser priests could be viewed as falling into three groups of personality organizations, as categorized in DSM-IV (American Psychiatric Association, 1994). The largest group includes individuals with dependent, avoidant, or obsessive personality disorders, all of which involve, to some degree, the need to be perceived as socially desirable and the need for approval and acceptance. He portrayed these priests as "naïve and socially immature" and as individuals who sought in a church vocation gratification of their need to be "idealized, admired, and loved"—characteristics often attributed to narcissistic individuals.

Lothstein also described a smaller number of priests from his sample as having more primitive personality organizations, including antisocial, narcissistic, borderline, and histrionic personality disorders. Individuals with these personality traits, depending on the admixture, can be exploitative, extremely manipulative, charismatic, and/or grandiose, with intense needs to be admired and loved. Individuals with these personality organizations have been found by other researchers to represent a significant subgroup of people in a variety of professions who have violated professional boundaries through exploitative sexual relationships (Garfinkel et al., 1997; and Celenza, 2004).

Bryant (2002) supports Lothstein's findings by emphasizing that, despite their "apparent normality … many priest offenders have traits consistent with narcissism or dependent personality disorders." Fagan et al. (2002) in a review of the literature on pedophilia across the general population, reported findings (by Raymond et al., 1999) that "sixty percent of their sample of sex offenders met the criterion for personality disorders," lending additional support to Lothstein's and Bryant's observations. The Raymond et al. review revealed that these personality disorders included obsessive-compulsive (25%), antisocial (22.5%), narcissistic (20%), and avoidant (20%) behaviors. Fagan et al. emphasized, contrary to Bryant, the relatively *small* proportion of pedophile sex offenders diagnosed as having narcissistic personality disorders.

The last subgroup described by Lothstein, the smallest in size, included individuals with paranoid, schizoid, and schizotypal features or disorders. According to Lothstein, these men were often very limited in their interpersonal functioning, were quite isolated, and had primitive sexual and/or aggressive fantasies. All of these priests, by his account, "were very negativistic and compulsive and had angry irritable depressions."

Finally, while direct references to the significance of identity problems among priests who sexually exploit male minors are rare, some of the characteristics discussed here can be understood as manifestations of identity disturbances (e.g., sexual orientation confusion). A recent attempt to explore whether pedophiles have a "weaker identity structure" than nonsexual offenders, using the Rorschach, MMPI-2, and the Ego Identity Scale (Tardi and Van Gijseghem, 2001), indicated that pedophiles who abused females and those who abused males both have "more fragile body image limits ... and present a higher level of social introversion than do nonsexual offenders." The latter finding is highly consistent with the multiple references to the social problems characteristic of many priests who sexualize children. Tardi and Van Gijseghem also found that pedophiles who abused males "have a weaker ego (Es scale) than do pedophiles who abused females and nonsexual offenders." If these findings are replicated and confirmed clinically, they would also point to the greater vulnerability of such priests to experience stressful life events more negatively than individuals with higher levels of ego identity, a finding described by Sammon et al. (1985) in a study of the psychosocial development and perceptions of stressful life events of a general sample of Roman Catholic "religious professional men."

To summarize, clinicians who have had considerable experience in evaluating and treating priests who sexualize male minors agree that on the surface these priests appear to be similar in many ways to their peers who do not. On deeper examination, however, certain common observations and hypotheses emerge: (a) priests who sexualize minors have clearly preferred pubescent or postpubescent male minors–not prepubescent boys or girls; (b) many of these priests have themselves been subjected to premature sexual interactions with an adult as minors, which can promote certain psychodynamic processes and defensive operations, especially repetition compulsions and identification with the aggressor, phenomena often seen in people who sexually abuse minors; (c) these offending priests often display social-skill deficits or social "immaturity," with associated inadequate object relationships; and (d) they often show evidence of various disturbances in psychosexual development, including sexual orientation confusion, heterosexual inhibition or blockage, or deficits in "sexual knowledge."

With regard to commonly occurring personality disorders, in their evaluations and treatment of offending priests the clinicians whose work we have cited have noted those involving passivity, dependence, and narcissism.

NARCISSISM IN INDIVIDUAL PRIESTS AND IN CLERICAL CULTURE: SOME OBSERVATIONS FROM CLINICAL PRACTICE

As described in Kochansky and Herrmann (2004), a significant number of the seminarians and priests treated by Dr. Kochansky in psychotherapy—whatever their personality organizations, symptoms, or diagnoses—presented with personality features and psychodynamics associated with significant narcissistic wounds and vulnerabilities resulting in insufficient levels, or an instability, of self-esteem. The majority of this subgroup of clerical patients struggled with self-representations/self-images marked by very negative components and associated negative affective states. They tended to view themselves as inadequate or critically defective, despite their various abilities and talents, and often struggled with self-perceptions (sometimes primitively elaborated in more or less accessible negative fantasies) that evoked distressing levels of shame, anxiety (including exaggerated fear of being embarrassed or humiliated), depressive affects, or various combinations of these emotions. As is characteristic of persons with narcissistic personality organizations or traits, these men were hypersensitive to even mild criticism, which often left "them feeling humiliated, degraded, hollow, and empty" and/or led to aggressive postures masked by "an appearance of humility" (p. 302).

The affect of shame—which differs from guilt in that its focus is the self rather than others—is central to the problem of narcissism and to *perfectionism,* a related phenomenon. In their study, Kochansky and Herrmann focused on how the role of the ego ideal, as described by Freud (1914) and later by Gabbard (2000), in *prescribing* what one should be stands out as critically important in the emotional functioning of many men in "formation" for priesthood or already ordained as priests: those who experience themselves as failing to live up to their internalized standards or "narcissistic aspirations," as described by Bibring (1953), struggle with a sense of themselves as defective and inferior and with the resulting painful affect of shame. The authors proposed that this subgroup of narcissistically fragile individuals can be viewed as "failed narcissists," in that they are unable to mobilize or sustain narcissistic defenses (self-idealization, devaluation of others, etc.) despite chronic and intense longings to achieve perfection and superiority, to be perceived and treated as special, and to be admired by all. Unable to achieve these intrapsychic and social states, they instead are often plagued by varying degrees of anxiety, depression, and envy of others.

A smaller group of seminarians and priests who had been in treatment for a variety of reasons but also shared narcissistic personality features might, the authors suggested, be classified as "grandiose narcissists." These men, consistent with DSM-IV descriptions and with Sipe's (1990) description of priests with these traits, lack the virtue of humility held as an ideal by the church, and instead have inflated self-representations, crave admiration, and lack empathy. Their sense of specialness and entitlement can promote the exploitation of others. And, "while feelings of inadequacy, defectiveness, and low self-esteem ... are usually kept at bay by this kind of defensive grandiosity, these defenses can be unstable, and the individual may periodically feel a sense of emptiness, and/or waves of self doubt and humiliation" (Kochansky & Herrmann, 2004).

FAMILY PATTERNS: THE IDEALIZING MOTHER AND THE ABSENT OR SCORNFUL FATHER

In the course of the treatment of seminarians and priests with these narcissistic character features or full-blown disorders, Kochansky and Herrmann reported certain family themes and patterns emerged in their histories. These involved relatively repressive parental attitudes toward sexual and aggressive impulses as well as developmental experiences in childhood and adolescence that involved painful narcissistic injuries with consequent damage to the child's evolving self-image and capacity to establish and maintain adequate levels of self-esteem.

In many cases, while the mothers of these men idealized their sons, promoting inflated self-representations, these self-representations were simultaneously "under attack" and frequently deflated and/or rendered unstable by their fathers, through excessive, sometimes sadistic criticism, direct rejection, or more subtle disengagement for a variety of what the fathers perceived as their sons' shortcomings, often including the child's being insufficiently masculine or even effeminate. The mothers of these boys, in turn, often felt and conveyed disappointment in their husbands, whom they portrayed as emotionally distant and insensitive and/or weak, and they often sought and established a special, sometimes relatively overtly eroticized closeness with their sons, a closeness which they tacitly or manifestly conveyed had to be concealed from the husbands/fathers. Peers often responded to these children in ways that reenacted their fathers' negative responses to them, promoting a sense of isolation and loneliness, thereby reinforcing feelings of deficiency and defectiveness or inadequacy. Boys from families like these who later went on to pursue the priesthood often found in the church, through parish youth groups and the benevolent attentions of their pastors, a haven extending their mothers' protective affective envelope and countering the sense of painful distance, passive neglect, and/or direct hostility they experienced in their interactions with fathers and peers.

These kinds of experiences in childhood and adolescence, in various combinations, can interfere with the development of the ability to experience empathy and the capacity to establish and maintain mature and satisfying relationships with others. Kochansky and Herrmann hypothesized that individuals raised in families that exhibit these dynamics "may be drawn to the priesthood to counter or neutralize feelings of inadequacy, impotence, and inferiority through a social role that allows them instead to feel superior, special, admired, and powerful" (p. 302), feelings that they did experience at some level, however inconsistently, through their attachments to their mothers. This conclusion is consistent with the formulations of Meloy (1986), who proposed "that narcissistic character disorders are prevalent among members of the clergy precisely because the profession provides strong reinforcement for such personality problems," and with those of Celenza (2004), who has been impressed in her clinical work with clergy who have engaged in sexual misconduct by the ways in which the hierarchy of the Catholic Church and the demand for celibacy "can offer pathological solutions for [people with] problems with sexuality, power, and narcissistic vulnerability."

With regard to the role of the father, some of the potential negative consequences of unavailable effective paternal authority in a family have been described by Herzog (2004), a child psychoanalyst who theorized that "narcissistic pathology featuring perverse sexuality" may result from that absence, especially if it is the result of a relationship between parents in which a boy's mother demeans her husband and his authority. This family pattern can promote the development of an arrogance which impairs the boy's—and later the man's—relationships with others. Rather than relating to others with empathy and mutuality, the need to control others will prevail. And it is relevant to our main topic that the possibility of gratifying this need is clearly greater when a man—empowered by the special role of the priest as mediator between the human and divine—attends to the needs of an adolescent who may have experienced parallel deficits in his own life than it is likely to be in relationships with well-functioning, autonomous adult men or women.

While the Church can gratify some of the defensive needs of narcissistically vulnerable priests, it often paradoxically reinforces some of their critical deficits as well. For many years, for example, seminarians were warned against developing "particular friendships" or "PFs." They were instead encouraged to respond to all of their peers with equal interest and affection. While based at one level upon the ideal of being fully available to, if not loving toward, all people, this unrealistic expectation was also an attempt to limit the possibility of homosexual interactions among seminarians. Apparently abandoned as an explicit seminary policy, it has endured covertly and continues to limit the opportunities for seminarians to form and sustain gratifying close attachments with *age-appropriate peers.*

In a similar manner, certain demands of the institutional Church, such as the promise of celibacy, reinforce the preexisting and longstanding oedipal bond with their mothers that characterizes a certain subgroup of priests. Informal practices function similarly, as in a previously described tradition (also abandoned) in which the mother of a priest was presented with the anointed linen with which her son's hands had been wrapped during ordination, a memento she would literally take with her to the grave and which would help ensure her entry into heaven (Kochansky & Herrmann, 2004). More recently, a priest–patient reported to Kochansky that in the past some mothers of men about to be ordained would present their sons with diamonds from their engagement rings, which could then be set in the chalices to be used for priestly functions. This patient exclaimed that he "couldn't imagine accepting this kind of chalice and then having to repeatedly 'take my mother' to the altar!'"

SOME FORMULATIONS ABOUT THE PSYCHODYNAMICS OF EPHEBOPHILE PRIESTS

Although there are great variations in developmentally significant occurrences in their early lives as men with histories of erotic attachments to adolescent boys, the extensive experience of Cohen and his colleagues in evaluating and treating such men reveal some familial patterns that have occurred in the lives of most, if not all, such men—familial experiences remarkably similar to those observed by Kochansky in the priests previously described. Cohen and his colleagues (Seghorn, Cohen, and Prentky, 1984; Cohen and Seghorn, 1987; Cohen et al., 1969, 1971; Seghorn and Cohen, 1980) have found that men with tendencies toward or histories of erotic attachments to adolescent boys report growing up in families that involve an essentially loving, admiring mother and a relatively absent father. The father may or may not have been physically absent, but was unresponsive to the needs of his son at significant points in early childhood—needs of the child for acknowledgment, warmth, attention, admiration, and love. This absence, never fully grieved, continues to be hungered for throughout the adult's relationships with men, and plays a major role in the sexual attachment to adolescent boys. This unmet longing then contributes to further deficit. The present but "absent" father is disabling to the development of a healthy resolution of the mother-father-son triangle (the oedipal phenomenon), which would have the son, in early childhood, begin to identify with the father on the road to developing into an adult male. What seems to occur instead with men who later become erotically attracted to adolescent boys is that parts of the child extend into adulthood—the legacy of unfulfilled longings.

The combined clinical experience of the authors of this chapter leads us to hypothesize that, along with the profound spiritual sense of a religious calling, for some the decision to become a priest may be further motivated by the centrality of the concept of "father," in both self and object spheres, in the institutional Church and its priests, thereby providing an opportunity for filling this developmental gap. The longing for the love and approval of a benevolent father may be at least partially gratified at relatively direct intraspsychic levels in a seminarian's relationships with priests during formation, and later by fellow priests and superiors (pastors, rectors, bishops, etc.) who may treat them with warm paternalism once ordained. One priest-patient in Kochansky's practice stated in a matter-of-fact manner that men who seek the priesthood are often escaping from their fathers' (controlling, aggressive) arms (when their fathers were engaged enough for that degree of connection) with the hope of being embraced by more loving fathers in seminary and after ordination.

Through more indirect and complex psychodynamic processes, the emotional function of the "father" for ephebophile priests in particular (though it may also be a factor in the behavior of noncleric offenders) is evident in the definite paternal quality of some of their eroticized interactions with adolescent boys, interactions that go beyond serving purely manipulative ends. The ephebophile often teaches the adolescent about sex, about fellatio, and masturbation; shows him pornography to help explain sexual activity; and offers pictures of naked women to arouse sexual feelings and to focus on sexual anatomy. Within all of this, through unconscious identification with the boy, the adult is living out conscious and unconscious fantasies regarding his own father. On the one hand, there is the experience of "I am caring for you, being with you, giving to you, as you wish and need your father to be and do." On the other hand, there is the experience of "I am (he is) giving you (me) that caring which you (I) long for and never fully obtained from your (my) father while you were (I was) growing up."

Another aspect of this kind of identification is seen in the features, character, and behavior of the adolescents who are selected for sexual involvement. Not just in ephebophilia, but in all of the paraphilias, there are very precise attributes that must be present in the object (or person) in order for sexual excitement to occur. For the shoe fetishist, the shoe must have a certain type of heel and must be of a specific color and shape. For the sadomasochist, the belt must be a chain or of leather and the wielder must have a particular facial sneer or vicious look. For men who sexualize boys, the boy must have a particular body shape, a certain personality, or special mannerisms in order to serve as a representation either of the self as perceived or an idealized self. The boy that is sought out must be an available source for identification. To further this identification, the adult may claim an absence of his own sexual excitement, needs, or demands. The message is: "We are not doing this because of any sexual desires that I have but because of my desire to be of help to you in learning about sexuality."

In addition, in this kind of relationship there is no conscious experience of exploitation on the part of the man of the power of his status as an adult or of the even greater power of the priesthood, although each is made use of in the solicitation and the sexual behavior. The internal defense against these factors is reflected in urging the adolescent, "And do not tell anyone of what *we* are doing, of the different things *we* do. This is *our* secret. We must keep this to *ourselves.*" This is clearly an effort to create equality, mutuality, or sharing between the adult and the adolescent boy. However, contained within this effort, at a somewhat conscious level, but mostly unconscious, there is an erotic identification on the part of the adult with the boy's awe, sense of dependence, and the need for adoration, to be desired, to be wanted. The use of the phrase "our secret" severs the boy from his parents, especially from the actual father, since the relationship is between an adult male (an alternate father) and a boy. There is also an enactment here of the ephebophile's unconscious rage at his own father for his withholding, extended to the larger "family." This perhaps gives particular meaning to the reports of instances in which adolescents were molested by priests in their family homes, after being enticed to go into a playroom or the boy's bedroom for sexual play.

In normal development, in adolescence the objects of sexual fantasies frequently involve boys as well as girls. In the ephebophile, however, in part through the processes of unfulfilled longings, the fixation of some structures of the self as child, and an identification with children in his surround, these sexual fantasies include younger boys as well as peers. For a variety of reasons related to social and cultural factors, and because of the problems these men had in adolescence in the formation of peer relationships where some of these feelings could be talked about, the conflicts associated with these desires had to be actively denied conscious reflection. It is our clinical judgment that for some of these men who eventually entered the priesthood—however sincere their religious commitment and scholastic calling may have been—their embrace of a vow of sexual abstinence was part of the effort to resolve such conflicts. Clearly, the priests who lived out their ephebophilic fantasies and desires failed in that effort.

We stated above that the typical ephebophile, with the exception of the perversion, is a relatively healthy person. He is not psychotic. And although he has some difficulties in forming close, intimate, connected relationships, and may therefore be somewhat asocial, he is not psychopathically *anti*social. Since he is fully aware of the social and legal unacceptability of his sexual behavior with adolescents, fully aware of society's and the Church's position on homosexuality, and fully aware of his own freely given promise or vow of sexual abstinence, how does he justify such explicit sexual behavior to himself? We believe that Freud's concept of *splitting* is most relevant here (Freud, 1940). He proposed that when there is a conflict between the demands of desire and the prohibitions of reality, some people take neither course, or rather take both courses simultaneously. He theorized that

> On the one hand, with the help of certain mechanisms, [the individual] rejects reality and refuses to accept any prohibition; on the other hand, in the same breath he recognizes the danger of reality, takes over the fear of that danger as a pathological symptom and tries to divest himself of the fear ... the instinct is allowed to retain its satisfaction and proper respect is shown to reality. (p. 275)

The ephebophile is then able to give direct expression to his sexual wishes while at the same time denying to himself that he is serving those wishes, bolstering that denial by maintaining to himself that what is happening is an educational service for the young boy.

There is no doubt that ephebophiles select boys to a far greater extent than they do girls. Our clinical theory does not attribute this to normal homosexuality. Most men (and women) who select someone of their same gender for the expression of their sexuality choose peers, just as most heterosexual men and women do. We have indicated above some of the meanings of the choice of adolescent boys as sexual objects—narcissistic injury, sustained grieving, and identification—but our clinical experience suggests an additional component, one involving the anxiety that many of these men experience in relation to the female body and the relationship of that unease to oedipal castration anxiety. (In fact, traditional psychoanalytic theory proposed that castration anxiety was central to *all* of the perversions [Fenichel, 1945]).

With some of these clinical theoretical formulations in mind, we have chosen the case presented below as an illustration of many of the characteristics of men who have erotic attachments to adolescent boys as we have described those characteristics in this paper. The individual in question is not a priest, but his spiritual beliefs, his commitment to the Catholic Church, his work within the Church, and his sexualization of the young parishioners under his supervision all parallel, in very specific ways, the emotional and psychological factors seen in the behavior of priests who molest minors.

AN ILLUSTRATIVE CASE

Mr. X was first seen when he was 33 years old and in prison awaiting trial on over a hundred counts of various charges involving his sexual activities with young adolescent boys. He was married, and had been so for over a year, but the sexual acts with the youngsters were the only interpersonal sexual life he had ever had. His marriage was—according to him, by mutual consent—asexual.

Mr. X had been a Catholic youth counselor at a Catholic Church in a small community in the Midwest. The sexuality involved exposing the boys to magazine and Internet pornography, separate and mutual masturbation, and fellatio (as both the performer and the recipient). Although there were many occasions when these acts took place with just one boy in his office at the church or in his home, the largest number of events took place in more public settings at a local athletic center—the pool, the tennis court, the exercise room—with small groups of boys. In all instances, the intent, as expressed to the children, was his effort as a counselor to teach them about sexuality.

Despite the fact that there was some conscious awareness on Mr. X's part that adolescent boys were the sole objects of his sexual desires, he was able to deceive himself about the nature of his proclivities by convincing himself that he was in fact living out his role as counselor. Significantly, his behavior with the boys—his manner, his way of being—was not authoritarian. He was not "Mr. X" to them; he was "one of the boys," to such a degree that he was called "Dougie." This identification with the young boys, together with Mr. X's neutralization or effort at desexualization of his erotic feelings under the guise of "teaching," reflects what we have described above as one of the dynamics often involved in ephebophilia: an attempt to satisfy an unfulfilled longing for love and closeness with the father.

Unconscious castration anxiety, another dynamic we have found to be characteristic of ephebophiles, was represented in Mr. X's case in a number of ways: in an intense involvement in neatness, cleanliness, and orderliness in his immediate surround; in an inhibition in all forms of intimate relations with women—no touching, fondling, or sexual intercourse with women; and in the peculiarities of his attachment to young boys. Regarding the latter, from early adulthood, Mr. X had been obsessively attentive to the bodies of young boys. He had loose-leaf folders containing hundreds of names of boys with whom he was acquainted through his meeting with them at the athletic center. For each boy on the list there was a description of the size and attractiveness of his penis and a statement about aspects of his personality. Mr. X also kept folders with many hundreds of photographs from magazines, books, newspapers, and medical journals of boys of all ages, from infancy to adolescence, who were seriously deformed—disabled or disfigured—in multiple ways. These were kept hidden and secret, secret to the extent that their disclosure came not from him to his clinician, but from the prosecution at his trial.

Although the content of the lists and the collecting was unknown to others, within the family Mr. X was described as being "so much like his mother" in his collecting of things and making of lists, and in his maintaining of objects even when they were no longer needed or part of his daily life. And indeed he reported that during his childhood he'd had a much closer and more intimate relationship with his mother than he had with his father.

In regard to his sexual behavior with boys, Mr. X stated that this had begun only three years before his arrest. Although the storm of publicity in his small community following his arrest led to many youngsters coming forward with reports of having been involved in some of the sexual episodes, none gave dates prior to three years before. Therefore, we can hypothesize that it may well be that the overt expression of his erotic attachment occurred only after the formation of his relationship with his future wife—that is, as an expression of defense against the sexual woman and her genitals.

FINAL REFLECTIONS

With regard to ephebophiles in general and priests who sexually abuse minors in particular, our independent observations and formulations as clinicians and illustrated in the case of Mr. X, point to the developmental role in the histories of these men of inordinately intense, not infrequently eroticized, maternal attachment combined with painful paternal deprivations involving emotional rejection through a father's distancing and/or devaluation of his son. We hypothesize that this pattern of relationship between a boy and his parents often results in narcissistic vulnerabilities and defenses involving unrealistic self-representations and an instability of self-esteem, with underlying feelings of inferiority, defect, and shame, and longings to achieve and maintain a sense of specialness and superiority.

This family pattern, we believe, also obstructs the development of the son's capacity to form comfortable and gratifying intimate relationships with women. Such relationships can evoke intense anxiety associated with oedipal threats, including castration anxiety. In addition to being beset with powerful longings for the warmth, admiration, and love of paternal figures, men who have this kind of history within a family may seek a resolution of those longings in the priesthood—under the mentorship of "Fathers" and as "Fathers" themselves. And for some of these men, identification and other mechanisms result in eroticized relationships with pubescent and postpubescent boys, many of whom may themselves have suffered from deficient relationships with their own fathers. These attachments—which ephebophile priests often view as purely benevolent while denying the power inequities and their own sexual and aggressive motives—also protect the instigators from the risk of being exposed as inadequate in intimate relationships with peers.

While other psychological factors surely are associated with the sexualization of minors, we have concluded that the narcissistic and oedipal factors described in this chapter can produce vulnerabilities and psychodynamics that significantly contribute to a tendency on the part of a small subgroup of priests to engage in sexual relationships with minors.

REFERENCES

American Psychiatric Association (1994), *Diagnostic and Statistical Manual of Mental Disorders* (4th ed.). Washington, DC: American Psychiatric Association.

Bibring, E. (1953), The mechanism of depression. In: *Affective Disorders,* ed. P. Greenacre. New York: Doubleday, pp. 13–48.

Bryant, C. (2002), Psychological treatment of priest sex offenders. *America*, April 1, pp. 14–17.

Celenza, A. (1998), Precursors to sexual misconduct: Preliminary findings. *Psychoanal. Psychol., 15*:378–395.

—— (2004), Sexual misconduct in the clergy: The search for the father. *Stud. in Gender & Sexual., 5*:213–232.

—— & Hilsenroth, M. (1997), A Rorschach investigation of sexualized dual relationships. *Bull. Menn. Clin., 61*:1–20.

Cohen, M. L., Garofalo, R., Boucher, R. & Seghorn, T. K. (1971), The psychology of the rapist. *Semin. Psychiatry, 3*:307–327.

Cohen, M. L. & Seghorn, T. K. (1987), *Sexualization of the Child and the Intactness of the Family*. New England Medical Center, Department of Psychiatry, Boston, Massachusetts, May 8.

Cohen, M. L., Seghorn, T. K. & Calmas, W. (1969), Sociometric study of the sex offender. *J. Abnormal Psychol., 74*:249–255.

Exner, J. (1993), *The Rorschach: A comprehensive system, Vol. I, Basic Foundations*. New York: Wiley.

Fagan, P., Wise, T., Schmidt, C. & Berlin, F. (2002), Pedophilia. *J. Amer. Med. Assoc., 288*:2458–2465.

Fenichel, O. (1945), *The Psychoanalytic Theory of the Neuroses*. New York: Norton.

Freud, A. (1937). The ego and the mechanisms of defense. London: Hogarth Press, 1962.

Freud, S. (1914), On narcissism: An introduction. *Standard Edition, 14*:67–102. London: Hogarth Press, 1957.

—— (1921), *Beyond the Pleasure Principle*. Standard Edition, Vol. XVIII:7–64. London: Hogarth Press, 1955.

—— (1940). Splitting of the ego in the process of defense. *Standard Edition, 23*:275–278. London: Hogarth Press, 1964.

Gabbard, G. (2000), Theories of personality and psychopathology: Psychoanalysis. In: *Kaplan and Sadok's comprehensive Textbook of Psychiatry, Vol. I* (7th ed.), ed. B. J. Sadok & V. A. Sadok. Philadelphia, PA: Lippincott Williams and Wilkins, pp. 563–607.

Gacano, C., Meloy, R. & Bridges, M. (2000), A Rorchach comparison of psychopaths, sexual homicide perpetrators, and nonviolent pedophiles: Where angels fear to tread. *J. Clin. Psychol.*, 56:757–777.

Garfinkel, P., Bagby, R., Waring, E. & Dorian, B. (1997), Boundary violations and personality traits among psychiatrists. *Canad. J. Psychiat.*, 42:758–763.

Haywood, T., Kravitz, H., Grossman, L., Wasyliw, O. & Hardy, D. (1996), Psychological aspects of sexual functioning among cleric and noncleric sex offenders. *Child Abuse & Neglect*, 20:527–536.

Herzog, J. (2004), Father hunger and narcissistic deformation. *Psychoanal. Quart.*, 73:893–914.

Kochansky, G. E. & Herrmann, F. (2004), Shame and scandal: Clinical and canon law perspectives on the crisis in priesthood. *International Journal of Law and Psychiatry*, 27:299–319.

Lothstein, L. (1994), Psychological theories of pedophilia and ephebophilia. In: *Slayer of the Soul*, ed. S. Rossetti. Mystic, CT: Twenty-Third Publications, pp. 19–43.

——— (2004), Men of the flesh: The evaluation and treatment of sexually abusing priests. *Stud. in Gender & Sexual.*, 5:167–195.

Meloy, R. (1986), Narcissistic psychopathology and the clergy. *J. Pastoral Psychol.*, 35:50–55.

Prentky, R., Knight, R. & Lee, A. (1997), Risk factors associated with recidivism among extrafamilial child molesters. *J. Consult. & Clin. Psychol.*, 65:141–149.

Raymond, N., Coleman, E., Ohierking, F., Christensen, G. & Miner, M. (1999), Psychiatric Comorbidity in pedophilic sex offenders. *Amer. J. Psychiat.*, 156:786–788.

Research Staff (2004), Summary Report: the Nature and Scope of the Problem of Sexual Abuse of Minors by Catholic Priests and Deacons in the United States. *Study commissioned by the Review Board for the Protection of Children and Young People of the United States Conference of Catholic Bishops.*

Rossetti, S. (1994), *Slayer of the Soul*. Mystic, CT: Twenty-Third Publications.

——— (1996), *A tragic grace*. Collegeville, MN: The Liturgical Press.

Sammon, S., Reznikoff, M. & Geisinger, K. (1985), Psychosocial development and stressful life events among religious professionals. *J. Personal. & Social Psychol.*, 48:676–687.

Seghorn, T. K. & Cohen, M. L. (1980), The psychology of rape assailant. In: *Modern Legal Medicine, Psychiatry and Forensic Science*, ed. W. Curran, A. Louis McGarry & C. S. Petty. Philadelphia: F. A. Davis Company.

Seghorn, T., Cohen, M. & Prentky, R. (1984), Development of a rational taxonomy for the classification of child molesters. Presented at the Third National Conference on Sexual Victimization of Children.

Sipe, A. (1990), *A Secret World: Sexuality and the Search for Celibacy*. New York: Brunner/Mazel.

Tardi, M. & Van Gijseghem, H. (2001), Do pedophiles have a weaker identity structure compared with nonsexual offenders? *Child Abuse & Neglect, 25*:1381–1394.

Wasyliw, O. E., Benn, A. F., Grossman, L. S. & Haywood, T. W. (1998), Detection of minimilization of psychopathology on the Rorschach in cleric and non-cleric alleged sex offenders. *Assessment, 5*:389–397.

Wasyliw, O., Grossman, L. & Haywood, T. (1994), Denial of hostility and psychopathology in the evaluation of child molesters. *J. Personal. Assess., 63*:185–190.

4

A Love Addiction: Psychoanalytic Psychotherapy with an Offending Priest

Andrea Celenza

The helping professions do not lack for wounded healers. This may be especially so for clergy, whose spiritual calling is based on the search for a mysterious, unseen, intangible reality. Such a calling requires a perseverance that is, for some, only sustainable when derived from profound, unmet need.

The following is a composite case constructed from several psychoanalytically-oriented psychotherapies that I have conducted with Christian or Catholic priests. None are pedophile predators. I present this composite to illustrate a more common type of exploitation (see Celenza, 2004), that being sexual misconduct in the context of an intense "love" affair with a parishioner. The essence of the misconduct derives from the asymmetric power distribution in the relationship and the priest's opportunity to exploit that imbalance.

Fr. J, a priest in his 60s, came to his first session stating that he is a sex addict. I noted the obvious irony of his self-description com-

ing from an avowed celibate, and I speculated that his vow probably arose as a desperate attempt to control a voracious and
repugnant (to him) appetite, an attempt to erect external fences
where internal controls were weak. But that was before I knew
what he meant by addiction and, indeed, before I knew what he
meant by sex.

In our initial meeting, Fr. J spoke of the extensive support system
that Sex/Love Addicts Anonymous (SLAA) provided him and wondered if my psychoanalytic treatment would be compatible with it. I
wondered the same thing, knowing that part of my goal was to help
him become more tolerant of his desire, to do this on both emotional
and intellectual levels, and hopefully, on a spiritual plane as well. I
knew the addiction model included a more prohibitory approach;
triggers were to be avoided and controlled rather than explored and
mined for meaning. We wondered together if his sponsor and I
would be working at cross purposes.

Fr. J told me he assiduously followed the 12-step program and was
wholly committed to the addiction model. He was worried that our
psychoanalytic treatment might loosen his moorings and sever as
well his ties to his much needed sponsor and support groups in favor
of a wholesale commitment *to me*. At this time, he had been immersed in the SLAA network for over a year and—beyond having
made much progress in his "sex addiction,"—he felt a deep bond
with other addicts, especially with his sponsor whom he could not
imagine living without.

I noted his either/or way of constructing our project and wondered if his assumption that I would require total and insular dedi-
cation had something to do with his sex addiction. I wondered if
he enslaved himself to a love object who might deprive him of
needed nutrients, requiring him to plunge into oceanic depths
and ultimately deprive him of air. I told him there was no need for
him to sever his ties to these important sources of support; I
hoped our work would add to his internal strength, not become
another form of deprivation. We would figure out a way to combine our efforts—and I sensed new areas of learning in this for me
as well.

SEX ADDICTION?

Fr. J told me that his sex addiction consisted of a series of relationships with women after he had been ordained. Though all were adults and some were married, most of them were parishioners when they met. He was monogamous when involved with each of these women and celibate in between. A few of these relationships lasted for several years. He said he had been unable to be celibate for more than a year at a time. He always prompted the ending of the relationship when the collision between his vow of celibacy and his commitment to the woman became intolerable. At these times, he would be overcome with guilt and increasingly more convinced that God would punish him for his infidelity to Him. He feared God might cause the end of the relationship with the woman (either she would reject him or God would bring about her death) or would condemn Fr. J's love for her and reject him.

Fr. J told me that he did not seek out these relationships; each one had been instigated by the woman. I was relieved when he added, "I know I am responsible no matter who initiates the relationship and that it is expectable that parishioners will idealize me or whomever is their pastor. So I am not holding them responsible." (With this statement, my picture of our work together took a giant leap forward.) He then added, "But I am unable to say 'no' to anyone who wants me in any way."

Fr. J said that with the help of his SLAA program he was trying a new tack toward celibacy that seemed to be working best for him. He was trying not to masturbate at all and had not even had an erection in over a year. He told me that he had tried other ways of maintaining celibacy in the past that had obviously failed. One included allowing himself to masturbate whenever he felt the need, but he found that when he did this his fantasies fed on themselves and his desire only increased to the point that he was masturbating "all the time." Feeling suddenly plunged into a Woody Allen movie, I asked him what he meant by "all the time." I am glad I asked, recalling that scene from the film *Annie Hall*—three times a week is either "all the time" or "hardly ever" depending on the person. He explained that during this time of free masturbation, he found himself going at it as much as once a month.

I commented that I didn't think masturbating at that frequency qualified as addictive behavior. He responded, "I guess it's not sex I'm addicted to, it's love" to which I responded, "Aren't we all?"

EMPATHY AS A DEFENSE

I knew at this point it was time I heard more about Fr. J's past. I was not surprised when he reported that he had not had a sexual relationship until he was in his late 20s. He considered himself totally repressed as a child and adolescent, then paused, stating there would be more to tell at some future point. I slowly nodded, letting him know that he was free to take his time.

Fr. J recounted his history with great compassion for those who had been cruel to him. He told me he thought his mother was a trauma victim—he didn't know the nature of the trauma because she was unable to talk about it, but he suspected she was abused as a child, at least physically and probably sexually too. He knew stories about her family from his father, who had told him that they were a mean bunch and did not deserve to know him. These meager comments were all he knew and were revealed only when Fr. J asked his father why his maternal grandparents never visited. Otherwise, there was a strict code of silence about them.

Fr. J's suspicions of abuse on the maternal side of his family made sense to me, but I was aware that I was learning more about his family and, in particular, his mother than I was about *him*. He had yet to make a single statement from his own subjective standpoint. I shared this impression with him and he said his mother had always been remote, even cold, toward him. She was unable to cuddle or hold him when he was young. He has no memories of being hugged or held on his mother's lap. (I am convinced now, after knowing him for over five years, that this is not a memory lapse or repression, but is a fact of his history.) He explained, again from her point of view, that her unaffectionate, emotional unavailability resulted from her trauma, making her "emotionally frozen."

I asked, "And you?" He became tearful and said he had a bottomless need for approval and felt in some basic way that he was unlovable except by God. He said this is a lifelong, deep wound. He stated, "I have the irrational sense that I do not have equal rights." Referring to his diocesan order, he said, "I feel like I joined a group that on some level I don't feel good enough to be a part of." We discussed his use of empathy for others as a defense against his own trauma and feelings of exclusion. I saw the treatment as a process where he might develop greater empathy for himself, in other words, a more elaborated internal experience derived from his own subjectivity.

THE MOTHER OR THE FATHER

Fr. J's recounting of his childhood history did not reference his father beyond stating that he was a distant figure in his life. In this way, his father's influence was conspicuous by its absence. Getting caught up in Fr. J's apparent but denied pain from his mother's unavailability caused a temporary blind spot in my own radar, so at first I did not particularly notice the absence of paternal images in Fr. J's recounting. (Interestingly, aspects of Fr. J's family history are consistent with the common findings in priests who have sexualized male minors—see Kochansky & Cohen, this volume).

Fr. J also related that he had had a homosexual relationship in his adolescence, adding that he has never before spoken of it. Though he knew it was not uncommon for men to have such experiences, especially in adolescence, his memory of the incident was fraught with profound anxiety and guilt. After all, he said, *the relationship involved a priest in his neighborhood church.*

Fr. J was an altar boy. One day, after Mass, while they were disrobing, the priest stood before him with an erect penis and guided Fr. J's hands to bring him to orgasm. Not a word was spoken and there was a tacit agreement that they would continue in this way, after Mass, each week.

Fr. J does not remember thinking about what was happening at the time, only that he felt like something was "coming over him" (his words). A baptismal image came to me. Fr. J felt no choice in the matter and never consciously thought about it between incidents. He realizes in retrospect, however, that a pit of dread was growing in his body, coincident with his sexual desire. As we explored his memories and feelings, it became clear to us that he would enter a dissociated state and relegate these experiences to a "not me" category in his mind.

The abuse thus became split off from Fr. J's conscious self-experience and identity, although it contributed greatly to an unconscious self-contempt and the conviction that he was evil. He came to see that he had gotten caught up in a vicious cycle of cleansing, sinning, and needing to be cleansed again. He felt drawn to the abuse because he was, at bottom, a sinner (defined simply by having sexual desire). The masturbation was enticing, gratifying, but then immediately repugnant, so that he needed to be cleansed by it in this quasi-purifying, baptismal rite—the ejaculate represented staining/cleansing, holy/evil water. Yet this very same cleansing ritual ignited his desire to sin again. All of this became entangled with his sexual longing, his need for love, his need for paternal approval, his masculine identity, and finally, his spirituality.

During our treatment, Fr. J gained greater access to the memories and feelings surrounding this relationship. I noticed and repeatedly interpreted his tendency to attribute all the evil and aggression to himself while absolving the priest of any trace of exploitation, sin, or corruption. Fr. J became more comfortable holding his aggression and seeing the abuse for what it was. He realized that the relationship with this priest was completely one-sided; it was always the priest's sexual pleasure that was the focus. Fr. J remembered that he would become aroused, would masturbate later, privately, and then would be overcome with shame and homosexual anxiety. Not surprisingly, severe doubts about his masculinity became a constant preoccupation and internal battle. We surmised that his seduction of women functioned, in part, as a reassurance that he was not gay.

BETTER A CRUEL GOD THAN THE DEVIL

I asked Fr. J his thoughts about this priest in light of the current crisis in the Catholic Church. True to his style, Fr. J said he knew this priest was a trauma victim himself and understood that he needed to repeat the act to master his own feelings of exploitation and subjugation. He added that he welcomed the notoriety of the current crisis in the Catholic Church, although it was painful. He saw it as a much-needed penance for all Catholic priests that would result in cleansing the church.

Fr. J's psychologically informed explanation of the priest's psychology, the predator who was excused as a trauma victim himself, was a familiar defense. His defensive use of empathy was something we had recognized and discussed before. But I was beginning to see this as an occupational hazard for me too; the valorization of empathic understanding of the other's subjective position could serve to sidestep my holding the other responsible and to see them as agentic.

By circumventing my own subjectivity, I saw how my psychoanalytically honed ear was primed to hear the experience of the other, and to experience myself from the other's point of view. While empathic attunement is essential to clinical work, I came to see it as overriding too easily my immediate, subjective, momentarily *"self-centered"* position. This made it difficult for me to see—and to help Fr. J see and own—his sexually predatory impulses and behavior, and to recognize his own aggression.

I realized Fr. J and I were in this together—it was a mutual blind spot that I, of course, identified first in him. I said, "But what about *you?* He did this *to you!"* I realized that there was vehemence in my tone and I was anything but evenhanded. Fr. J restated, "I forgive him. He didn't know what he was doing," and I heard the echo of Jesus's statement on the cross, "Forgive them, Father, for they know not what they do."

I have always loved what Jesus said on the cross, considering it the finest example of Christian belief. At this point in Fr. J.'s treatment, however, the statement felt premature, indeed *pre-emptive*. I assumed he was defending against a murderous rage toward this priest; a rage he was then prone to act out predatorily, perhaps in a dissociated state. In order to protect this predatory priest and his own need to preserve a loving, paternal image of him, Fr. J unconsciously shifted his focus from subjective to objective positions, that is, from self/victim to other/victim. Avoidance of aggression once again masqueraded as empathy. In other words, Fr. J's statement, "He didn't know what he was doing" could be equally applied to himself. He did not want to recognize what he fundamentally wanted to do with this priest's penis and what he did do with the women he exploited.

Fr. J said he understood the logic of my reasoning, but he just did not see the priest as anything but a victim of his own trauma. I said, "You would rather live in a world with a cruel God than the devil." This became an idea we would consider and reconsider for some time; it revolved around the question of whether Fr. J could envision a world with evil in it, that is, in himself and in others.

LOVING OR BECOMING

A few years into our treatment, Fr. J remembered, or was able to admit to himself, that on one occasion he tried to put the priest's penis into his mouth. He didn't know why he had that urge and the priest would not allow him to continue, but the longing (at the time, frustration) to take in the phallus became an unbidden masturbatory fantasy that greatly frightened and disgusted Fr. J. He had no idea why he wanted to do this with such intensity and, prior to our treatment, was wholly absorbed in trying to prevent the thought, fantasy, and impulse from coming to the surface.

One day Fr. J verbalized that he always had trouble establishing a boundary between loving and becoming. He said he was afraid that the way he loved felt too much like taking over or being taken over. He continued that he always knew that he was so hungry, he would love someone so much that he could "gobble a woman up." We noted the oral destructive imagery. What was the desire to consume and destroy the woman? Did this desire reverse a desire to merge or be consumed? We wondered if his desire "to take in the phallus" reflected his desire to take in masculinity, to empower himself in a concrete way, and confirm himself as a man, to remain hard in relation to his hunger for the enticing but potentially consuming mothers. Being hard was his inoculation against being consumed by his own need or devoured by the other.

Fr. J noted that his life in the priesthood was a way to surround himself with brothers and fathers. He recognized a longing to be accepted by a father figure, yet felt he never achieved it in a lasting way: "Everyone is called father, never dad. There is no intimacy. I spend a lot of psychic energy trying to please father figures from this distance. I'm always saying to myself, 'I hope I'm doing this the way they want…. I hope this won't displease.' My sexual acting-out, in part, was a way to free myself. But something was going on between me and God because I sought this woman out in the first place. I was running away from God."

VICTIM OR PERPETRATOR

It is always difficult to access the part of the offender that is the perpetrator. Many treatments founder at this point or are prematurely terminated (even after years of very sound and beneficial work) when the treatment edges toward the patient's sadism or capacity for exploitation. It is ironic that this aspect of the treatment tends to come last despite the fact that the exploitation is the leading edge of what brings the patient to treatment in the first place. Yet there is no effective way of recognizing, accepting, and integrating "the perpetrator within" without first shoring up "the self as victim" and expanding the patient's capacity to empathize with those he himself has victimized.

For Fr. J it was not difficult to begin the treatment by helping him expand his empathy for those who had been hurt, including himself. His evident compassion for others as victims was near enough to the surface and was a central way he already organized his experience. But when his reflections later on suggested that *he* had hurt others, he would be drawn (defensively) to the cruelty he had wrought and become overwhelmed with self-criticism and guilt such that processing and owning his potential for sadism or exploitation became a self-victimizing vicious cycle that he could not, in the end, accept. (This, by the way, is a common iatrogenic by-product of confrontational treatment methods that attempt to "break down defenses of denial and resistance" without enhancing the patient's capacity to integrate such self-perceptions and empathize with himself or his victims. It is a last-resort measure often thought to be the only way to get at more sociopathic offenders who take little or no responsibility, but probably is more reflective of our own anger and frustration at their impermeability than a truly effective treatment strategy.)

Ultimately, a helpful dialectic was established in the treatment of Fr. J that captured the tension between victim and perpetrator in such a way that internally held each position. Fr. J would reflect on his past exploitation of women and grasp his use of them for his own purposes (an understanding derived from our previous work on his struggle with his sexual desires). He then would become appalled at his selfishness and cruelty, especially when he empathically resonated with their intense love for him. This capacity reflected his ability to empathize with their vulnerability, derived from his emerging capacity to identify with his own.

The other side of the dialectic revolved around Fr. J's ability to see his own cruelty that he directed toward himself. He would admonish himself for his sins, in effect using the recognition of his exploitation as a weapon against himself, thus furthering his conviction that he was evil at the core. He then began to recognize his self-condemnation and feel the profound ways in which he was enacting an unforgiving retribution against himself. He was gradually able to set this vicious cycle aside, resolving that he is neither powerful enough to totally condemn himself nor to fully transcend his desire to subjugate others to his own will.

A new relationship with his own omnipotence emerged that in some ways can be seen as mirroring the tension between the God of the Old Testament and the God of the New.

A NEW RESOLUTION

A female parishioner, Beth, approached Fr. J one day after Mass. He recognized Beth as a new member of the congregation. She said she was going through a divorce and teared up, saying she needed guidance and support. Fr. J felt an impulse to hug her, but he did not, knowing that this scenario had gotten him into trouble in the past. (Though hugging is an accepted practice upon leaving a service, Fr. J recognized that a hug in this context would be sexually tinged, at least for him, and would likely become the beginning of a seduction he would soon feel unable to control.)

Beth and Fr. J agreed to meet that afternoon in Fr. J's office. In the ensuing hours before the meeting, Fr. J felt a familiar feeling of anticipation mixed with anxiety, along with a temptation to dimly light the room and a hope that "something dramatic" would happen. He turned on all the lights and called his sponsor.

In the past, Fr. J would have eventually offered to counsel Beth, picturing himself as Christ the Savior, and setting himself up to be everything she could possibly need from anyone. On a more conscious level, he would rationalize that he was only trying to help her cope with her loneliness, hurt, and confusion. He now knew that he had been profoundly seduced by the omnipotent wish to be *the only man* who could heal her and within whom she would find the embodied God. He now said, "My purpose is to bring God to others, not *to be* God."

Fr. J also recognized that in the past he had been partly seduced by the love and acceptance he would feel from a woman like Beth. He succinctly stated, "The arms of a lover comprise a drug that kills the pain of being born under a dark cloud." He now felt more in control of, and less enslaved by, her passion for him. He felt he could maintain his commitment to other aspects of himself, including his own marriage to Christ, in the face of his longing to be loved by a woman. He recalled that in the past

> I was afraid to devote myself to a woman for fear I would lose her. This felt inevitable because she might leave me or she would eventually die. I believed God might kill her because he was angry with me for betraying him ... I decided to make God my primary love object ... He is always there. I am never alone.

When Beth finally arrived, she poignantly described her struggle to get back on her feet, both financially and emotionally, after her husband left. She told Fr. J her husband had been emotionally unavailable and abusive. She told him that she had been a victim of incest as a child. Fr. J was intensely moved by her suffering and felt a need to be generous with his time, compassion, and kindness; however, he was also aware that this was a "trigger" for him. He recognized her as the current embodiment of his "frozen mother" who was *becoming unfrozen*. He knew the seductive power of this long-held wish was almost irresistible. But the idea that his mother would unfreeze was only one wish; the more intense longing was the idea that it *would be him* that would unfreeze her. He smiled at the recognition of his omnipotence. Uncharacteristically, he referred Beth to a psychotherapist.

REFERENCES

Celenza, A. (2004), Sexual misconduct in the Clergy: The search for the father. *Studies in Gender & Sexual.,* 5:213–232.

Kochansky, G. E. & Cohen, M. (2007), Priests who sexualize minors: Psychodynamic, characterological, and clerical considerations. In: *Predatory Priests, Silenced Victims: The Sexual Abuse Crisis and the Catholic Church,* ed. M. G. Frawley-O'Dea & V. Goldner. Mahwah, NJ: The Analytic Press.

II

Victims and Survivors:
The Clinical Picture

5

Can You Imagine?*

Mary Gail Frawley-O'Dea

When a child or adolescent is sexually abused, the aftereffects can be seriously disruptive and long-lasting. Our examination of the consequences for victims of clergy sexual abuse begins with a true story told in my consultation room by a 30-something-year-old man. I have presented his case to Catholic clergy, asking them to imagine themselves as my patient; to listen more with their bodies, guts, and emotions than with their heads so that they can connect with the victim more than with their fellow priests if even for a day. I ask the reader to do the same, since we all want to naturally distance ourselves from the tumultuous internal states evoked by intimacy with sexual abuse.

Imagine, then, that you are eight years old and have just become an altar boy. Your parents, struggling with marital problems and alcoholism, are not very available to you so you are especially proud to have a place in the family of your parish. It is a bright, cold February

*Portions of this chapter appear in Frawley-O'Dea, Mary Gail. *Perversion of Power: Sexual Abuse in the Catholic Church*. Vanderbilt University Press, 2007.

Sunday and you have just finished helping Fr. Bill, your favorite priest, serve Mass. As you enter the sacristy, Fr. Bill tells you that you did a great job and you can feel the pride and happiness filling you up. The priest—your priest—offers to help you pull the cassock over your head, joking that he still can't get used to wearing a dress. But, as Fr. Bill lifts the cassock up, he holds it over your face with one hand, unzips his trousers with the other, and pushes his erect penis into your back. You sense him moving back and forth and back and forth against you. Blindfolded by the cassock, you can only stand still until, after moaning and leaning into you one more time, Fr. Bill loosens his grip. You feel moisture on your back but, as he pulls the cassock all the way off, he is wiping your back with a towel and mumbling about the steam radiator heat making you sweaty. He pats you on the back and tells you to turn the lights off before you leave for the day. Not a word is said about what just happened. What did just happen you wonder? You feel funny—scared but not really sure if you have any reason to be. It's Fr. Bill after all. Your favorite priest. Can you imagine?

For the next three years, Fr. Bill repeats the act in many places at many times. Empty classrooms, the sacristy, the small school chapel, the nurse's office, and the rectory all become sexualized spaces. He tells your parents he'd like to take you to his summer place at the beach and they are relieved not to have to worry about you. There, the abuse, during which you always are blindfolded, meshes with daily fishing expeditions, movies, riding the ocean waves, clam digging, and other seashore activities that a lonely only child living in a city apartment building with drunk and arguing parents finds amazing. Fun and adventure fill your days, but your nights find Fr. Bill rubbing his penis between your buttocks, caressing and sucking on your now erect penis, tongue kissing you, and pushing your blindfolded face onto his penis. You clench your teeth tightly and, as far as you can remember, never let him get inside your mouth. It is a small but important act of defiance and self-protection. Imagine.

You are now 11 and prepubescent acne spurts on your face. On the first day of sixth grade, Fr. Bill pulls you into a storage room and, as he tries to kiss you, he tells you that your "badness" is coming out all over your face. This time, you push him off and run. He never touches you again. Can you imagine?

Such was the life of this young boy from ages eight through 11. And afterward? He never spoke of the abuse until beginning treatment. He had read in the newspaper that Fr. Bill was accused of sexually molesting boys 30 years earlier in another parish. Although removed from ministry, Fr. Bill denied all the charges and claimed that he was being scapegoated and had never even known his accusers by name when they were boys. At that point, my patient contacted other men that he suspected had been molested by Fr. Bill in their parish and a number of them went to the press with their stories. My patient is not suing anyone nor does he plan to. He says the abuse:

> is something that I have thought about every day of my life, yet have always been far too ashamed to talk about. I am still ashamed. After reading Fr. Bill's denials in the papers, though, I decided I couldn't hide my story any longer. I was robbed of my youth and my faith at a very young age. If I can prevent this from happening to other children, then perhaps I am on the right track. I am not a practicing Catholic, and I certainly don't need the Catholic Church to teach my children morals and values and right from wrong. In fact, it will probably be years before I have to answer the question, "Hey, Daddy, what's a priest?"

Can you Imagine?

Like my patient, sexual abuse victims often are young people for whom something or someone is missing. They yearn for an adult who sees them, hears them, understands them, makes time for them, and enjoys their company. Unfortunately, the sexual predator is exquisitely attuned to the emotional and relational needs of potential victims; he ingratiates himself into the lives of his victims, evoking respect, trust, and dependency long before the first touch takes place.

There are those who devalue survivors of childhood—and especially adolescent—sexual abuse for not disclosing their victimizations when they were occurring. Secrecy, however, is the acknowledged cornerstone of sexual abuse. Some perpetrators overtly extract secrecy by suggesting that the victim will be blamed for the abuse, then taken from his or her home and placed in an orphanage. Or they threaten that if the victim discloses, the perpetrator will harm him or her or members of the family. Sexual abusers may also blame the victim, accusing him or her of seducing the predator, thus filling the victim with the shame and self-loathing more appropriately experienced by the victimizer. In a more covert covenant of secrecy, the abuser provides the victim with gifts and special privileges that both buy silence and instill terrible and long-lasting guilt.

In addition, many abused minors maintain silence because they accurately perceive that there is no one in their environment who will help them if they disclose. It is more hopeful for a child to pre-serve a fantasy that *if* he told, someone would protect him than it is to reveal the abuse to another who ignores, blames, or reabuses him. Many children and teenagers do not disclose the sexual abuse secret because they care for the perpetrator. A central cruelty of sexual abuse, in fact, is the perpetrator's trampling of the young person's generously and freely bestowed affection and respect. It is from this epicenter of betrayed trust that the mind-splitting impact of sexual abuse ripples outward.

Let me now guide you on a tour through the corridors of a psyche twisted by sexual transgression. It is a trip through a traumato-genically constructed, psychological House of Horrors in which ex-periences of self and other are grotesquely distorted and terrifying images unexpectedly pop out from seemingly safe places. The visitor lurches from one emotional shock to another in an interior atmo-sphere of darkness punctuated only by frightening flashing lights and nightmarish unreality. As we travel, hang on to your reactions to abuser Fr. Bill and my victim patient. They will make our tour even more meaningful to you. Our first stop is at the victim's images of self and others.

When a young person is being abused, the psychological shock is so great that the normal self cannot absorb or make sense of what is happening to it. In a valiant attempt to cope with the overwhelming overstimulation and sense of betrayal literally embodied in sexual trauma, the self splits using the psychic mechanism of dissociation. The normal operation of dissociation allows each of us to drive 10 miles, for example, and then "come to" with no memory of the road just traveled. For the victim of child or adolescent sexual violation, however, dissociation is an exponentially more dramatic process, one that serves as both a blessing and a curse.

On the one hand, by entering into an entirely different state of consciousness while being abused, the victim preserves a functional and safe self who is removed from the trauma and is therefore able learn, grow, play, and work. Many a patient has reported, for instance, that the self recognized as "I" floated above the bed on which that "other kid"—the alienated victim self—was being abused. On the other hand, the curse of dissociation condemns the self who experienced the abuse to a trapped existence in the inner world of the survivor, a place dominated by terror, impotent but seething rage, and grief for which there literally are no words. Because trauma impels the brain to process events quickly and in a state of organismic hyperarousal, verbalizing pathways are bypassed. Instead, the sexual violations are encoded by the child and retrieved by the survivor as nonverbal, often highly disorganizing feelings, somatic states, anxieties, recurring nightmares, flashbacks, and sometimes dangerous behaviors.

Often, the adult survivor's life is wracked by unexpected regressions to his victimized self that are triggered by seemingly neutral stimuli. Much as the Vietnam veteran who hits the floor during a thunderstorm is, in a very real way, back in the Mekong Delta seconds before his buddy's skull is blown off, so too the sexual abuse survivor may be triggered into a regression by something or someone reminiscent of his earlier traumas. No longer firmly located in the present, the survivor thinks, feels, experiences his body, and behaves as the victim he once was, badly confusing himself and those around him. For victims of priest abuse, a Roman collar, the scent of incense, light streaming through stained glass at a certain time of day, organ music, or most certainly, interacting with priests and bishops about their abuse may well evoke the appearance of usually dissociated self-states.

Coexisting with the violated, terrorized, grief-stricken victim self, the adult survivor of sexual abuse has a state of being within that is identified with the perpetrator. Through this unconscious ongoing bond to the predator, the survivor preserves his or her attachment to the abuser by becoming like him in some ways. When threatened by experiences of helplessness, vulnerability, or anticipated betrayal, the survivor unconsciously accesses this self-state to gain a sense of empowerment. Subjectively experiencing herself as righteously indignant, the survivor may enact at times breathtaking boundary smashing, cold contempt, and red-hot rage. Not surprisingly, survivors are sickened by the thought that they resemble in any way their perpetrators and therefore avert their gaze from these aspects of self for long periods of time lest they fragment even further at the sight of their own abusive tendencies.

I am not talking here about the victim becoming sexually abusive. While that can happen, it is exceedingly rare. Rather, the survivor enacts with some frequency some aspects of the perpetrator's lack of respect for others. It is important to recognize that the clay of the survivor's abuser self was molded quite literally by the hands of a master—the sexual and relational victimizer. While those in relationships with survivors can set limits on what they will tolerate, an empathic understanding of the source of the survivor's sometimes outrageous behavior is essential to remember.

Finally, the sexual abuse survivor sometimes may enact a long-split-off aspect of self that is greedy, grandiose, and insatiably entitled. In addition to representing another identification with the abuser whose appetites were insatiable, this aspect of self gives voice to demands for restitution. There comes a day in every survivor's recovery upon which he fully comprehends what was so cruelly taken from him. Further personal growth and healing requires that the survivor then mourn the childhood or adolescence that never was, the defensively idealized caretakers who never existed, and, perhaps most poignantly, the self that could have been had trust, hope, and possibility not been so brutally shattered.

I cannot exaggerate nor adequately convey the soul-searing pain of this phase of recovery. One patient, at this point in treatment, cried,

> This is too much. I can't stand it—I won't—you can't make me. I can deal with the abuse—maybe. But the idea that I can't go back, that my childhood is broken forever—I can't live with that. I won't know that I never was and never will be just a kid. [Davies & Frawley, 1994]

Quite understandably, the sexual abuse survivor may act to avoid the ultimate mourning necessary to move on from the abuse and all that was stolen from him. Launching a lawsuit against the perpetrator or against those who abetted the abuser may be one way to deny unrecoverable loss and pursue an illusion of full restitution of that which, tragically, can never be restored. No matter the amount of financial settlement, a residue of emptiness and lost hope persists. At the core of the survivor's being, the worst has happened yet again; he has been paid off to go away while life goes on relatively untouched for the perpetrator and those who shielded him.

However, money can be a little better than nothing, and nothing is mostly what the Church historically offered victims. Many survivors, in fact, resorted to lawsuits only after being stonewalled in their quest for more personal reparative gestures. Legal action, in this situation, represents a last-ditch effort by the survivor to become an agent in his own life. Further, a lawsuit, when all else has failed, enacts an understandable demand that the truth be told one way or another. In addition, many survivors need financial assistance for therapy, substance abuse rehabilitation, and educational or vocational training previously unattainable because of posttraumatic stress symptoms plaguing the victims.

Leaving the realm of the sexual abuse survivor's organization of self, we enter a related corridor on our tour, one in which we explore typical characteristics of the victim's interpersonal relationships.

Survivors' relationships with other people are colored and shaded by expectations and anxieties forged during their traumatic experiences. Approaching others from within the psychological confines of posttraumatic stress disorder, the trauma survivor exhibits rapidly shifting relational stances, painfully lurching from periods of extremely dependent clinging to vicious rage. Stark terror and tears can turn in an instant to cold aloofness, while warmth and vivacity may turn kaleidoscopically to paranoid suspicion. All of this leads to many chaotically unstable relationships, often alternating with stretches of the loneliest isolation.

Needless to say, normal sexual functioning is almost impossible for most survivors until well into their recovery. Too often, sex, even with a trusted other, triggers terrifyingly disorganizing flashbacks during which survivors sometimes literally see the face of their abuser superimposed on the visage of their sexual partner and experience dreadful relivings of their sexual traumas. In addition, survivors frequently are disgusted by and ashamed of their own bodies and sexual strivings. Unfairly blaming their abuse on their own sexuality, they often desperately insist that it never would have happened were it not for their self-perceived horribly seductive bodies and deplorable sexual desires. Heterosexual boys abused by men are additionally tormented, wondering what it was about them that attracted the perpetrator.

Sexual abuse survivors of all genders and sexual orientations are deprived of the right to gradually grow into a mature sexuality and, instead, are forced or seduced into premature sexual encounters they are emotionally ill equipped to handle. As adults, therefore, these men and women often spin between periods of promiscuous and self-destructive sexual acting out and complete sexual shutdown during which, like burn victims, they experience the gentlest physical contact as excruciatingly painful.

Finally, many sexual abuse survivors assume a characteristic relational stance that is particularly germane to the Church. It involves those who did not abuse them but also did not protect them.

If it takes a community to raise a child, it also takes one to allow the abuse; whenever a minor is sexually violated, someone's eyes are closed. Throughout history and across every segment of society, the most common response to the suspicion or even the disclosure of childhood sexual abuse has been self-defensive denial and dissociation. No one finds it easy to stand in the overwhelming and destabilizing reality of sexual abuse. Blindness, deafness, and elective mutism are responses endemic to many confronted by a victimized child, an adult survivor, or a perpetrating adult. What is important to recognize is that adult survivors of sexual abuse frequently are, at least initially, even angrier with adults who failed to protect them than they are with the perpetrator himself. Because the survivor's internal relationship with his abuser is organized around paradoxical feelings of attachment and hate, he often feels freer to turn the full blast of his long pent-up rage and bitterness on those who did not protect him and who, in addition, failed to provide for him in ways the perpetrator seemed to, albeit at an unholy cost to the exploited child or adolescent.

Turning down another corridor on our tour of a sexually traumatized psyche, we will examine the impact of sexual abuse on the cognitive functioning of the victim and survivor. Part of what is overwhelmed during sexual abuse is the young person's ability to cognitively contain, process, and express the enormity of the relational betrayal and physical impingement with which he is faced. It is striking and often bewildering to observe in adult survivors completely contradictory thought processes that ebb and flow with little predictability. One moment you are speaking with an intelligent adult, capable of complex, flexible, abstract, and self-decentered thinking. Under sufficient internal or external stress, however, or in situations somehow reminiscent of the abuse, the cognitive integrity of the survivor shatters and he or she becomes locked in rigidly inflexible, self-centered thought patterns, simplistic black-and-white opinions devoid of nuance, and an immutable conviction that the future is destined to be both short and unalterably empty.

If a survivor's cognitive functioning is severely ruptured by sexual abuse, his or her affective life, the next stop on our tour, is even more impaired. When a young person is sexually traumatized, the hyperarousal of the autonomic nervous system and the body's subsequent attempt to restore order disrupt the brain's neurochemical regulation of emotion. In addition, we are now learning that attachment relationships also impact upon the brain's ability to modulate feelings, with traumatic attachment experiences interfering with effective neuropsychological regulation of affect. The brain of the sexually abused minor thus suffers a double assault. Both the sexual traumas themselves and the betrayal of an attachment relationship assail the flow of affect-modulating neurochemicals.

As an adult, the survivor shifts—sometimes quite rapidly—between states of chaotically intense hyperarousal and deadened states of psychic numbing. This inability to modulate emotional arousal often leads to interpersonally inappropriate verbal or motoric actions when the survivor is hyperstimulated, and to similarly inappropriate emotional and psychomotor constriction as the individual moves into psychic numbing. Further, autonomic arousal becomes a generalized reaction to stress in the midst of which the sexual abuse survivor is unable to discern realistically the severity of a perceived threat. Instead of reacting at the actual level of psychological danger, the survivor may engage in seemingly irrational behaviors like temper tantrums or terrified withdrawal. These behaviors do no fit the present-day situation but are perfectly complimentary to the now affectively revived earlier trauma. Because of the damage done by sexual abuse to affective brain functioning, adult survivors often need psychotropic medications for some period of time during recovery. For some, their impairments are sufficiently intractable to require lifelong medication.

Almost finished with our psychological tour, we are now about to enter what can be the most shocking corridor of all. Partly due to disrupted brain functioning, sexual abuse survivors often display a truly spectacular array of self-destructive behaviors. They slice their arms, thighs, and genitalia with knives, razors, or shards of broken glass. They burn themselves with cigarettes, pull hair from their heads and pubic areas, walk through Central Park alone at night, play chicken with trains at railroad crossings, pick up strangers in bars to have unprotected and anonymous sex, drive recklessly at high speeds, gamble compulsively, and/or further destroy their minds and bodies with alcohol and the whole range of street drugs. Both male and female prostitutes tend to have backgrounds of early sexual abuse. Survivors also are two to three times more likely than adults without abuse histories to make at least one suicide attempt in their lives. Sometimes they die.

Survivor self-abuse performs a myriad of functions too complex to address adequately in this context. A quick inventory of a survivor's motivations to act self-destructively includes: punishment for the abuse he blames himself for; mastering victimization by taking charge of the timing and execution of harm; self-medication of turbulent affective storms; and unconsciously seeking states of hyperarousal that then trigger the release of brain opioids, providing the survivor with a temporary sense of calm. At an even more deeply unconscious level, frighteningly self-destructive sexual abuse survivors want to turn the table on present-day stand-ins for those who violated and neglected them. Unconsciously, they long to see their own terror, helplessness, impotent rage, and shocked recognition of utter betrayal reflected now on the face of someone in their lives. Who can blame them?

As we end our tour of the terrifyingly disorienting psychological House of Horrors constructed during sexual abuse and maintained by its aftermath, it should be clear that a survivor's recovery is a long, complicated, sometimes treacherous process. Psychoanalyst Leonard Shengold (1989) entitled his book on the effects of childhood sexual abuse, *Soul Murder*. I do not think that early sexual trauma necessarily has to result in soul *murder*, but it most surely batters and deadens the soul of the young victim and the adult survivor. That this ravaging of souls has been administered by priests entrusted with a sacred covenant to protect and enliven souls is despicable. That bishops and other clerical leaders have covered up and lied about the sexual crimes committed by priests in their charge is as bad, or worse; it is evil itself.

The Catholic Church and its American leaders are at a crossroads. Like the recovering victim of sexual abuse, those in authority can choose to defend, deny, retrench, and rigidify. They can turn away from all their decency, all their love and generosity, all their arrogance and indifference. When a survivor takes that familiar and well-worn road, further fragmentation and diminished integrity of mind and soul ensues. But, as is the case for so many sexual abuse survivors, another road can be chosen. The Catholic Church, pushed and prodded by its leadership, rank and file priests, laity, and competent professionals can decide on a path of recovery, growth, and restored faith. This horrible scandal could become a new epicenter that changes, revitalizes, and restores souls. Which road is taken is a matter of will.

REFERENCES

Davies, J. M. & Frawley, M. G. (1994), *Treating the Adult Survivor of Childhood Sexual Abuse: A Psychoanalytic Perspective*. New York: Basic Books, Inc.

Shengold, L. (1989), *Soul Murder: The Effects of Childhood Abuse and Deprivation*. New Haven: Yale University Press.

6

Failed "Fathers,"
Boys Betrayed*

Richard B. Gartner

The controversy surrounding the scandalous abuse of children by priests has churned throughout our culture and boiled over into bitterness and vindictiveness. Too often, the media, like the Church, paid far more attention to the effects of the scandals on the Church than to the effects of the abuse on its victims.

While there have been some reports of abuse of girls by priests, the largest number of cases have involved boys. I will therefore only track the effects of sexual abuse on boys, with particular attention to the aftermath of abuse by priests.

EFFECTS OF BOYHOOD SEXUAL ABUSE

Some common aftereffects of boyhood sexual trauma include dissociation, isolation, addiction, prostitution, rage, suicide, denial, and

---

*Portions of this paper have been previously published (Gartner, 1999a, 2002, 2005).

the possibility of becoming an abuser. (See Gartner, 1996, 1997a,b, 1999a,c,d, 2005; Holmes & Slap, 1998, for lengthy descriptions of these aftereffects.)

Sexual abuse is an interpersonal experience with ominous implications for a boy's future relational frame of reference. In this betrayal, seemingly indissoluble ties are shattered. Abusers use power relationships to satisfy their own needs without regard to the needs of their victims. When the abuser is someone the boy has believed he could count on implicitly, "treachery is introduced into the most private, personal, and trusting relationships" (Gartner, 1999a, p. 13).

During childhood molestation, dissociation is an effective way for victims to defend against psychic disintegration. Eventually, dissociation may become a victim's chief way of dealing with any uncomfortable situation. What started out as a useful, perhaps even lifesaving, way to deal with trauma ends up as a principal mode of being in the world.

But dissociation is not an appropriate reaction to all stress. The dissociative "cure" for anxiety can itself become a problem (Bromberg, 1998). For example, sexually abused men may develop compulsive behaviors, like substance abuse, incessant masturbation, or anonymous, unpleasurable sexual activity through which they self-hypnotically return to a dissociated state that once was protective but now interferes with adaptive adult functioning.

Interpersonally, these boys often grow up distrusting power and authority. Their ability to form attachments to authorities is severely compromised because they have internalized people in power as untrustworthy, malevolent, and undependable.

But the interpersonal effects go beyond relationships with authority figures. Feeling all relationships include a power differential, a sexually abused man may have a constant need to be in control. He cannot understand equal partnership, which bodes ill for his intimate love relationships in adulthood. Power also can become eroticized, possibly leading to sadistic and masochistic sexual and love relationships. Phobic about emotional attachment, a man with a boyhood sexual abuse history often maintains an interpersonal distance in relationships. This may alternate with a sense of merging with a loved one so that he hardly knows where he ends and the other begins.

Confused about what is affection and what is abuse, what is desire and what is tenderness (Ferenczi, 1933), such a man may have great difficulty differentiating sex, love, nurturance, affection, and abuse. Interpersonal approaches from others that are simply friendly may be experienced as seductive and exploitative. Conversely, he may not notice when exploitative demands are being made on him, for he has learned to accept such demands as usual in his interpersonal world.

An adult male survivor of sexual abuse may at times be phobic about sex and feel smothered by its forced intimacy. As one man said to me, only half-joking, "The trouble with sex is there's always someone in your face." This survivor is likely to feel isolated during interpersonal sex. In addition, he may feel ambivalent about sexual pleasure, since a certain amount of physical pleasure may have accompanied the traumatic abuse. Another man put it, "All pleasure is bad. It's bad that my father touches my penis. His touching my penis gives me pleasure. Therefore, pleasure is bad."

On the other hand, interpersonal relatedness may become eroticized because sex is the only way for the man to feel intimate (or seemingly intimate). Hungry for interpersonal contact but phobic about it, believing that sexual closeness is his chief opportunity to feel loved but experiencing love as abuse, a sexually abused man who allows himself to be sexual at all often solves his dilemma by engaging in frequent, indiscriminate, and dissociated sexual encounters (Gartner, 1999a, pp. 202–203).

Compulsive sexuality strengthens the dissociation that sexually abused men need to deal with anxiety. It soothes momentarily, just as abusing alcohol or engaging in other compulsive behaviors like gambling, eating, drug taking, shopping, overworking, and overexercising, provide relief. However, compulsive sex recreates the sexual-abuse situation where dissociation first developed and therefore is a particularly effective way to summon up familiar dissociative trance states.

These sexually compulsive acts are not free or joyous expressions of erotic, passionate sensuality. Rather, they demonstrate a man's imprisonment in an empty behavioral circuit from which he feels there is no exit. Although he pursues sex incessantly, he achieves little intimacy. He desires love but "he does not feel loved once the sex act is concluded. These incidents leave him feeling empty and lonely, while the idea of fully pursuing interpersonal relatedness fills him with a dread of repeating his abuse history" (Gartner, 1999a, p. 203).

An abused child learns that sexuality and seduction constitute his interpersonal currency, his chief means of getting what he needs in life. Having learned that his sexuality is valuable to others, he may become seductive in diverse relationships, often inappropriately so.

Another aftermath of boyhood sexual victimization is that relationships may become exploitative, even sadistic or masochistic. It is commonly believed that sexually abused boys almost inevitably become sexually abusive men. While it is true that most male abusers were themselves abused as boys, it appears that relatively few sexually abused boys become abusers (Lisak, Hopper, and Song, 1996). Because of this myth, however, many men fear that they will become abusive or worry that others will think they are abusers should they disclose their history.

Two major issues differentiate sexually abused boys and girls. Both complicate boys' capacities to integrate sexual abuse. First, socialized masculine gender roles dictate that boys and men are not victims and that they may express rage but not the "softer" emotions. These norms also dictate that men are competitive, resilient, self-reliant, independent, and certainly not emotionally needy. Also, "real" men always want and are the initiators of sexual activity. Sexually abused men may be driven to deny their reality in the service of maintaining these norms.

Masculine-gender norms often interfere with a man's ability to process sexual victimization. As a result, many men identify victimhood with femaleness. They then believe, consciously or unconsciously, that only sissies and weaklings allow abuse: victims can only be women or feminized men (often seen as gay). Being victimized or acquiescing to victimization is "not male." Therefore, men often can neither acknowledge sexual victimization nor allow themselves to say they were traumatized and emotionally devastated by a sexual encounter (especially with a woman) without giving up some sense of manhood.

Masculine-gender norms also make it difficult for men to develop or use the psychological resources necessary to recover from trauma. Unable to be emotionally needy or to process emotional trauma, they may have counterphobic reactions to feeling feminized by abuse. They become aggressive or "hypermasculine." If they thus become action oriented rather than self-reflective, they are more likely to become abusive themselves.

A second major factor differentiates boys from girls as they process sexual victimization. When the abuser is male (and even sometimes when she is female), many boys and men—whether straight or gay—worry about sexual orientation. Conventional wisdom dictates that a sexually abused boy is likely to become gay, although there is in fact no persuasive evidence that premature sexual activity with either men or women fundamentally changes a boy's sexual orientation.

Nevertheless, a boy who was headed toward heterosexuality before his abuse is likely to doubt himself, wondering why he was chosen by a man as a sexual object. A boy headed toward homosexuality may feel prematurely rushed into defining himself as gay, or may hate his homosexuality, believing that it was caused by his abuse. Even boys who say that their early experiences were not abusive were introduced to sex by a more powerful person exploiting a less powerful one. Whether the boys are gay or straight, this exploitative introduction to sexuality has implications their future intimate relationships.

SEXUAL ABUSE BY PRIESTS[1]

Priests certainly have no monopoly on being sexual predators. I have known victims who were sexually abused by family members, teachers, coaches, scoutmasters, babysitters, neighbors, and doctors, not to mention non-Catholic clergy.

Yet there are special implications for victims abused by priests. Catholic children are told to call the clergy Father, Mother, Sister, Brother. There is a concerted effort, usually benign, to make Catholic clergy part of a parishioner's "family." Children can be quite literal in their understanding of such adult ideas. Furthermore, a priest is not simply "a" father. He is a direct representative of "the" Father, a living

---

[1]I urge any reader who wants to understand this issue to see *The Boys of St. Vincent* (1994), a film depicting long-term, brutal sexual, physical, and emotional abuse of boys in a Catholic orphanage. Based on true events in a Newfoundland Catholic home for boys, it addresses sexual abuse of boys and conveys the boys' complex reactions to it. I consider it a paradigm for what happens when boys are sexually abused by priests (Gartner, 1999b).

representation of Christ. One priest/abuser actually told a child that to resist molestation would be a direct defiance of God's wishes.

Encouraged to consider clergy as special family members with immediate links to God, how are children to understand when Father, Mother, Sister, or Brother makes sexual overtures? A sacrosanct family member has betrayed them in a fundamental way. The more they believe in a link to God through a priest, the more horrific the betrayal. The more they accept the familial implications of calling someone Father, Mother, Sister, or Brother, the more incestuous the sexual abuse. So many victims of priests are psychologically dealing with incest.

When a child is abused by a priest, he may not simply have a crisis of faith; he may literally feel he is betraying God. He knows his abuser has taken a vow of chastity. Even if he is sure he never desired the priest sexually, he may still feel he somehow tempted the priest to break those vows. He is particularly likely to think so if his abuser tells him they are engaging in sexual behavior because the boy is special or beautiful. Whatever the adult's intent in saying such a thing, the boy may well conclude the abuse was his own fault.

As he discerns that he was exploited by someone he considered a direct link to God, a boy's whole spiritual world may begin to crumble. Boys most easily preyed upon by priests are likely to come from families with deep religious convictions. They may be altar boys or choir boys; they are likely to feel engaged in their religious lives and to have idealized views of their spiritual mentors. Also, they may come from troubled families and be looking for parental figures in the Church to act as role models and provide the structure that they lack at home.

Elsewhere (Gartner, 1999a, 2005) I have discussed two men who were sexually abused as boys by priests. The circumstances of their abuse were different: Julian was abused by a priest/mentor from ages 12 to 15. Lorenzo had been abused by a number of men before a sexual encounter with a priest at age 15.

TWO SURVIVORS: LORENZO AND JULIAN

Both Lorenzo and Julian came from large families in which tenderness was almost unknown and violence was the norm. Starved for affection and guidance, they looked to priests for help, making them easy prey for the priests they idealized.

Following their abuse, both teens became sexually compulsive, and each had vast reserves of rage and problems with older authorities. As an adult, Lorenzo, a gay man, had never had a relationship of any depth. Julian, a married straight man, found ongoing intimacy with his wife nearly impossible to achieve. Both had crises of faith superimposed on the other sequelae of boyhood sexual abuse.

By age 15, Lorenzo had numerous exploitative and callous sexual encounters in which he sexually serviced men, all of whom publicly identified themselves as heterosexual and many of whom were married. Confused about the meaning of his own behavior and only vaguely knowledgeable about sexual orientation, Lorenzo began to wonder if he were gay. He had no one with whom to talk about this in the working-class mill town where he grew up. One of 10 children in a physically abusive lower-middle-class family, he knew better than to discuss gay sex at home. Feeling desperate about his sexual feelings, he contacted a priest he considered "cool" and told him about his sexual experiences and his concern that he was gay.

> The priest looked at me and said, 'I knew you were gay the minute I laid eyes on you!' At first he was good about it—he invited me to visit him, and when I did he took me around the city and showed me gay neighborhoods, gay bars, gay shops. But then we went back to the house he lived in with other priests, and I wanted to get high—I was a crazy kid in those days—so I asked him where to get grass. He said, 'No problem, just go upstairs and ask Fr. Donald.' So I went upstairs, and there was nice Fr. Donald, and we got high together, and then he made a pass at me. It was the first time anyone serviced *me*, and I really liked it. When I went downstairs and told the first priest about it, he said, 'Oh, sure, Father Donald does that with everyone.' Can you believe this? He *knew* what was going to happen when he sent me up there!

Lorenzo was talking faster and faster. I asked him how he felt about all this. "I thought it was funny. And exciting. But, you know, I'm 35 now, about the age Fr. Donald was then. I have no interest in 15-year-olds. My nephews are that age! I'd *never* go near them for sex." For the first time, he seemed reflective. "It was a terrible thing to do. They knew how fucked up I was about sex with all those men and how unsure I was about being gay. I went to them for sanctuary! And they just helped me party with them." Lorenzo looked sad. "In those days I really believed in the Catholic Church. No more."

Julian was deeply ambivalent about the man who simultaneously mentored, loved, and abused him. From the time he was 12, Julian was abused for three years by Fr. Scott, a parish priest who required that he come for special counseling sessions in order to get confirmed. Fr. Scott made Julian his special altar boy, invited him to visit him in his rooms, and educated him in classical texts, languages, and music. Julian came from a psychologically and physically invasive large family in which emotions and boundaries were ignored. Although he flunked out of school after Fr. Scott began to abuse him, he became an A student once the abuse stopped, largely, he believes, because of the earlier influence of the priest. Julian eventually went on to get an advanced degree in another field.

Fr. Scott taught Julian to idealize the male relationships described in ancient Greek texts. These idyllic relationships included physical sexuality as well as intellectual mentoring, deep commitment, and interpersonal intimacy. Julian's abuse began a few months after Fr. Scott started counseling him. Fr. Scott groomed him for "seduction" by asking him to talk about the pain of being in a physically abusive but otherwise unresponsive family. Then the priest would hug Julian. These hugs were precious to the boy, who was starved for physical affection and, indeed, any positive response from an adult.

With time, the hugs got longer. One day Fr. Scott kissed Julian, putting his tongue in the boy's mouth. Julian was startled and confused. After the kiss, Fr. Scott said, *"I know you want more,* but that's all for now." As a man, Julian said, "So right from the beginning he made the abuse *my* idea. I felt guilty even though I had no concept of men kissing other men at the time, and certainly no interest in it." Shortly thereafter, the priest introduced Julian to anal sex, and for two years they had regular sexual encounters that included anal sex and mutual masturbation.

The priest said their relationship existed on the highest plane possible for two human beings, that they had attained the ideal glorified by the greatest poets of the ancient world. He reiterated that they experienced all forms of love together: love of beauty, love of thought, love of logic, love of art, and love of one another that was intellectual, sensual, and emotional.

Julian did love Fr. Scott and craved the priest's companionship and deep interest in him. Still, he was confused and conflicted about the sex that accompanied that interest. "He did so much for me! Anyone would think he was the best mentor a boy could ever have, and, except for the sex, he was."

Julian put a stop to the sex when he was 15. He started to excel in school and entered seminary to become a priest, but he dropped out when he realized that this path was actually an outgrowth of his relationship with the priest. He married, but remained ashamed, conflicted, and secretive about his abuse. He continued to be grateful for the intellectual and emotional expansion the relationship with Fr. Scott had afforded him. At the same time, Julian was covertly furious about the exploitation and mystification in their sexual activity. As an adult, he became a compulsive masturbator who furtively viewed peep shows and was consumed by female pornography when he was anxious. When he began treatment, he felt out of control, caught in the grip of the sexual impulses that flooded him.

In their treatments, both Julian and Lorenzo became increasingly aware of the extent of their rage at their priest/abusers. But they also realized, sadly, how much they still hoped for from these inadequate men. Lorenzo phoned the priest who sent him to the abusing priest. He found this man receptive until he realized that Lorenzo wanted to talk to him about how hurt he was. The priest then abruptly terminated the conversation. He never returned other phone calls. Nor did he respond to a letter in which Lorenzo told him he wanted to understand what happened, not to hurt the priest.

At age 30, Julian saw Fr. Scott at a funeral. He felt furious but paralyzed, wanting to shame and hurt the priest but barely able to speak to him. The priest drew him into a corner and whispered, "You may feel better than the rest of us now, but you and I know that all I have to do is rub your belly and you'll squeal like a puppy!" Feeling helpless and ashamed once again, Julian finally got in touch with his rage at his former mentor. Yet he was never able to confront Fr. Scott and maintained a fantasy of reconciling with him.

I believe that many suits against the Church were brought by men who, like Lorenzo, initially sought some kind of healing pastoral experience. Met with silence or denial, they chose legal means to get acknowledgment of the wrong done to them.

Both Lorenzo and Julian entertained thoughts of legal redress long before the Church scandals became public. Lorenzo considered writing the diocese where the priests were now serving to warn of the danger the men might still pose. But he reasoned that the Church was unlikely to do anything about the situation. This conclusion was later confirmed, of course, by the many stories made public about abusive priests who were transferred by Church authorities from one parish to another. Eventually, Lorenzo decided that to write to Church authorities would only give new life to the devastating conflicts that he had largely worked through in his lengthy analysis.

Julian considered suing to have his analysis paid for either by the Church or the estate of his now-deceased abuser. He felt justified in such a demand but decided that entering into a lengthy legal battle would do him more harm than good. It would keep him stuck in his anger and in his memories for at least the additional five or six years it would take to pursue a court case. He also recognized that in a legal battle he would risk reexperiencing the psychological fragmentation he had felt before he began treatment and that there was no guarantee that he would gain anything at all from the process.

Lorenzo and Julian each recognized that the Church would offer neither justice nor solace. Both men seem to have been correct in assessing that their most fruitful path would be to mourn their childhood and innocence, and that this was better accomplished in the consulting room than in the courtroom. When the Church scandal broke, Julian and Lorenzo felt liberated by having their torment validated. They were very glad that the Church was forced to acknowledge the extent of abuse by priests.

At the same time, however, their shame recurred. Furthermore, they were conflicted about not having come forward as other victims had, a struggle that was retriggered by each new report of abuse in the Church. Lorenzo said that he had to monitor tightly what he allowed himself to read or hear in the media in order to keep himself from being overwhelmed by anxiety. And Julian noted sadly that he was a religious man without a church:

> I went to seminary because Catholicism means something to me. But now I can't go into a church without feeling I will vomit. My wife says, "Let's go to an Episcopalian Church—it's almost the same!" But it's

not the same. I'm not an Episcopalian, I'm a *Catholic*. And there's no-where I can go to be one.

DR. X

The theme of religious betrayal overlaying betrayal by a trusted adult is underlined by a third man who spoke to me about his abuse by a priest. Dr. X[2] is a mental health professional, married and now in his 50s, who had personal therapy for over 20 years and who has treated numerous male victims of sexual abuse. He has in many ways successfully dealt with his boyhood trauma. But he is left with a cold fury at the Church and all it stands for, as well as a bleak contempt for organized religion.

Dr. X was raised in the rural American heartland, the son of a devout Catholic mother and a less religious father who nevertheless "went along with the program." A pious child who always wanted to please his mother, Dr. X was a very literal believer in Church doctrine. He absolutely believed that a priest was God's representative on earth.

Of his mother, he says, "To her dying day she was a praying, God-fearing woman. She was the ultimate Catholic, and she wanted me to be one, too." He paints a mixed picture of his father: workaholic, sometimes dangerous, unpredictable, demeaning, and physically abusive; at other times, a strong, capable, and "centering" presence. Dr. X says his sense of self-esteem and goodness came not from his parents but from two men close to his family. One was a friend of his father's who stayed with the family occasionally and seems to have been a near-ideal role model. The other was the family's parish priest.

The priest came from New York and was viewed by Dr. X and his parents as worldly and wise. He visited the family frequently and often stayed the night, even though he lived only three blocks away. He slept on a couch outside Dr. X's room. Starting when Dr. X was five years old, the priest would take the boy out of his bed and bring him onto the couch, placing the boy on top of himself. Dr. X could feel

---

[2]I am indebted to Dr. X for his willingness to speak so frankly to me about his painful history and permit me to write about him.

the priest's erection through the sheet that separated them. The priest moved under him, pressing the boy's moving body against his erection until he reached orgasm. He would also fondle Dr. X's genitals, sometimes with an ice cube. As far as Dr. X can recall, there was never any oral or anal contact. He notes, however, that there are numerous gaps in his memory about the priest's actions.

After a few years, the priest moved to another parish in the same state. He would visit the family every few months and take Dr. X away for the weekend. At these times they went to a suburban house that Dr. X believed at the time was where the priest lived with other priests. He now believes it was a house that the priests kept for their encounters with young boys, since all the other priests also brought boys with them on these weekends. There were many incidents that Dr. X remembers only vaguely. From within his dissociated state, he recalled one in particular. Watching from above, he sees himself step out of the shower while the priest squats down and rubs shaving cream all over his genitals, then "lovingly" wipes it off. Dr. X's younger brother accompanied him on at least one of these weekend trips; this brother recalls clinging to a maid as the other priests tried to bring him into the bathroom with their "special boys" to watch Dr. X being fondled.

These incidents continued until Dr. X was 15.

As I grew older, the guilt intensified. I sensed that things were off, but I felt it was only me, that I was not able to exercise self-control. I didn't want him to take me with him anymore and I grew increasingly wary of his visits. I dreaded them but felt obliged to be "good"—a good Catholic, a good, compliant boy in both his eyes and my parents'. I could not disappoint him.

When he was in his late teens, Dr. X's mother told him that there were rumors about the priest being sexually involved with children. "I became enraged. I'd thought I was special to him. I told her what he'd done to me, but, amazingly, she stayed in touch with him, and *so did I!* I didn't truly realize that I'd been abused. It was just something that happened."

When Dr. X moved to New York as a young adult, the priest, who had left the priesthood, lived there also. For a while, Dr. X stayed with him. The priest tried to seduce him again "for old times sake," but Dr. X fended him off. A year later, Dr. X began therapy and started to identify his experience as abusive. He decided to confront the priest and, taking a "huge friend" along for protection, went to see him. "I told him, 'You abused me,' but he said, 'What I did was just love. It was good for you.' He never acknowledged any wrongdoing."

Dr. X exclaimed, "I felt so betrayed! It went on for 10 years, from a person who seemed to love me and whom I loved. That reduces the trauma, I suppose, but 10 years adds up to a lot of trauma in itself." He noted that only after 20-odd years of therapy was he aware of how enraged he had been all his life. He had always felt anger toward his father, and even his mother, a seemingly more passive figure. "My rage was always under the surface, and I knew that. But there was more, and I knew that, too. Only now do I affix it to him as well."

As a boy, Dr. X never considered telling anyone about his abuse. The priest had said, "This is between you and me. *God thinks it's OK. You don't have to tell your mommy and daddy.*" In retrospect, Dr. X believes his mother was in love with the priest, albeit from a worshipful distance. In any case, he felt sure that all hell would break loose if he told about the abuse, and that he, not the priest, would be the loser. "He was awesome. He would not be blamed. He was Godlike."

As a boy, Dr. X had been ambivalent about what the priest was doing. While he had an underlying sense of disgust, he now feels that he was somehow seduced into thinking that participating in these acts was good and noble. "I remember once, at age six or so, laying there, expecting him to come in. I lay there in the form of a crucifix. I thought he'd see me as Jesus. I'd please him. I *so* wanted his attention!" Dr. X's self-esteem depended on the priest's coming in and making him feel special. "I had a love affair with him in my heart, even at age five."

In addition, Dr. X felt, as Julian had, that his priest could help him become worldly and well-read. "I somehow thought he would show me how to be intelligent and sophisticated, how to live in a better way, not like my redneck family. I don't know how much of that was my fantasy, but certainly his manner reinforced the idea—he was on a pedestal, aloof, someone to be in awe of."

Differentiating between the physical and psychological abuse by his father and the sexual abuse by the priest, Dr. X said,

I had no power in either situation, but somehow my connection to my father remained. I could actively hate him as a counterpart to my love. He was a man. A sick, scary, fucked-up, angry, mean, heartless man at times, but loving, strong, safe, and capable of protecting me, too. The priest was lascivious, stomach sickening, confusing, obligatory, awesome, and desirable. My relationship with him did not carry the attachment, dependency, and love that I felt with my father. Yet I was more powerless with him in a way, given his religious status.

Noting how vulnerable he was, Dr. X at first said that his trauma would have been of an equal magnitude had his abuser been someone other than a priest.

Perhaps if my dad had sex with me I would feel the same way about him, but it was the priest, in his Godlike position and his misuse of it, that soured me to ultimate authority. Although today I think that is a good thing, at that time it left me hopeless, angry, rebellious, hostile, and running in circles. I survived. I did not live.

But the religious underpinnings of abuse by a priest created an additional trauma. Even though he says he is now glad that his eyes were opened to the "hypocrisy" of religion through his abuse, Dr. X makes clear that he had a painful crisis of faith because of the specific nature of his relationship to his abuser: "I felt it was God's representative on earth that opened my eyes to God's failing. I don't believe in God today at all anymore." Reconsidering, he went on:

I am angry at God. To the degree God exists for me I am angry at Him. The idea of a Supreme Being was shattered for me by this man. He introduced evidence to me that God failed, that God won't protect you or prevent bad things from happening to you. The fact that it was a priest was cataclysmic. It taught me that there is a lie in the world. I developed a slowly evolving cynicism. As I got older and gave up on my piety, I grew to hate the smells, sounds, feelings of the Church—the incense, the collars, the robes. My spirituality and ability to believe in a higher power were destroyed.

Wrestling with whether and how priest abuse is different from abuse by others, especially fathers, Dr. X said, "What is unique is that one's connection to religious belief, trust in God, belief in a higher power all becomes skewed, confused, shaken, questioned, tainted.

And that might be a good thing, ultimately. I think it was for me." Yet, he went on to say,

> The fact of his "priestness" had little real specific contribution. It was more the betrayal, the stigmatization, the powerlessness, the frustration. His priestness just gave him the right of way. Being a priest was his ticket to taking advantage. His tool. Like anyone who abuses a child. They all have some tool.

CONCLUSION

Why do the media focus more on the effect of the scandals on the Catholic Church than on the effect of sexual abuse by priests on young children? Perhaps we all would like to have faith in the basic goodness of the Church. Focusing on how the Church is affected by scandal somehow forces us to consider how the Church might regain its exalted state. Obviously, such concerns are legitimate, and it is crucial that Church practices in relation to predatory priests be reformed.

But I think a more fundamental cause of neglect of victims by the media is the taboo many of us continue to have about boys being sexual abuse victims. Although the media are faced with hundreds of hurting male victims of priests, they seem unable to consider for long the effects of these betrayals. I have personally found this to be true when being interviewed by reporters about the sexual abuse of boys. The reporters, of course, want to know about numbers and facts. But when I talk about the specific outrageous acts of sexual abuse on boys, or the long-term negative effects of these acts, the reporters sometimes gasp in horror and disbelief, then move the interview to a less toxic focus. None of us wants to hear such stories.

If a parent betrays a child in a fundamental way, the child's resulting wounds are profound. To the extent that a priest is experienced as a father, he will likewise be the object of conflicting, complex feelings. Therefore, if a priest is a child's Father, his betrayal affects the child to his core.

Each of the men I have described was in a vulnerable psychological state. Indeed, their vulnerability is what made them easy targets for the priest/predators. As boys, they looked to their abusers for solace and support, and they were betrayed. The trauma in all three cases was shattering.

Overlaying the betrayal of Lorenzo, Julian, and Dr. X was the specific effect on each boy's spiritual life following his abuse by a representative of God. They all had a terrible crisis of faith. Their religious feelings were destroyed, further alienating them from their religiously observant families. Although the boys survived, they were truly victims of what Shengold (1989) has aptly called "soul murder."

REFERENCES

Bromberg, P. M. (1998), *Standing in the Spaces: Essays on Clinical Process, Trauma, and Dissociation.* Hillsdale, NJ: Analytic Press.

Ferenczi, S. (1933), Confusion of tongues between adults and the child. In: *Final Contributions to the Problems and Methods of Psycho-Analysis,* ed. M. Balint (trans. E. Mosbacher). London: Karnac Books, 1980, pp. 156–167.

Gartner, R. B. (1996), Incestuous boundary violations in families of borderline patients. *Contemp. Psychoanal, 32*:73–80.

——— (1997a), Considerations in the psychoanalytic treatment of men who were sexually abused as children. *Psychoanal. Psychol., 14*:13–41.

——— (1997b), An analytic group for sexually abused men. *Internat. J. Group Psychother., 47*:373–383.

——— (1999a), *Betrayed as Boys: Psychodynamic Treatment of Sexually Abused Men.* New York: Guilford Press.

——— (1999b), Cinematic depictions of boyhood sexual victimization. *Gender & Psychoanal,, 4*:253–289.

——— (1999c), Relational aftereffects in manhood of boyhood sexual abuse. *J. Contemp. Psychother., 29*:319–353.

——— (1999d), Sexual victimization of boys by men: Meanings and consequences. *J. Gay & Lesbian Psychother., 3*:1–33.

——— (2002), Effects on boys of priest abuse. *Psychol.-Psychoanal., 22*:15–17.

——— (2005), *Beyond Betrayal: Taking Charge of Your Life after Boyhood Sexual Abuse.* New York:: Wiley.

Holmes, W. & Slap, G. (1998), Sexual abuse of boys: Definition, prevalence, correlates, sequelae, and management. *J. Amer. Med. Assoc., 280*:1855–1862.

Lisak, D., Hopper, J. & Song, P. (1996), Factors in the cycle of violence: Gender rigidity and emotional constriction. *J. Traumat. Stress, 9*:721–743.

Shengold, L. (1989). *Soul Murder.* New York: Fawcett Columbine.

III

Victims and Survivors:
Survivor's Stories

7

Surviving Is What I Know; Living Is What I Am Learning

Kathleen M. Dwyer

I remember staring out the kitchen window the night my husband left. I was 37 years old and feeling very sad. I wanted to cry, but the tears could not quite make it over my eyelids. Crying was something I rarely did. Suddenly, I realized that my tears were not because he had left, which was something I had asked him to do, but because I was feeling far less alone with him gone than when he was physically there. I knew then that I had felt that way for as long as I could remember.

Three weeks later I had my first appointment with a therapist. I had come to get help to support my children through the separation and divorce. But I was also aware that while I kept trying to make wonderful memories for my children to carry into adulthood, I seemed to have few, if any, memories of my own childhood.

Six weeks later, I found myself on the floor of the therapist's office, shaking in terror at the first of many memories of incest. During this first round of therapy, my focus was the long-term sexual abuse committed against me by my father, the occasional sexual violations by my grandfather, and a onetime assault by neighborhood boys.

My father was a "functioning" alcoholic who was abusive to the entire family. I still am not sure exactly how young I was when my father began sexually abusing me, but it was always said that we had a "special relationship." To add to my confusion, I knew in some ways that we did. In the beginning, what my father did to me was not violent. He claimed what "we" did was what "God" wanted "us" to do and he used the commandment, "Honor thy father and mother" to further support his behaviors.

As I got older, however, he did become violent. He began to rape me and make me do to him things that would please him. I remember trying to crawl into the wall or to leave my body by going up to the ceiling to escape the fear of being thrown out the window by the force of his back and forth motion. Once he stopped, I would quietly wait for him to "sleep breathe"[1] so that I could carefully make my way out of the room and into the bathroom. Often, with my head held down, I would pass my mother and siblings on the way.

I was about 14 when my father stopped raping me. It was then, and again in God's name, he began masturbating what he called the "evil" out of me. Because of the many times there was blood in my underpants, I have no idea when I actually began to menstruate; however, I believe it must have been close to when he did his "masturbation ritual," having realized he could no longer safely rape me. (Today, I understand that he did not masturbate the evil out of me but rather, until I was 40 years old, he masturbated my ability to orgasm.)

In addition to working on my abuse history with my first therapist, I also began to address the legacy of having a mother who was depressed and emotionally unavailable. After her death, I learned that she too was an incest survivor. I suspect that my father also was abused, and so I grew up with two parents who passed their trauma to another generation.

---

[1]The consequences for leaving the room prematurely were great. I had to learn to tell the difference between being almost asleep and being really asleep. How he was breathing became the indicator.

In my own life, the self-hate that resulted from the abuse was masked by risk taking. Self-cutting was masked by jeans and long sleeved shirts. Drinking was masked by my being in the closet. Feeling evil was masked by devotion to God. Being a lesbian was masked by claiming heterosexuality. And suicidal ideation was masked by silence.

I grew up in a white, very religious, poor, working class, Irish Catholic family whose Catholicism mattered more than anything else. Church was family and family was Church. Someone who attended Mass was good, someone who was involved in the community must have good character, someone who had amassed some wealth had "made it." As I began to questions these cultural and religious assumptions, I thought about breaking the silence about my abuse, but I was terrified. I still believed somehow that my parents could and would kill me if I talked.

At some point, I read an essay by Audre Lorde (1984), who wrote:

> And it [speaking] is never without fear; of visibility, of the harsh light of scrutiny and perhaps judgment, of pain, of death. But we have lived through all of those already, in silence, except death. And I remind myself all the time now, that if I were to have been born mute, and had maintained an oath of silence my whole life for safety, I would still have suffered, and I would still die. It is very good for establishing perspective.

Lorde emboldened me. Each time I spoke my truth, I felt more empowered and less helpless. I began to cautiously take my story from the office of my therapist and tell it to the larger community through writing, conversations, and presentations.

At the end of my first therapy, my therapist and I felt that I had grown enough to "fly" a little. I graduated from college, celebrated my third anniversary of sobriety, and eventually became the director of two residential substance abuse treatment programs for women, 90% of whom were survivors of sexual abuse. I continued writing and drawing, activities I had done since childhood, and some of my poetry was published. I also entered my first relationship with a woman and became a social justice activist committed to doing "anti-ism" work.

I am not sure when the downward spiral started again, or for that matter if it ever really stopped. But gradually a strong desire to cut returned, as did many of the behaviors I had previously worked on. I knew that if I didn't get help I would definitely commit suicide.

In 1995 I began therapy again. Nine months into the work, a variety of distinct self-states began to emerge. Eventually, I drew a picture of my inner world; it included 11 parts/alters, some of whom were standing on a padlocked box where two other parts/alters lived. I told my therapist that the box must never be opened as it held things I (we) must never talk about. But quickly, the padlock was opened and memories of priest abuse came flooding in. Flashbacks and body and smell memories filled my days. As the abuse resurfaced, my multiplicity surfaced as well. Each part/alter reported what had happened,, and my life again became touch and go, with cutting and other self-destructive behaviors returning.

The Church where I was abused was the same Church where priests took confessions and where penances were assigned. It was the Church where the Brownies met, where one of my brothers became an altar boy, and where my sister and I sang in the choir. This was the Church where all the children in my family were married, some grandchildren were baptized, and where my parents are buried.

The messages I received in my Church were supported by my family. I was taught that God was father and that father was God and that God knew and saw everything and would punish me for all the wrong and bad things I had done. I was taught that the priest/father was next to God and only he knew how to help me be less sinful, evil, and more worthy of God. I was to do anything and everything he might tell me to do.

So when my father, on two or three occasions, took my hand and brought me to the church at a time when it was not Mass, not Brownies, not choir, not First Friday, not the paper drive, the ritual, sexual, and spiritual abuse I will now describe by my church family formed a seamless continuum between my personal and cultural families and the "fathers" in them.

It is important to stress that the abuse to which I was subjected was not satanic abuse (devil worship) but ritual, sexual, and spiritual abuse done in the Catholic God's name, a perverted version of liturgical rite. I remember my father taking me to the side door of our church, bringing me to the lower level and into a room I had never been in before. The room was all white and had a long, high white marble table in the middle. He placed me on the floor in front of the table and left. I waited a long time for him to return and then he quietly walked through the door. Soon after, a priest and two members of the Knights of Columbus came in wearing white robes with the hoods up on their heads. The robes looked like the robes monks wore in Robin Hood days but they were white.

Without a word, my father took off my clothes and put something like a white slip on me. It was very cold in the room. After that, I was placed on the altar, where they removed my slip. They said some words and then put me on the floor in front of the altar and made me kneel down and bend over, and raped me. Increasing the terror and horrifying images of that night were the memories of my kitten, Snowball, being sacrificed in a perverted version of the Eucharistic sacrifice.

I knew I couldn't tell and so I prayed to God to either make me a boy or to at least make me not be. I think that was the first time "God" helped me, even before I asked, because somehow, all of a sudden one day *we*[2] were just out playing again.

As my therapist and I continued to work on these new memories and their psychic meanings, depression was my constant companion and suicide often seemed a better alternative than the process of recovery. Just as I had earlier feared my parents' wrath, I now was afraid that "they"—the Church, the priest, the Knights of Columbus, and my father—would get me.

Moreover, some of my alters did not know the abuse had ended, and others believed that the abusers had spiritual powers ordained by God that would allow them to reach out from the grave and kill *us* for telling the "secret." Most of me felt that we had deserved everything that had happened, that *we* were in fact evil, and that they had only, in God's name, tried to remove such evil.

On January 21, 2002, the *Boston Globe* broke the story of the crimes of sexual abuse in the Archdiocese of Boston. I heard victims speak and identified so strongly with them that when I would listen

---

[2]As a way to recognize and honor all the parts of who I am, I often use pronouns. For the purpose of this writing, I put them in italics.

to news of these events in the car, I would have to pull over to the side of the road to sob.

But the only survivor voices *we* heard were male, and I thus decided to come forward. In time, and with pressure, the abuse of girls began to be acknowledged, not by the Church, but by the media.

I reported my abuse to the Archdiocese of Boston. Their initial response was highly disrespectful. I described my experiences orally and in writing, and provided the name of the priest who had abused me. Three months later, after leaving phone messages and writing a letter, I finally got a response that there was no priest with the name I had given at the parish where I claimed the abuse had happened. I was devastated and, of course, began questioning my own experiences.

Fortunately, I had started to attend Survivors Network for those Abused by Priests (SNAP) meetings. At one of the meetings, I met an old neighborhood friend who had been abused in the same church by another priest. My friend clearly remembered the priest I named and also remembered being very afraid of him.

About six months later, the Boston archdiocese hired another person to handle victims' allegations. In a meeting with her and accompanied by my therapist, I asked if any other people had come forward with reports of abuse similar to mine. Sadly she said, "Yes, others have reported the same type of abuse, but by other priests." A week later, I was told that the priest in question had been in fact at the parish I named, and had died in the late 1950s. Shortly after that, my own research led me to a copy of an article about his death and funeral. In it he was listed as the "Chaplain of the Braintree Knights of Columbus and in charge of parish Christian Doctrine Classes." It went onto say that he was also the "Spiritual Director for the Braintree Catholic Youth Organization and the Ladies Sodality." At the end of the article his pallbearers were reported, with their appropriate titles. Feeling horrified and validated, I saw listed as pallbearers and 4th-degree members of the Knights of Columbus the two other men who had participated in my abuse.

I wish I could close by saying that I am healed and that both secular and religious communities have changed. Unfortunately, neither has happened. Yet, some things have changed. Many of us have moved from victim to survivor to activist, as many have moved from victim blaming to victim believing. It is my hope and challenge that together we will use the past to inform us rather than immobilize us as we work toward creating a safer and more sacred world for those yet to come.

8

Severed Selves and Unbridged Truths

Father M.

"If you bring forth what is within you, what you bring forth will save you. If you do not bring forth what is within you, what you do not bring forth will destroy you."

—Jesus, The Gospel of Thomas

"That which we do not bring to consciousness appears in our lives as fate."

—C. G. Jung

The preceding words of Jesus and Jung have particular relevance for me. The Greek word for truth, *alethia,* means "unforgetting." It is often understood in the context of myth where a river of forgetfulness had to be crossed in order to enter into the underworld, that place where unforgetting occurs and meaning is applied to the truths of a life.

For most of my adulthood, I have lived on various islands of self that kept significant truths of my life segregated. Remaining "forgetful" protected me from consciously experiencing the pain, betrayal, secrecy, and shame that had been central to my life. Here, I want to try to bridge some of these islands by telling parts of my story.

I bring a unique perspective to the sexual abuse crisis in the Catholic Church. I have experienced the scandal on several levels—as a Catholic priest who is a victim/survivor of other priests, as a gay man, and as a sexual transgressor. My story is of secrets imposed on me, secrets told, secrets still held, and secrets not yet unforgotten. It is a story of islands of selves that remained unbridged and compartmentalized for many years. It is also a story with pockets of unforeseen grace and redemption. Not cheap grace, mind you; rather, grace that has come at a very high cost, to myself and to others.

Paradoxically, I have chosen to share my story pseudonymously. Revealing myself at this time and in public could jeopardize my priesthood, as the institutional church discourages self-disclosure by its clergy. Using my name also could derail processes of restitution and reconciliation that still are unfolding.

VICTIM

The first island I bring you to is that of my abused self. My initial abuser is the person I looked up to the most as a child, my Uncle Joe. He was admired and respected by my entire family. He always came bearing lollipops so big that they would last into the next day. He had a contagious laugh and would brighten up whatever room he was in. My brother and I were raised to respect him, which was easy given his personality, the gifts he brought us, and the closeness he had with our mom and dad. But, my uncle betrayed that trust and corrupted the love and respect I had for him.

The first betrayal was relatively innocuous. I still believed in Santa Claus at age 6. One Sunday evening close to Christmas, after the dinner we shared around my grandparent's dining room table, Uncle Joe invited me to his house. He told me that he was going to share a secret with me that I could not discuss with anyone. He then explained that Santa Claus didn't exist and, in fact, he dressed as Santa on Christmas Eve. I am sure he saw the pain and disappointment on my face. He assured me that knowing this and keeping the secret was part of becoming an adult.

The following year, I traveled on vacation with my grandparents and uncle and shared a hotel room with him. When we got ready for bed that evening, Joe stripped naked and told me to do the same. I can remember being frightened and feeling aroused at the same time. Sometime during that night, I remember my uncle pressing his naked body into mine. He kept rubbing up against me. It was frightening and yet it excited me. He didn't say anything—nor did I—and eventually I must have fallen asleep. The next morning we showered and dressed and he acted as if nothing had happened. I knew my world had changed—I was confused and shaken but had no one to talk to about it. I kept that night's activities to myself—a secret that proved to be good training for the many secretive acts that were to follow.

Four years later, when I was 12, and a few months before his marriage, I had another sleepover with Joe, this time at his new house. He again stripped naked and invited me into his bed to "jerk off." I told him I didn't know what that was. Without any explanation, he masturbated me. It felt both terrifying and sensational at the same time. He also masturbated himself as I looked on. The next evening it happened again. It felt both great and sneaky. The following week I was back at his house and this time he introduced me to oral sex.

Joe married that summer and I was an altar boy, along with my brother, at his wedding. A few months later, I was invited to stay overnight so that I could go to his store, where I worked on Saturday mornings. I thought, "He is married now, surely our sexual escapades will not continue." But, after his wife went to bed, he invited me to sit next to him on the couch, where we had sex. I was terrified that she would hear us or come downstairs and find us. The intense fear of getting caught, mixed with the pleasure of sex, took root in me and began to taste good. This became a predictable routine, and, unfortunately, I developed an appetite for sex mixed with fear of getting caught that remained with me for many years.

My uncle's store was near my grandparent's house. Joe and I ate lunch there while they watched the store. Dessert usually included a quickie in my grandparent's living room. There was nothing passionate or affectionate about the sex—it was purely about getting off. I didn't want to think about Joe's wife or the children they were bringing into the world. Although I felt deceitful and ashamed, I put these thoughts into a closet in my head because they were too painful to acknowledge.

Our sexual encounters at his house evolved. We showered together in the morning "to save time." Eventually, his wife began leaving the house in the morning while we were in the shower. Some part of her must have known what was happening. These sexual experiences continued regularly until I was in college and found the strength to keep away from him.

I grew up Catholic and was proud to be an altar boy. The summer I turned 12, my favorite priest left the parish and another priest replaced him. I had grown close to the priest who was leaving and was honored to serve his last Mass at the parish. During the Mass, I began to cry and had to leave the sanctuary. As I wept, the new priest came to comfort me. As the summer drew on, a relationship developed between me, this new priest, and my family. He came for dinner and began to spend increasing amounts of time at our home. We played catch and saw movies together. Over the summer, he became my best friend. He also gave me a taste for the priesthood that was tangible and savory. Yet, from that first summer, the seeds of confusion were sewn into the fabric of the relationship. For example, depending on the circumstances, sometimes I called him Father and sometimes I used his first name, Larry. He and I began to spend more and more time together. We discussed the Church and the priesthood, and eventually our discussions became more personal and intimate.

I never told him about the sexual relationship I was having with my uncle and, although he knew him, there was never a hint that he suspected anything peculiar going on between us. Eventually we began to talk about sex and I told him that I was attracted more to boys than girls. He disclosed his orientation as bisexual and told me about some of the friendships he had with homosexual men. The following spring, when I graduated from eighth grade, I told him that I loved him. He told me that he loved me too and that I was a very special person in his life.

The relationship became more and more physical and seductive over time. We would wrestle and play games that involved touching each other. Our wrestling often ended up with one of us on top of the other with our groins touching. Watching television with my family, Fr. Larry and I would sit behind everyone and hold hands. This eventually led to more intimate touching. At first it seemed like a game, but eventually became very stressful since it occurred extremely close to my family.

One evening Fr. Larry pulled down his pants and asked me to touch his genitals. I was fourteen years old. I was frightened and aroused at the same time, by then a familiar admixture of reactions. He left before we could talk about it.

The next evening, Fr. Larry slept over in my room and masturbated me. A few days later, we began engaging in more extensive sex. My most dreadful memories are of us having sex and then immediately going downstairs to join my family for dinner. Fr. Larry would offer the blessing while I prayed silently that my family wouldn't know what had just happened upstairs.

The relationship and the sex with him were both pleasurable and shameful. As a teenager, I thought I was "lucky" to be in an intimate relationship with a person that so many people looked up to. At the same time, I knew that our relationship was wrong and sinful because Larry was a priest and no one else could know about it.

Although we expressed our love for each other, there was a familiar feeling of deceit. The layers of shame continued to smother me while I felt more and more alone. There were many evenings I cried myself to sleep because Larry had threatened to abandon me. I loved him deeply and yet I couldn't understand his behavior. I blamed myself, thinking that the problem was my inadequacy in giving and receiving love.

My relationship with Fr. Larry continued into my first year of college. He came to visit. He was very interested in my new life as a college student, especially in my relationships. His jealousy hindered my ability to develop close relationships with others.

I met a priest friend of Fr. Larry's on a retreat during high school. My first contact with Fr. Fred was during the sacrament of confession. After granting absolution, he stood up and gave me a long hug that included pressing his groin into mine. I thought this was a pass but didn't want to believe it because it occurred in the context of the sacrament. The next evening he asked me to meet him in his room where we talked about my vocation to the priesthood. He called me after a couple of weeks to go out for dinner.

At the restaurant he made several sexual advances that led us to a motel before he drove me home. Fr. Fred was very sexually aggressive and much more experienced than I was. There was no affection and little concern for my needs. He continued calling me, but I tried to dodge his calls. My parents didn't understand my avoidance and encouraged me to see him again. They knew he was a friend of Fr. Larry's and another fine priest who could help me discern my vocation. I felt doomed by how trapped I was in secrets and lies.

This island of my abused self left me feeling cheap and dirty over and over again. I felt as if I was betraying every relationship I had: parents, family, friends, priests, church, God, myself. The secrecy and shame were so overwhelming I could not face them and shelved them in another compartment of self.

GAY MAN

I knew I was more attracted to boys than girls since grade school. I occasionally played sexually with boys my own age from elementary school onward. My family had relatives who were in the theater and who spoke about their friendships with gay men.

I grew up post-Vatican II and post-Stonewall. I was taught that God "doesn't make junk." Rather, God creates each of us in His own image out of love, for love, and with love as our destiny. The Church's teaching on homosexuality, that we are "intrinsically disordered," never made sense to me.

It was in college that I fell in love with a man my own age. By this time, Fr. Larry was out of my head and out of my heart, or so I thought. Being in love at this time in my life was full of rich graces and complexity. Looking back I can see how the seeds sewn into my being from the abuse were already poisoning my ability to relate intimately. I had little ability to trust, forgive, and compromise, and I was extremely possessive. The relationship echoed my earlier fear that I was inadequate in giving and receiving love.

I found myself being drawn deeper and deeper into a subculture of the gay community that centered on drugs and music. The club drugs induced a trance state that was familiar and also had to be hidden.

After college, I entered the seminary. I moved from dancing all night with my friends to praying in the early mornings with my fellow seminarians. It is startling to realize just how compartmentalized my life had become. The transition happened almost overnight and generated no inner conflict. Today, I see how the seeds of secrecy and shame sewn into my vocational call by my priest abusers supported these splits.

PRIEST

From a very early age I felt close to God. My call into the priesthood, mysterious and graced as it is, was present from boyhood and continues today. Entering seminary was something I simply had to do.

I made the choice to enter the seminary after several years of therapy and discernment. The inner work helped me to acknowledge the fact that men I loved and trusted had abused me. And although I divulged the abuse in spiritual direction, a forum where you can speak the truth to another priest in secret, there was no inner healing. Not one of my spiritual directors throughout discernment and seminary invited me to probe deeper into my abusive experiences. When I revealed in confession that I had a difficult time adhering to the Church's definition of celibacy, one of my directors suggested I was a sex addict and that I should pursue a 12-step spiritual practice to keep from engaging in sexual activity. Certainly there was some compulsivity to my sexual appetite but suggesting that this was merely an addiction fueled the shame that surrounded my sexuality.

As a priest, I lived a double life. There was my life in the parish where I practiced ministry and there was my life outside the parish where I lived among my gay friends and was sometimes sexually active. The great capacity I had developed to compartmentalize helped keep me from becoming too emotionally overwhelmed by this incredible divide.

TRANSGRESSOR

I knew very little about Fr. Bernard when the bishop assigned him to the parish where I was pastor to minister to the growing Hmong population from southern China. Soon after Fr. Bernard's arrival, he was accused of having sex with one of the teenage boys in the Hmong community. A small team interviewed those involved and concluded that the accusations could not be true. The boy's parents did not want to believe the allegations either, and their teenage son vehemently denied anything inappropriate had taken place. I later learned that Fr. Bernard had a history of inappropriate touching with teenage boys in his previous assignment and I was angry that my bishop had not shared this with me.

Fr. Bernard knew I was a gay man. Months after the investigation, he asked me for a massage to help him with back pain. It felt both erotic and terrifying at the same time; a toxic mixture that I had grown to savor in an earlier diet of sexual desire and fear. Over the next few months, the massages became reciprocal. I felt as if I were on familiar turf; the feelings of deceit, shame, and secrecy mixed with sexual arousal were all too familiar.

The massages eventually turned into some genital activity. It was mutual, but I knew we had crossed a critical boundary and that it was a grave mistake. Now Fr. Bernard could blackmail me if I ever was confronted with further sexual misconduct on his part. Further from awareness then was the serious transgression I was enacting in a fiduciary relationship with a subordinate.

Over the next few months, more evidence surfaced of an inappropriate relationship between Fr. Bernard and the teenage boy. I chose to report the information to the bishop, knowing that doing so would probably expose my own transgression. Fr. Bernard was sent off to treatment and I was instructed to lie to my parishioners about his abrupt departure because the bishop did not want to make the scandal public.

Predictably, Fr. Bernard reported me to the bishop for sexual harassment. This time I was instructed to leave the parish immediately, with no explanation given to parishioners. Again, the bishop did not want the truth to be told and I agreed with him at the time. It saved me from further embarrassment, but it did not afford my parishioners access to the truth or an opportunity to express a range of reactions.

RECOVERY BEGINS

I entered a Catholic treatment center that included clergy as patients. There, I found a community of men and women, including some who had sexually abused minors, who were deeply engaged in the painful process of their own unforgetting.

A big piece of my work in those months was to confront my memories of the priests who had sexually abused me and to look more closely at the aftereffects of those experiences. This work became far more painful and complicated after the sexual abuse scandal erupted in Boston. As a priest, I disagreed with the bishops' policy of zero tolerance, which I consider un-Christian and devoid of the complexity that each and every sexual abuse case deserves. Eating and praying and journeying with sexual abusers who were now fellow travelers in a recovery process exposed me to the humiliation they experienced when their misbehavior became public. I heard their stories; I knew the pain they felt as a result of leaving their assignment and public ministry oftentimes, like myself, in the middle of the night.

Yet, as a survivor, I knew that "justice served in secrecy is not justice." These men needed to be held responsible so that other young people should not be put at risk. I wrestled with finding some way to hold my abusers accountable that could shield them from public humiliation. In the end, I met with the bishop to share my story, leaving it to him to handle the priests involved. He heard me—believed me—and he acted swiftly, removing both priests from ministry and placing them on administrative leave.

It hurt to learn that only one of the priests admitted to the abuse. Perhaps unrealistically, I wanted to hear from them that they were sorry for betraying my trust and sexually exploiting me. I wanted them to acknowledge that they had some inkling of the pain they caused me. Instead, the bishop offered me a financial settlement. Although I am grateful for that form of restitution, it feels as if they are replacing with money the opportunity for restorative justice and reconciliation.

From 2000 through 2002 I had the following recurring dream:

> I am driving in a car and begin to lose control of the vehicle as I drive over a bridge. The car is moving very fast and I don't have power over the steering wheel. I am terrified because the car is racing out of control—off the bridge—into a large body of water.

In preparing to write this piece, the dream resurfaced and I began to look at its meaning through the lens of un-forgetting. My life was terribly out of control, moving down a highway at high speed in sometimes opposing directions. There were few bridges connecting one configuration of self to another. My "vehicle" did crash into the waters of unconscious processes and unprocessed memories. Today, I am working to ride the waves of healing while still delving into deep wounds, wounds that are the very openings that allow the salve of God's healing grace to transform and redeem. Through my relationships, I am beginning to construct vital bridges that help connect my journey with the fact that when we speak our truth, when we unforget, individually and communally, we heal not only ourselves, we help heal the world.

REFERENCE

Jung, C. G. (1953–1979), Christ: A symbol of the self. *The Collected Works* (Bollinger Series XX), trans. R. F. C. Hull, ed. H. Read, M. Fordham, G. Adler & W. McGuire. Princeton, NJ: Princeton University Press, 9ii, par. 126.

9

Sexual Abuse, Spiritual Formation, and Psychoanalysis

Tom Lewis

Sexual abuse, once an event in fearful silence, is now seen as a civil wrong or crime. Participants are stereotyped as perpetrators, victims, or enablers, the simplifications of an adversarial legal system. I suggest a more complex view. As an altar boy, I was abused in church by the senior acolyte who was training me. The abuse taught me to lie and lose trust in adults and myself. For survival, I learned to invent provisional selves without knowing these would become confusions of identity, sexuality, and purpose, lifelong sources of anxiety and depression. Through a recovery of my spiritual life and a psychoanalysis that together amounted to a metanoia, "a change of heart," I was able to reconcile with myself and my history, and with my elderly father, whom I saw as having failed to protect me years before.

Memory is the most complex element of one's inner life. Behavior, which we generally think of as complex, is relatively consistent over

time if closely observed. Memory seems disorderly and unpredictable. The forms of fiction—novels, films, plays—are mostly about
memory and nearly always convert memory to behavior in order to
observe and record. Intuitively and experientially, one's own memories are cryptic and unreliable, dreamlike. Memory seems to define
human complexity.

Memory can be trained but mostly simply occurs, an almost autonomic function of the body–mind, obviously a neurological function
in which sensory input is recorded and retained and ordered. It is as-
sociational. It is how we know a door is a door and a color a color;
memory enables us to remember why and how to stir the sugar into
our coffee. It is how we remember the scene in *The Brothers
Karamazov* in which Ivan describes to Alyosha, a dray horse being
beaten to death in the street (Dostoevsky, 1880), how we know others and how we know ourselves. Embedded in memory is the elusive
master narrative, if only we could recall it whole.

Now, at 62, I can't remember with certain accuracy what has happened in the time I have existed.[1] Nor can I differentiate my own,
original memories from stories taken in from others, or those
skin-to-skin experiences one has with close family and intimates—
mother, father, children, lovers, strangers—or chance encounters on
the sidewalk. It's all in there, the stuff of life that makes day-to-day life
depressing, frightening, overwhelming, exciting, delightful—the ac-
cretion of new memories and the editing or selection process that
seems to take place as one grows older.

When I was 10 and 11, I had my first sexual experiences. They
were at the hands, as it were, of an older boy. He was 17 or 18, the senior acolyte at the small Episcopal church I attended with my mother
and father. He was also a baby-sitter trusted by my parents. I won't
name him because he may still be alive and I have no wish for re-
venge, let alone legal action. I'll call him N, a sample of one.

Does naming matter? Accuracy? I am not taking N to court, where
standards of accuracy ("truth") are defining. I cannot now know accurately what happened. I probably cannot find out. N and I were the
only witnesses. There seems to me no such thing as forensic psychology or psychoanalysis; it would be inherently untruthful to say we

---

[1]The original article was written in late 2002.

know the truth about such distant events or even recent events, as reconstituted-memory cases have shown. Any cop or insurance adjuster can testify to the differing stories of eyewitnesses. See Kurosawa's *Rashomon* (1950).

But accuracy does matter because there is an ethics to how we act on our memories. We are not isolates. Our memories and actions always involve others; if they are intimates, our memories collide and mix with theirs. My memories of what happened in the basement men's room of St. Suburban's Church in Pittsburgh in 1951 and 1952 are, no doubt, similar to and different from N's memories.

I don't have access to any recollection he may have. Therefore I am solely responsible for this story. However, I don't know exactly what happened because I don't remember exactly. In *Light In August,* William Faulkner (1932) wrote: "Memory believes before knowing remembers" (p. 119).

I needn't define sexual abuse. There is a body of literature on the topic—psychoanalytic, legal, journalistic, autobiographical. I don't want to join the fraternity of abused boys. I do want to understand the effects of my experience with N. They were catalysts for the origins of my spiritual life and much of my psychic history.

I have been an autodidact all my life, from my reading of children's stories to the reading in boarding school and college that began an adult lifetime of reading. From reading and experience, I acquired the need and ability to make my own choices. I was taught and absorbed entire congeries of language, stories, terms of thought and argument, and models for behavior—what we interchangeably call values or culture.

I learned there were an amazing variety and number of choices available. Choices were required, could not be avoided. When I was eight, I began to make some of those choices. If spiritual formation is a matter of choice as much as inspiration, I was finding a spiritual path.

As a small boy in Pittsburgh in the late 1940s and early 1950s, my autodidactic formation began in an Episcopal baptism at age eight followed by catechism and confirmation at nine and concurrent training by N as an acolyte or altar boy. N was not ordained but acted as a de facto deacon trusted by the priest, who was himself a close friend of my father, responsible for my father's discovery of a life of faith and devotion.

N was a close friend of another boy who, along with the boy's older sister, baby-sat for me. One night, N and the other boy took me to see *King Solomon's Mines,* which was to me a marvelous movie. The other boy gave me a hand-me-down leather jacket that I wore for years. Made of pale, smooth deerskin, it had the efficacy for me of an Iroquois hunter's shirt made from his own kill. We learn to wear the behavior of others, as well as their clothes; we inhabit their lives, as their memories and behaviors inhabit us.

In this atmosphere of total trust, N seduced me—the only word that seems appropriate—one Saturday in the men's room in the basement of the church when we were preparing for a service the following morning. I remember standing next to him, clothed, facing the waist-high—chest-high for me—white urinals. I held his erect penis in my left hand—it seemed huge to me—while he held my little penis in his right hand and masturbated me. He came in a spasm that surprised me. I did not. That first happened some time later when I masturbated myself, sitting at my desk in my room in the house where I lived with my mother and father.

I remember one other sexual encounter with N, although I know there were several more. It was in a Ford coupe that belonged to his father. We were parked at the end of a dead-end road down a hollow not far from where I lived. Fully clothed, zippers open, small hand on big penis, big hand on small. There was no oral sex, none of the back-rubbing reported in contemporary stories of priestly seduction, none of the tense threats to keep silent. There was trust and talk. He talked about college, his ambition to be a priest. He talked about girls, not in the images of twisted fantasies, but in the most disembodied way, about ankle bracelets and what they signaled in the simple, binary code of the 1950s: available, taken.

The encounters, over a period of a year or somewhat less, were never discovered by my parents or anyone else. How it ended, I don't remember.

My sexual future? I remember a circle jerk with four or five other boys in someone's bedroom after school. There was no mutual touching. I was about 12. There was a lot of talk about masturbation then and in high school and boarding school, very little talk of it in college, none in the Army. I acquired a girlfriend in public high school, in ninth grade or the summer after, and discovered the ritu-

als and pleasures of making out. This was the 1950s. Teen sex was covert but also an open secret, as it probably always had been, at least
among blue-collar people and the white-collar classes into which
they rose, the classes of people I grew up among.

At 15, one summer night, I was taken to a whorehouse by the older
brothers of two pals of mine, five of us in a souped-up 1950 Mercury;
the place was up a back alley in one of the steel towns down the
Monongahela River from Pittsburgh. The women were African American. The price was two dollars. I was nervous but managed somehow with the help of a woman who was kind and patient and bored
all at once. That was all I knew of her life, which was certainly far
harder than I could imagine had I known to try. I was taken back several times that summer and took myself, after I learned to drive, a few
more times in the next year or two.

I grew up lying about sex and, therefore, lying about myself. I
learned to lie, I now believe, about sex with N and my girlfriend and
the prostitutes in Brick Alley because the truth shamed me and was
unacceptable to my mother and father. Thus, in the mind of a boy, I
was taught to lie by my parents. They had been, until then, all-powerful figures in my life. They embodied the culture in which I was
raised. To maintain their trust, I lied. To remain trusted and loved, I
had to become someone other than who I was. Lying to them without apparent penalty taught me they were not all powerful. For me,
the habit-forming part of lying was the sense of autonomous power it
conferred.

That was the damage done by N and by the culture in which I
grew up. I learned a malignant, enduring lesson: emotional
survival required the creation of false selves. "False" is what I
called them when I first discovered their existence at the age of 60
during psychoanalysis. I soon learned to call them provisional,
out of simple self-respect and with the help of my analyst. He
never suggested one adjective or another. Instead, he helped me
learn to honor and respect and begin to like myself for who I am,
not who the voices of those provisional selves told me I should or
could have been; not the person suggested by all the shoulda-
woulda-couldas directed at me by so many people over the years;
and not the person who heard so many shoulda-woulda-couldas
when they weren't intended.

Telling lies to my parents about where I'd been, what I'd done, and with whom metamorphosed into lies to myself about who I was. Not knowing who I was rapidly became the determining problem of my life, though I was unable for many years to give voice to or name the problem. The ability to create a provisional self for survival in any situation in which I found myself—abandoned by my parents at boarding school, at a university in which I could not find a congenial direction for my life, in various jobs over the years for which I was not suited or did not find satisfying—was a talent that plagued me. A psychiatrist once told me I was better at landing on my feet than anyone he'd known. "But don't get cocky," he said. If only he or I had understood the pun.

My repertoire of shifting identities was fundamentally confusing to me and often to the people with whom I worked or lived. The old selves were parasitic and sometimes reappeared on their own when they were not needed or wanted, not unlike inconvenient memories.[2]

When I was about 50, I saw a therapist for serious depression after a divorce. In one session, I asked for a diagnosis. The therapist's response? "Well, this won't help you but here is what I think. Your emotional development was arrested at the age of 15."

That was my age when I was sent to boarding school. He was partly right without knowing why. At the moment, his comment only confused me. It added nothing to the narrative I did not yet know I needed to construct.

Was I abused? Of course I was. I didn't know it at the time. I had no language for it. It didn't feel like abuse then; nor years later. Was I taken advantage of? Yes. N obtained pleasure and satisfied a need at my expense and without my consent. The age of consensual sex is different for different people. My girlfriend and I were old enough to consent mutually to have intercourse when we were 15. Different states legislate sexual consent at different ages. Experts and ordinary citizens can argue the age of consent, but we generally believe that it is important to set reasonable standards and make reasonable rules for living up to them. In no way did I consent to have sex with N.

---

[2] I am not talking about alters or multiple personalities here. I am neither a mental health professional nor writing in a professional language.

By current standards, I might have told my parents what happened with N, and my parents might have done something. The preferred remedies now involve lawyers and seem to be exposure, humiliation, litigation, and monetary reparation. Circa 1951, the preference was silence.

Was I harmed? Yes. My life was altered against my will and with no deliberate choice on my part. I did not know I had a choice. I lost trust in my mother and father because, although they did not know what had happened, they were unable to protect me against it or the consequences. I lost my trust in N—who was to me an adult—and in the adult world in general. I entered adolescence with little trust in anyone.

But life causes wounds and scars. Were I not injured by N, I would have been injured sooner or later in some other way by someone else. The consequences of that unknown injury are impossible to determine. I have learned to live with the consequences of my encounter with N. People I know with different sorts of psychic wounds have been very nearly crippled by them. I have scars from my dealings with N, but the wounds that caused them were not life-threatening or crippling. Trust and intimacy can be difficult for me. Damaging? Surely. Hurtful to me and others? Sometimes. But not fatal.

N set me on a path of many years of confusion, pain, and loss. What has been complicated—and has taken a long time and hard work to sort out—is the way the experience with N constellated with other experiences, the way new experiences mapped onto old, how these concatenated to form additional experiences, and how new provisional selves laminated over old selves and obscured and disguised the true self beneath.

Sexual pleasure came later and proved to be a complex thing. Complex with others and with myself alone. For example, I realized many years later, with a start, that I often masturbated over a white enamel sink in a bathroom. If, by that, N can be said to have taught me pleasure, it became not pleasurable but obsessional. This was no initiatory gift. It was a robbery.

During and after the sexual experience with N, my religious faith and practice continued to mature. N continued to play an important role in my life or that part of it that had to do with St. Suburban's. My time as an acolyte was one of the most influential of my life. In that role, I was useful, trusted, and relied on.

When I was 12 or 13, with my parents' permission, N took me for several weekend visits to a chapter house of the Order of St. Barnabas, a celibate, monastic order of the Episcopal Church that I am unsure still exists. Clearly, I was not afraid of N. For self-sufficiency, the order ran a small farm in a rural county north of Pittsburgh. The brothers worked on the farm and prayed and sang together in a small chapel. The visits formed in my mind a vivid image of a religious community. For me as a boy, it defined the idea of community.

At 15, I was sent away to Kent School, a decision in which I played no part. It was a place as socially unfamiliar to me as a foreign land. There were reasons: I was in serious trouble with the local police for vandalism and being "bad"; teachers had told my parents to find another school because I was "too bright" for the local high school; my parents suspected or knew I was having sex and didn't know what to do about it. They felt they were doing the right thing but, for me, it was an abandonment. I had literally no guidance or emotional support from them while I was at Kent. I told my father later that they might as well have sent me to sea as a midshipman in Nelson's navy.

The school was founded by a celibate priest in the Episcopal Order of the Holy Cross, on the principles of simplicity and self-reliance. It observed a vaguely monastic rule derived somehow from English public schools; the Sixth Form, or seniors, were responsible for the day-to-day running and discipline of the student body. When I arrived, the founder had died. His system of self-reliance had been corrupted into a petty system of power, control, and punishment.

Almost immediately on arrival, I lost the practice of my religious faith. I had imagined a more or less religious community like St. Suburban's with elements of the St. Barnabas chapter house. What I found was an institution with a lot of unwritten behavioral and social rules that seemed familiar to most of the students but not to me. I could not find a way to insinuate myself into the small group of boys who assisted in the chapel. They were somehow chosen by someone. Without knowing why, I was not chosen. For my three years at Kent, I sat in my assigned seat in the pews as a rote participant in the required daily services. I continued as an acolyte at St. Suburban's when I was home for Christmas, Easter, and summer breaks, but a thread was broken and the attachment gone. My spiritual life fell silent and disappeared under the surface of my daily life. It did not reappear for 25 years and then in a new guise.

In some respects, it was familiar. In my 40s, I became a Catholic, an impulse I'd had since the summer I was 17 and began dating a devout Catholic girl who did her best to convert me. She was a student at a school run by Franciscan nuns. She introduced me to her confessor, a Franciscan priest. I talked with him a few times but found that here also were many rules, not much discussion of them, and a powerful effort to enforce behavior. The Catholicism I encountered in 1958 seemed more authoritarian than Kent's social orthodoxy and encompassed far more than life on the campus of a small school. I lost interest.

Kent was a boys' school, an insular, all-male society. There were rules, nowhere written, about sex and physical contact. There was to be none. There was a muted homophobia. It was assumed by all that homosexual or any other sexual activity was grounds for expulsion. Boys made jokes and there were several teachers said to be queer, but other than masturbation and a lot of talk and joking about it, I wasn't aware of any sex among students or between teachers and students.

I made out with my girlfriend when I was home, but we were competing with Franciscan rules. We never went far because we understood that the burden of the penalty was on her. Instead, we talked about nearly everything. I could be more myself with a girlfriend or my pals at Kent than with my parents and the St. Suburban world that had once filled my life. A nearly permanent estrangement from my parents set in; they seemed unaware of it.

I was a changed person. To survive at Kent, in a briar patch of social and institutional conformity based on upper-class mores, I had imagined and constructed a new self. I learned how from the evasive self that emerged during the experience with N.

The survival self I evolved at Kent was more complete, more complex. I learned to mimic my social surroundings. This was more than the momentary camouflage one throws on and off in fleeting social situations.

It was a partial-self, residing not on me but within me. This self mimicked adaptation to the rules, stated and unstated, at Kent. It was at war with the lying self I invented after N and perfected in public high school, the self that mocked rules and rebelled. Now there was a good boy opposing the bad boy. I didn't understand that the good boy was also bad for me. This was no deerskin jacket. It was the shirt of Nessus.

I had lost all trust in grown-ups, so I had few relationships with the adults at Kent. I did well on the standardized tests that mostly determined college admission. I did well in some courses, but not in others. I got along with some coaches, not with others. I was picking and choosing. In my junior year, or the fifth form, I began to rebel. But Kent was no place for disobedience. In the fall term, I typed out a kind of broadside on the topic of hypocrisy and school spirit and pinned it to the main bulletin board. It was taken down. I was chastised rather than encouraged to find a useful outlet for my impulse to write. But rather than joining the school newspaper or literary magazine, I stifled the impulse. I knew the candidates were chosen somehow by someone. Here again, I was not chosen. The wound was greater than the desire. It was a syndrome that affected me for years and damaged me greatly later on.

I know now, or think I know, that this problem originated from my encounter with N. It was a triple whammy. I lost faith in someone I trusted but was unable to recognize the loss because I had no words for it; I lost trust in my parents for not protecting me; I lost trust in myself for not being someone else. Other adults were facsimiles of my mother and father. What other model was there? Perhaps I feared the older adolescents at Kent would be facsimiles of N. As it happened, some of the older men I found helpful as a freshman at Columbia were gay. I backed away. In those years, the only way there could be another person to trust was for me to invent that person, another provisional self, and so I did, several times over, then and in the years to come.

I experienced abandonment at age two (another story), again at 10 or 11; and then at 15 when I was sent to Kent—no wonder I became adept at inventing provisional selves. Now I have words for this history, part of the narrative constructed with the help of several years of difficult but useful analysis with a caring, competent analyst. I can relate these events without falling into the intense feelings of depression and anxiety that I experienced during most of my adult life. But, until recently, I was able only to write and rewrite, tell and retell, forget and remember, erase and fill in an elaborate palimpsest in the effort to locate myself. Mine was a restless, determined effort to remember, but the result was a superficial chronology that only increased my agitation and self-doubt. I was trapped in a mocking circle of selves. Like little Frankenstein monsters, they refused to lie down and die.

Falsity, loss of self, a fear of self, not wanting to know who I was, a rejection by myself and others of the little boy I had been—these were consequences of my experience with N. He was not the sole cause of my troubles. He was not, I don't believe, responsible at all as a young man, not the way a 40-year-old priest might be considered responsible. But the experience was a true catalyst. There were a before and after. Down Saul and up Paul, as I was taught. Down Tommy and up Tom.

Perhaps we should accept, even welcome, the persons we become as a result of the difficult or terrible experiences of life. But how?

As I passed from adolescence to young adulthood and discovered a more introspective language, I found I was experiencing a low-grade homophobia in myself and realized it was an image of the homophobia, as pervasive as racism though more subtle, in the places and cultures in which I grew up and matured—the black and white homophobias of a steel town and public schools, then the more shaded and complex homophobias of the all-male institutions I inhabited for a decade in the 1950s and 1960s: Kent, Columbia College, the Army. My own homophobia manifested as sexual self-doubt and demanded a more or less constant reaffirmation of my straight sexual desires.

I first recognized this when I was 20. My father bought me a suit at a men's store he liked in downtown Pittsburgh. Standing in front of the three-way mirrors, I was having the suit fitted. My father was elsewhere in the store. Kneeling behind me, the tailor measured and pinned the trouser cuffs and marked the seat. He said quietly, "You have a nice ass. You have the hips of a woman." I froze. I couldn't respond. I felt as though he had touched me. It was certainly his intention. I felt marked with the white chalk he used, as if for alteration. I have obviously not forgotten it. The unconscious feeds on such stuff and feeds it back to us in daily life and dreams.

I had, without knowing it, learned a specific mistrust of men. Nor did I trust women because I did not trust my mother not to abandon me. I could not trust myself because, as I learned while at Kent and Columbia, I was unable to control my behavior. I was acting out, although this was another phrase and idea I did not understand until many years later. I was nearly expelled from Kent for mischief. I was suspended and then expelled from Columbia for academic failure.

I enlisted in the Army, where my abilities were recognized and used. The simple rewards of acceptance and promotion, the paradoxical autonomy of taking and being given responsibilities, gave me the self-discipline to control my acting out. My acceptance and usefulness in the Army was similar to my experience as an acolyte a decade earlier. After the Army, I was readmitted to Columbia with the help of a sympathetic dean. I finished college and went on with my life.

In the middle years of my marriage, I began acting out again; this time it was sexual. I had several affairs that deeply hurt my wife and damaged our marriage. It was not until I spent two years rediscovering my spiritual life with the help of the best teacher I ever had, a retired Jesuit priest serving as chaplain of a retreat house run by the Catholic Order of the Holy Cross—these circularities are enough to make one a Jungian—that I found the self-knowledge and moral compass to stop acting out.

One night during years of spiritual recovery, I dreamed I was lying on my bed in an apartment I shared with my mother and father as a child. In the dream, I was in my early 40s. A young boy came into the room and lay down on the bed beside me. It was a child's single bed. The figure of the boy merged in a ghostly way into the body of the man. The boy was me. I woke up weeping, sobbing, unable to describe the dream to my wife, unable to speak at all. It was the greatest catharsis of my life. In the dream, the man was made whole. In life, the man began the healing that has only now, 20 years later, seemed complete enough for description as a metamorphosis.

Ovidian metamorphosis moves only forward, bare of the idea of redemption. Conventionally, as a Christian, one is made new through baptism, one of the original Christian sacraments, the most singular mark of a Christian. Baptism redeems sin, particularly Original Sin, the theological origins of one's humanity. Thus, it is a kind of reverse metamorphosis. The baptism of Jesus by John the Baptist is the paradigm, but there is another in the conversion of Saul described in Acts. It is violent in conception and in practice, as millions of people have found who are not the same religion as those conquering and killing them.

The priest—his name was Gregory Roy—who "witnessed," as he put it, at my becoming a Catholic taught me the idea of metanoia: a New Testament Greek word for change so complete that one is made new.[3] He explicitly rejected the use of the word conversion for my experience. Metanoia, I believe, can be achieved only by individuals. In my experience, the process has not been violent but painful, uncertain, and long. You can set out to find it, but you may not succeed. It may occur in a moment or take many years. My experience of metanoia began with Father Roy in 1982 and ended with Dr. Louis Lauro in 2002, two men I learned to trust and who cared for me and helped me identify and give voice to my inner life. Spiritual life and daily life—why do we think there is a difference? True self and the provisional selves created by the true self—why did I think they were different?

In analysis, the word "story" is avoided, perhaps because it suggests fiction. Is a narrative of self a story? I have written and published fiction and nonfiction. Did I ever think there were differences?

In my years at St. Surburban's, I was taught that forgiveness is a cardinal virtue for a Christian and a habit to be cultivated. Turn the other cheek, I was told. At eight, I had not turned the other cheek— which was when that lesson was first preached to me—nor did I later develop the practice. In the competitive, sometimes violent—always potentially violent—world of a boy growing up in a tough town in the 1950s, it was hard to understand how nonviolence could be practical.

It took 30 years for me to find the impulse to forgive N, which is to say it took 30 years to recognize there had been an injury. The impulse was triggered by accident. During a visit to my parents in 1984, I think, I found a church newsletter with a black and white photograph of Fr. N standing in front of a mission school in rural Africa. I read that he was back in the United States and resting for a while at a place not far from where I lived. I wrote to him, received an answer,

---

[3]From A Great Change of Heart, Papal Homily to the Young on Mount of Beatitudes Pope John Paul II, March 24, 2000 (*http://www.catholic-forum.com/saints/pope02461.htm*).

and went to visit him. It was a reunion warm with the familiarity and intensity of the associations of childhood. I did not say, "I forgive you." We did not talk about what had passed between us. We talked about what he'd done and where he'd been, about the 30 years of my life that had passed. I told him of my having become a Catholic. He taught me a little meditative prayer from his investigation of the liturgy and practices of the Russian Orthodox Church. It was enough to spend a few hours with him, to share a meal. We parted amiably. There were two or three letters back and forth, then silence.

For me, there is no question that the act of forgiving N by seeing him in person was a counterphobic catharsis, a deliberate recognition of self. It uplifted my spirit. I only then realized what a burden N had been for me, for so long.

There was another burden—the mild, self-doubting homophobia. This simply went away over time. The recognition of self that occurred at the time of my visit with N included a recognition that my homophobia was lodged within me, self-generated, no longer a function of the homophobia of the larger culture and my experience with N. The visit with N turned out to be a kind of naming ceremony. The anxiety atrophied, now something else: the anxiety about identity and selfhood and uncertainty about who I was. The primary, determining problem had been exposed.

Metanoia, for me, is the extreme change that heals the wound that does not heal. It is pain and healing and change all together, sometimes quick, sometimes agonizingly slow. It is not possible to choose it. One is, instead, chosen, not by a deity but at a crossroads. It is Sophoclean, oedipal, as it were.

There was another forgiveness for me to accomplish, of a very different kind, far more comprehensive and difficult. My father died at 92 in August of 2002. I would not have been able to write this before he died. Perhaps I was protecting him. Perhaps I was still lying to protect myself, not from N but from the recognition that my father was not the perfect father, that he had abandoned me at critical moments, that I had been deeply hurt by his absences and weaknesses, that I had, in effect, been forced to become an adult and live as an adult without the ability to see myself as an adult.

I was not fully adult because I did not fully know myself as an autonomous person. I was still lying to myself about who I was, the thing that began with N, when I lied to my mother and father when I was 10 about where I'd been, whom I was with, what I was doing. Not to protect N, but to protect myself and, later, to protect the little boy in drag as an adult.

It was not until my mother and father were in their late 80s, when my mother was an invalid in a wheelchair, finally incompetent, and my father was her caretaker, frail himself, that I was able to forgive him for abandoning me when I needed protection at age 10 and other times, particularly when I needed help or guidance at Kent and Columbia.

Only when he recognized that I had taken responsibility for his care and would show up when needed, no matter what, did I fully recognize the adult in myself. "The child is father of the man," he told his doctor. From the Greeks to Wordsworth. I was in my late 50s. I never forgave my mother because, when I was able to, her decline into mute senility had so completely absented her that I could not. With her, I needed to talk. She had taught me to talk.

With N, I did not need to talk of forgiveness. I did not want to; I did not wish to turn the other cheek. I forgave him in the silence of my heart only so I could forgive myself.

Prayer speaks to silence. My spiritual life is reduced to a matter of the mute rumblings of the heart, a phrase I remember, perhaps incorrectly, from one of Paul's letters read long ago. Father Roy made it possible for me to be comfortable with my mute spirituality, which is all I seem to need or want.

Starting with N or as a psychic aftershock, I began to seek a kind of oblivion in the acted-out self-destructions available to men: alcohol, sex, work, depression, anxiety, severally or all simultaneously. I mostly avoided violence and drugs and avoided entirely adult crime, war, and suicide. It would be fair to say that N taught me to act out. He showed me how.

Being an only child, I was comfortable in solitude but often lonely. N saw a vulnerability and took advantage of it. He taught me to not trust. From not trusting adults, I went to not trusting their institutions, not trusting others in general and, far worse, not trusting myself. I find now that I trust myself, my children, and a few others. I have trusted two male teachers, who were a priest and an analyst. I trust the voice that appears on the page when I write it: the voice tells the story of the transformation of an episode of abuse into a lifelong spiritual journey. It is the road N set me on. I am mostly content to be who I am and where I am but do not know for how long. I feel I have one more pilgrimage ahead.

REFERENCES

Dostoevsky, F. (1880), *The Brothers Karamazov*. New York: Knopf, 1992.
Kurosawa, A. (1950), *Rashomon*. RKO Radio Pictures.
Faulkner, W. (1932), *Light in August*. New York: Vintage, 1990.

IV

The Institutional Church
and The Pastoral Church

10

How Could It Happen?
An Analysis of the Catholic Sexual
Abuse Scandal

The Reverend James Martin, S.J.

Let me begin this chapter by publicly apologizing in the name of the Catholic Church to any and all victims of sexual abuse by priests. I know that may be cold comfort. I have never abused anyone, but since victim survivors were hurt by people ministering in the name of the Church, it is the least I can do.

The sexual abuse scandal has rightly been called the greatest and gravest crisis in the history of the Catholic Church in the United States, and we are still very much in the midst of it. All of us inside the Church must continue to work to better understand and confront the problem of sexual abuse by priests. We must begin to reflect on how to heal victims, hold the church accountable, and help prevent such crimes from occurring again in any organization, religious or otherwise.

I write for a weekly Catholic magazine, *America,* published by the Jesuits, a men's religious order. Since January 2001, we have featured dozens of articles on the sexual abuse crisis written by survivors of abuse, parents, and friends of abuse victims, psychiatrists, psychologists, lawyers, lay Catholics, priests, and bishops—all in an effort to shed light on the crisis. Jesus of Nazareth, after all, said, "There is nothing that is concealed that will not be revealed." Even more to the point, he said, "The truth will set you free." All of us must continue to pursue the truths inherent in the sexual violation of minors by priests.

In discussing some of the underlying causes of the Catholic scandal, I will draw on the work of the National Review Board, a group of lay people appointed by the United States Conference of Catholic Bishops, who researched the reasons for the crisis and reported their findings in early 2003. While there are critics who have questioned the independence of the Board, I think that their situational analysis contained many accurate and important observations.

There are, of course, no excuses for these crimes. Although I will discuss a number of reasons for the scandal here, none of them are exculpatory. Yet we must unearth and evaluate causal factors in order to ensure that we never again generate a crisis like this one.

The Board asked two main questions. First, why did so many priests abuse minors? Second, how could the bishops have dealt with the issue so poorly, or not at all?

Approximately 4.5% of all priests in active ministry between 1950 and 2000 have been accused of abuse. I believe that is slightly higher than in other professions. Any number, of course, is too high. But how could this happen in a religious organization committed to helping others and living out what Christians call "Gospel values"? The Board cited two primary factors contributing to the incidence of sexual abuse in the Catholic priesthood.

Improper Screening for Candidates in the Past

This is clearly accurate in my opinion. From many conversations with men who entered minor seminaries or religious orders in the 1940s and 1950s, I know that entrance requirements were relatively few. One priest explained to me that to enter his religious order one needed merely to submit a recommendation from another priest and meet with the local provincial superior. If the provincial gave his approval, the candidate was accepted.

By 1988, when I entered the Jesuits, things had changed considerably. To be accepted into the order, candidates were administered a battery of psychological tests and the order was provided with a lengthy report of the results. In addition, there were six face-to-face interviews and an eight-day retreat. Candidates also were required to submit a comprehensive autobiography, recommendations from six friends and coworkers, a physician's health evaluation, and more. Today, we have reason to believe that these screening procedures help to weed out prospective priests with serious psychological problems, including pedophilia and ephebophilia.

Poor Formation or Training of Candidates

Once again, it is important to note how very different formation and training are today than they were 30 or 40 years ago when many accused priests were in seminary. In the past, many priests were ordained with virtually no education or counseling about sexuality, celibacy, or appropriate boundary setting between himself and others. It is difficult now for a man to reach ordination without substantial exposure to discussions about sexuality, intimacy, and chastity. He also receives training about professional boundaries and sexual abuse.

The National Review Board's analysis of the second question—church leaders responded so poorly to the problem of sexually abusive priests for so many years—is particularly astute, and I concur with all the reasons they list.

**Some Bishops and Other Leaders Did Not Understand
the Broad Nature of the Problem, but Treated Incidents
as Extraordinary Episodes**

Prior to the early 1980s, when sexual abuse was identified as a serious problem in the wider culture, even educated men and women simply did not grasp the great prevalence of sexual abuse inside the family or outside of it. Megan's Law, for example, was passed only in 1996. The bishops were no better informed than the general public about the common occurrence or the long-term consequences of sexual abuse. They simply were at a loss to appreciate the magnitude of the problem.

Many Bishops Put Institutional Concerns above the Needs of the People

Historically, there has been a deep antipathy to "scandal" in the Catholic Church, where the community is seen as the "Body of Christ"—a visible representation of Christ's presence—and where tradition is seen as one way in which the Holy Spirit leads the Christian community over time. An attack on the Church often is interpreted as tantamount to an attack on the faith itself. Similarly, the notion that the faithful needed to be "protected" from scandal, lest it lessen their love and respect for the Church, made bishops less likely to admit even obvious problems with abusive priests. The horrible irony was that in protecting the faithful from scandal by concealing evidence of abusive priests and by shuffling them between parishes, many American bishops helped to create the greatest scandal in the history of their Church in this country.

The Threat of Litigation Caused Many Bishops to Adopt an Adversarial Stance

Protecting the church means more to a bishop than simply protecting the institution. The potential financial losses threatened by lawsuits were accurately assessed as losses that would damage the great many social services provided by the Catholic church: parishes, hospitals, schools, shelters. The bishops felt the need to defend this network of social service agencies and so followed the advice of lawyers who suggested adopting the most aggressive responses to lawsuits. Sadly, the bishops failed to realize that those institutions, noble as they are, were not the only entities needing protection.

Some Bishops Failed to Comprehend the Magnitude of the Harm Suffered by Victims

Needless to say, when some bishops failed even to meet with victims—a shockingly callous act—it was easy to remain ignorant of the suffering stemming form sexual abuse.

Many Bishops Relied Too Heavily on Psychiatrists, Psychologists, and Lawyers When Making Decisions

Still today—but particularly in the 1960s and 1970s when many of these cases first came to light—many bishops turned to mental health professionals who themselves had conflicting opinions about the treatability of pedophilia and other forms of sexual offending. It is curable? Is it genetic? Can a man be placed back in active ministry after treatment? What is the best type of treatment?

Bishops, hardly expert in these matters, often relied on advice that, in retrospect, was flawed. In other instances, they chose to believe experts who told them what they most wanted to hear—that the priest could be cured and returned to ministry. But none of this excuses the bishop who repeatedly moved a priest from one assignment to another where he just as repeatedly reabused. One need not be an expert of any kind to see the stupidity of such actions.

Many Bishops Avoided Confronting Abusive Priests

The simple inability to confront and appropriately engage with difficult situations, whether out of apathy, ignorance, or fear of conflict, seems to have played a major role in the bishops' behavior.

Many Bishops Placed the Interests of Priests above Those of Victims

The image of the bishop as a spiritual father who protects and guides his priests has deep roots in the Catholic tradition. Tragically overshadowed in too many cases of sexual abuse was the bishop's larger and more important role as pastor or shepherd of all the people of his diocese.

Canon Law Made Removal from Ministry Onerous

The process of laicization (returning a priest to lay status) includes stripping a man of all clerical rights that were conferred on him at ordination. No longer may he celebrate Mass, wear a Roman collar, or call himself "Father." Laicization is a cumbersome ecclesiastical process designed to provide due process to a priest and protect his right.

For some bishops, initiating laicization of an abusive priest may have seemed overwhelming.

Turning now from the findings of the National Review Board, I would like to add four additional reasons for the crisis that stem form my own experience as a priest.

Discomfort with Sexual Topics

Many bishops, who are mostly elderly men, were themselves uncomfortable with discussing *any* sexual matters. Whether because of personal, cultural, or familial backgrounds, or because their own formation did not educate them about psychosexual development and sexuality, they had no frame of reference within which they could think about, confront, and appropriately respond to abusive priests or abuse victims.

Fear of Change

Some bishops were hampered by their inability to entertain the possibility that the scandal would generate dramatic changes in the Church. If one fears even discussing difficult church issues like celibacy, the ordination of women, and the parameters of episcopal authority, one will naturally be more afraid of issues like sexual abuse that are potentially linked to these other topics.

Lack of Accountability

Some bishops, like Bernard Cardinal Law of Boston, were unable or unwilling to accept personal responsibility for their approaches to sexual abuse. From the beginning of the crisis, many of the bishops seemed to handle it as if they were corporate chief executive officers rather than Christian pastors. Many apparently forgot that an essential part of the sacrament of reconciliation, formerly known as confession, is the assignment of penance through which one makes amends for one's sins. It is not simply enough to confess, to admit sinfulness, and to beg for forgiveness from God and the person you offended. One *also* needs a "firm purpose of amendment" and the willingness to engage in some form of penance.

Around the time that the sexual abuse scandal first became public, a Catholic nun I know said that a corporate response to the crisis was at odds with a Christian response. Quoting from Jesus's parable of the prodigal son, she described what a Christian response from an offending bishop would have sounded like, "I have sinned against God and you and I no longer deserve to be called your bishop. I will resign and spend the rest of my life praying for victims." This was an action that Catholics would understand, and it is the least that offending bishops should have done. It is a tragedy that many bishops, consecrated to be teachers within their communities, often ignored the treasures of their own spirituality and Christian traditions.

Contempt for the Media

When cases of abuse were raised in the press prior to 2002, many bishops viewed the media as adversaries. For example, Cardinal Law was once quoted as saying that he called down the power of God against *The Boston Globe*. Despite some lingering anti-Catholicism in the media's overall coverage of the crisis, like their facile conflation of celibacy and pedophilia, the church needs to be grateful rather than resentful toward the media for revealing what the church had attempted to keep hidden.

These are just some reasons for the sexual abuse scandal in my Church. There may be additional causes that I, as a Catholic priest, am unable to see. Given the general myopia of the church, that would not surprise me at all.

Now allow me a more personal comment. Since the crisis began, many people have asked about my reaction as a Catholic priest to the sexual abuse scandal.

My primary reaction has been one of overwhelming sadness, for the victims, their families, and friends. The more I learn about the effects of sexual abuse, the more I see how corrosive a crime it is, and how enduring can be the damage. Many of the stories I hear are simply beyond description. Second, I find myself angry. I am furious at both the abusers and those bishops who, unbelievably, moved them from parish to parish, often after several credible accusations of abuse. In this case, I think anger is a natural emotion and can mark the beginning of a healthy desire to change the system that gave rise to these crimes. After all, the Gospel narratives tell us that Jesus of Nazareth was angry because of the same thing: his driving the moneychangers out of the temple was a response to the desecration of something holy. Desecration has happened here as well, and a righteous anger is our legitimate response.

Over the past few years, I have met several priests who have been removed from active ministry because of sexual abuse crimes. And I find myself angry, not only for their crimes, but for a more personal, perhaps more selfish reason. They have fixed in the public's mind the stereotype of a "pedophile priest." And now, even though just 4% or so of priests have been accused of abuse, *all* priests are suspect in the public eye. This means that simply putting on a collar makes one suspect. Also, as a younger priest, I know that much of my priestly life will be about making amends for someone else's crimes. So I am angry for selfish reasons.

I struggle daily with my feelings toward these abusive priests, these criminals. I know that someday, as a practicing Christian, I will be called upon to forgive them for the ways in which they have made my life difficult. Though it often seems impossible, forgiveness is at the absolute heart of the Christian message. At the same time, I cannot counsel victims or their families to follow my own personal path to forgiveness: their road to reconciliation will be far different than mine because their pain is infinitely greater than mine.

So I still struggle and still pray, for the victims and their families, and for a way to understand the Christian response to these terrible crimes.

11

Clericalism and Catholic Clergy Sexual Abuse

The Reverand Thomas P. Doyle

*C*lericalism is the radical misunderstanding of the place of clerics (deacons, priests, bishops) in the Catholic Church and in secular society. Clericalism is grounded in the erroneous belief that clerics form a special elite and, because of their powers as sacramental ministers, they are superior to the laity. Clericalism hues the self-perceptions of church officials, bishops, and priests and is enabled by laypeople who hold their clergy in awe, too often in a childish way. These spiritual powers have historically led to a variety of social privileges, which, in turn, have regularly resulted in different levels of corruption (Sanchez, 1972, p. 7).

Clericalism is sufficiently pernicious that it is correlated with many past and present problems within the Church. Catholic writer Russell Shaw says:

> Yet the clericalist mindset does fundamentally distort, disrupt, and poison the Christian lives of members of the church, clergy, and laity

alike, and weakens the church in her mission to the world. Clericalism is not the cause of every problem in the church, but it causes
many and is a factor in many more. Time and again ... it plays a role in
the debilitating controversies that today afflict the Catholic community in the United States and other countries. [Shaw, 1993, p. 13]

Following the Second Vatican Council, many progressive clergy
and members of the laity hoped that the power of clericalism would
wane, especially in light of the Council emphasis on the important
role of lay members in Church life (Cullinane, 1997, p. 182). Unfortunately, however, recent studies indicate that the present generation of young priests once again sees themselves as essentially
different from the laity and as men set apart by God (Hoge, 2002, p.
27). It appears therefore that the malignancy of Catholic clericalism
is alive and prospering.

Theologian Hans Kung asserts that there is no biblical evidence
that Jesus Christ intentionally founded an institutional church
(Kung, 2001, pp. 3, 19). Nevertheless, official Catholic dogma and
canon law both state that the institutional church is of divine origin,
founded by Jesus Christ acting on the will of the Father. The way of
life inspired by Jesus Christ, known for centuries as Christianity, thus
has evolved in tandem with a human political structure that is best
described as the institutional Church.

The institutional Catholic Church is made up of two groups: the
laity and the clergy. Constructions of the clergy as particularly fa-
vored by the Almighty began early on and led to a variety of social and
legal privileges, expected deference, and vast power that generated
fear within the laity. By the publication of the *Catechism of the Council of Trent* (1564), a theology of clericalism was entrenched:

In the first place, then, the faithful should be shown how great is the
dignity and excellence of this sacrament considered in its highest degree, the priesthood. Bishops and priests being, as they are, God in-
terpreters and ambassadors, empowered in his name to teach
mankind the divine law and the rules of conduct and holding, as they
do, His place on earth, it is evident that no nobler function than theirs
can be imagined. Justly therefore are they called not only Angels, but
even gods, because of the fact that they exercise in our midst the
power and prerogatives of the immortal God. In all ages priests have
been held in the highest honor; yet the priests of the New Testament

far exceed all others. For the power of consecrating and offering the body and blood of our Lord and of forgiving sins, which has been conferred on them, not only has nothing equal or like it on earth, but even surpasses human reason and understanding. [McHugh & Callen, 1923, p. 318]

In 1906, Pope Pius X echoed these sentiments in an Encyclical Letter to the French bishops supporting their opposition to the separation of Church and State:

It follows that the Church is essentially an unequal society, that is, a society comprising two categories of persons, the Pastors and the flock, those who occupy a rank in the different degrees of the hierarchy and multitude of the faithful. So distinct are these categories that with the pastoral body only rests the necessary right and authority for promoting the end of the society and directing all its members towards that end; the one duty of the multitude is to allow themselves to be led and, like docile flock, to follow the Pastor. [Pope Pius X, 1906]

Even today, canon law emphasizes the ostensibly divinely inspired division of Catholics into groups:

Canon 207, 1. Among the Christian faithful by divine institution there exist in the Church sacred ministers, who are also called clerics in law, and other Christian faithful, who are also called laity. [Code of Canon law, c. 207, p. 130]

The "sacred ministers" referred to here are deacons, priests, and bishops, including the Pope. Although these clergy constitute a minuscule fraction (.00042%) of the world's Catholic population, they wield all of the power in the Church. The Church's governmental structure therefore is both hierarchical and monarchical by definition and, according to official Catholic teaching, intended so by divine will. The pope embodies the fullness of all judicial, executive, and legislative power for the worldwide church. His power extends over the entire Church but also reaches directly into each diocese or geographic region. In their respective dioceses, the bishops too hold a similar fullness of power subject only to limitations included in general law or imposed by the Pope.

The central focus of clerical attention historically has been the "good of the church" which, in reality, has generally meant the good of the hierarchy. As in most aristocracies, the church's leadership elite has equated its own individual and caste needs with the needs of the Church itself.

Early on, the institutional church began to construct a theology of sacred orders (deacon, priest, bishop) that supported the isolation of clerics into a special caste and easily led to the theology that bishops are direct descendants of the apostles. Here, it is held that both priests and bishops, including the pope, are ontologically different from laypersons because they have been singled out by God to take the place of Jesus Christ on earth. There is no concrete historical evidence of such singularity. Rather, this construction is supported by hierarchical rationales based on continuities of man-made, rather than divinely directed, tradition. And man-made is the correct term. The vast majority of the approximately 430,000 Catholic clerics worldwide are celibate males. No married clerics, married laypeople, and much less women, hold any positions of power anywhere in the Catholic Church.

Although there is ample historical evidence demonstrating that priests, bishops, cardinals, and popes remain human in spite of the sacred ceremonies that elevate them to their clerical positions, there persists a belief that erring clerics are somehow above the law and beyond most forms of accountability. That trope, in turn, enables the ecclesiastical caste to slip into deep denial when faced with the possibility that clerics really are no different and no better than other mortals.

CELIBACY AND CLERICALISM

One common misconception about the clergy sexual abuse is that it is caused by mandatory celibacy. It is much too simplistic to assume that the inability to turn to women for sexual release causes clerics to prey on children or adolescents. Mandatory celibacy alone does not *cause* sexual dysfunction of any kind. Even scholarly critics of the Church's celibate tradition agree that healthy celibacy is possible for those who freely choose it.

There is, however, a relationship between celibacy and the clericalist mystique. It resides in the tortured reasoning used to justify mandatory celibacy and in the formation processes in which prospective celibate clerics were immersed until quite recently. Although celibacy is a church law, neither grounded in scripture nor universally imposed until the Second Lateran Council in 1139, it has been framed by the hierarchy as essential to authentic priesthood (Pope John Paul II, 2002). In spite of 20 centuries of documented evidence of violations of clerical celibacy, and constant but unsuccessful official attempts at curbing them, the papacy has resisted serious reconsideration of the wisdom of mandatory celibacy. Indeed, as recently as January 2004, Pope John Paul II told a group of French bishops that celibacy is an essential dimension of the priesthood (Pope John Paul II, 2004).

The Church teaches that celibacy is necessary because the priest-cleric must be removed from all distractions and totally dedicated to God's service. Furthermore, since Catholic ministry is centered in the priesthood, the most important part of which is the celebration of the Eucharist, there are historic and contemporary appeals to the concept of ritual purity.

In the early 1990s, Cardinal Francis Stafford delivered a paper entitled "The Eucharistic Foundation of Sacerdotal Celibacy" (Stafford, 1993). In this essay the author postulates the astonishing theory that a priest must be celibate because he takes the place of Christ as he celebrates the Eucharist and, in so doing, takes part in an irrevocable covenant union with what Stafford calls the "New Eve," meaning the Church:

> It is because of the priest's own nuptial integration into the sacrifice he offers that only a man is capable of acting in the person of the head and can be a priest ... He cannot marry without that betrayal of his own nuptiality, which is analogously adulterous; his exclusive dedication to the bride of Christ bars any secondary self-donation. [Stafford, 1993]

Stafford's argument is a direct reflection of John Paul's doctrine on celibacy, set forth in his 1992 letter, *Pastores Dabo Vobis*. As a theoretical justification for mandatory celibacy, it forges an essential dependency relationship between the concept of priesthood and the sexually pure state. In the process, it ignores the married popes, bishops, and priests who populated significant periods of Church history. It also turns a blind eye to the contemporary reality of married Eastern rite priests and married former Anglican priests. John Paul and Stafford offer this theology as the divinely inspired justification, not only for mandatory celibacy, but also for an all-male priesthood.

Despite the historical and contemporary rationales given for mandatory celibacy, historical studies reveal other, much more pragmatic reasons for it: the retention of clerics' property by the church, the elimination of clerics' progeny as a challenge to hierarchical authority, and the centralization of power within the Church.

In addition to the dubious theological bases for mandatory celibacy, candidates for the priesthood received little assistance in learning to achieve celibacy. Traditional preparation for clerical celibacy involved the exaltation of virginity and total continence, a devaluation of intimacy and marriage, and the surrounding of human sexuality with a blanket of sin. Many of the clerical abusers of the past two decades were products of this seminary system, which often began when a young adolescent entered a high-school seminary. Here we find males who were entering puberty, isolated in an all-male environment with an institutionalized negativity (or even hostility) toward marriage, sexual contacts, intimate relationships, and women. All sexuality was considered from the context of morality and all violations of sexual continence—in thought, word, or deed—were, for clerics, a double mortal sin. They were sins against the Church's sexual mandates for all Catholics *and* they were sinful abrogations of celibacy.

The idea of seminary formation was that men (or boys) could best prepare to accept and live a celibate life if they were cut off from all contact with, or even discussion of, the sexual dimension of humanity. Upon completion of their formation, these men were thrust into the world and expected to live a totally chaste life. Studies have shown, however, that this traditional formation system produced a significant degree of emotional and sexual immaturity (Baars, 1971; Cozzens, 2000, 2002; Kennedy & Heckler, 1972; Sipe, 1990, 1995, 2003). Kennedy and Heckler (1972), for example, found that 66% of U.S. priests were underdeveloped and 8% were maldeveloped. The authors stated that these men had not resolved the psychosexual developmental milestones and challenges usually worked through in adolescence (p. 11). Many were what one priest referred to as "the best educated 14-year-olds in our society ... young teenagers on the bodies of men." They had been given no guidance for maturing into a life whereby chaste celibacy would be a freely made choice (Cozzens, 2000; Frawley-O'Dea, 2004).

Even after the contemporary sexual abuse crisis rolled out in countries throughout the world, Pope John Paul II defended mandatory celibacy, indirectly supporting the caste system it upholds. The pope presented celibacy as an *antidote* to sexual abuse and scandal rather than as a dynamic, albeit indirect, component of the clerical system within which sexual abuse was tolerated and covered up. In an address to the bishops of Ireland, a country as rocked with sexual abuse scandal as the United States, John Paul said:

> These scandals, and a sociological rather than a theological concept of the Church, sometimes lead to calls for a change in the discipline of celibacy. However we cannot overlook the fact that the Church recognizes God's will through the interior guidance of the Holy Spirit and that the Church's living tradition constitutes a clear affirmation of the consonance of celibacy, for profound theological and anthropological reasons, with the sacramental character of the priesthood. [Pope John Paul II, 1999]

Even in the face of an enormous scandal involving the sexual and spiritual violation of tens of thousands of young people, the institutional church cannot acknowledge the problems inherent in celibacy. It serves the interests of a clerical culture too well. It is a kind of clerical garb that sets those who wear it apart and above all others. The sacrifice of celibacy and the aura of mystery surrounding it help promote the celibate belief that he is ontologically superior to others. His celibacy, he believes, symbolizes the higher worth he possesses, one that gains him entry to the Holy of Holies where he communicates directly with the Almighty. Dispense with celibacy and the house of clericalism begins to crumble. One then is left "only" with Jesus of Nazareth, who ministered not from above the masses but in the midst of them, arrayed not in fine Roman lace, satin, and silk but in clothing indistinguishable from his flock, eating and drinking not in finely appointed homes of the aristocracy but out on the road as he preached.

CLERICAL NARCISSISM

The clerical culture of the Catholic Church supports enactment of narcissistic personality features by its priests. Grandiosity, an inflated sense of self-importance, interpersonal exploitation of others, the absence of empathy, a defensive structure privileging the use of projection, primitive idealization and devaluation, and denial—especially of one's own shortcomings, haughty behaviors, and attitudes, all accepted symptoms of narcissism (American Psychiatric Association, 2000)—are syntonic to an organizational culture infected with clericalism. During the sexual abuse crisis, clerical narcissism infused the clergy's approach to their problems.

It has been particularly painful to witness the narcissistic relationships clergy established with sexual abuse victims/survivors. The perpetrator, of course, seldom grasped the devastation his actions caused his victims, their families, and his wider Church community. Many victims have testified that their perpetrators convinced them that the sexual activity was special, even divinely approved, because it was with "Father." Others have testified that perpetrators actually threatened them with retribution from God for speaking ill of a priest. Whether the perpetrator was openly contemptuous of his victims or was acting more from psychosexual immaturity, his narcissism ensured that he focused only on himself.

The narcissistic foundation of clericalism was particularly evident and appalling in the reaction of the hierarchy, including Vatican officials and Pope John Paul II, to victims and other critics.

John Paul II, who reigned over most of the sexual abuse scandal until his death in April 2005, was consistently more sympathetic to the episcopacy and the lower clergy than he was to victims/survivors and their families. He had been fully aware of the parameters of the crisis from its inception in the 80s and surely also knew the centuries-old saga of clergy sexual abuse of minors, but he made no public statements about the subject until June 1993. In a letter to the American bishops that year, he expressed sympathy for *their* suffering during the scandal, anchoring the sexual abuse phenomenon in the context of sin. The pope told the bishops, "… I fully share your sorrow and concern … especially … for the victims so seriously hurt by these misdeeds" (Pope John Paul II, 1993). In 1993, there was little evidence that many bishops lost sleep at night over the plights of sexual abuse victims/survivors. While John Paul II mentions the victims in this letter, he neither instructs his bishops to reach out pastorally to them nor to involve civil authorities in their cases. In fact, the Pope's letter goes on to recommend canonical, rather than civil or criminal, penalties for the offenders. The most remarkable section of the papal missive, however, is the longest paragraph in which John Paul II shifts the cause of the sexual abuse problem from the Church to the secular media:

> I would also draw your attention to another aspect of this whole question. While acknowledging the right to due freedom of information, one cannot acquiesce in treating moral evil as an occasion for sensationalism. Public opinion often feeds on sensationalism and the mass media play a particular role therein. In fact, the search for sensationalism leads to the loss of something which is essential to the morality of society. [Pope John Paul, 1993]

The Pope prescribes prayer as the preferred response to the sexual abuse of minors and closes with a condescending admonition, "... Yes dear brothers, America needs much prayer, lest it lose its soul (Pope John Paul II, 1993).

The Pope set a tone with this first pronouncement about the crisis and effectively disowned any institutional responsibility causing the scandal.

The Pope's next utterance on the subject was also clericalist in tone yet with a different focus. This time he talked about sex abuse during an address to Irish bishops. Here, John Paul II commended the victims to the bishops' prayers but emphasized sympathy for priests who suffer "... due to the pressure of the surrounding culture and the terrible scandal given by some of their brother priests ..." (John Paul II, 1999).

The fury unleashed by the *Boston Globe*'s January 2002 revelations about sexual abuse of minors in the Archdiocese of Boston prompted the Vatican to take the historically unprecedented step of summoning the American cardinals to Rome for a meeting. When the Pope addressed the assembly of cardinals and other U.S. and Vatican prelates, he added two new elements to the projective defenses already at work in the Vatican. First, John Paul II reinforced one of the bishops' standard themes: that they had acted as they had because they had insufficient knowledge about the nature of the problem and therefore had responded to flawed medical and mental health advice. The pope said, "It is true that a generalized lack of knowledge of the nature of the problem and also at times the advice of clinical experts led bishops to make decisions which subsequent events showed to be wrong" (John Paul II, 2002). In the next paragraph, he returns to the theme of the secular culture's responsibility for the clergy sex abuse scandal, saying, "The abuse of the young is a grave symptom of a crisis affecting not only the church but society as a whole. It is a deep-seated crisis of sexual morality, even human relationships, and its prime victims are the family and the young."

John Paul II's rationales are difficult to reconcile with Church history and secular laws. First, there are 18 centuries of official church pronouncements condemning clergy sexual abuse of the young, suggesting that sexual abuse of minors has been a problem within the Church for a very long time. Moreover, while it may be true that some bishops were given problematic professional advice about some perpetrators, it is also true that other bishops obstructed the ability of clinicians to do their jobs well. For example, at least two clinicians from The Institute for Living, a Hartford, Connecticut, facility that treated many abusive priests, publicly asserted that bishops regularly withheld essential information about referred priests and then either intentionally misinterpreted professional recommendations or simply ignored them (DiGiulio, 2002; Rich and Hamilton, 2002). Regarding secular culture, surely the Vatican and the American bishops knew that in even sexually liberal Western societies, the ones most lambasted by the Pope for contributing to the crisis, sexual abuse of minors is a serious crime. In fact, over the same decades that these cultures became more liberal in their sexual attitudes regarding consenting adults, they became more intolerant of sexual crimes against minors. The Vatican, however, had its story and was sticking to it.

Other Church officials continued to criticize society's angry response to the scandal. Cardinal Maradiaga of Honduras, for example, compared American press coverage to ancient Roman persecutions and to the modern persecutions under Hitler and Stalin. Back home, retired Cardinal Avery Dulles, a lifelong academic who never held a pastoral position of any kind, was reported by the *Boston Her-*

ald to have said, "I don't think there is any great crisis in the U.S. It's practically no news. To the extent it's a crisis, it's created by the news media" (Sullivan and Convey, 2002). Even Wilton Gregory, President of the U.S. Conference of Catholic Bishops and a man presumably better informed about the abuse crisis than any prelate in the Vatican or abroad, reinforced the aura of narcissistic projection with a statement in 2003:

> I think the media last year did help the Church to take some steps that will bring this terrible stain out of her life…. However the way the story was so obsessively covered resulted in unnecessary damage to the bishops and the entire Catholic community.

Like the Pope and Vatican officials, bishops also consistently failed to embrace clergy sexual abuse victims/survivors as brothers and sisters in Christ. Rather, their reactions to victims bespoke self-absorbed administrators and bureaucrats instead of caring pastors. Most bishops have had little if any meaningful contact with victims, often appearing afraid of the confrontations. One Midwestern archbishop, speaking through his Vicar General, offered to meet with victims. All they had to do was call his secretary to arrange for an appointment. Another archbishop rejected advice that he meet with individuals and small groups of victims because he feared they would not respect him and display their anger. Yet another cardinal archbishop admitted before a grand jury that he had never met a victim face to face. When asked why not, he replied that it would not be an efficient use of his time. Such responses reflect a callous, businesslike attitude, devoid of even the slightest insight into the role a bishop *should* play when one of his flock has been severely damaged by a priest. They also suggest clerical narcissism at work in the episcopacy.

Bishops used two other narcissistic defenses that deeply hurt victims and their supporters and also backfired in the legal arena. One involved trying to reverse the victim–victimizer role and the other was devaluing critics as enemies of Catholicism. The reversal technique has been employed by bishops attempting to portray themselves as unfairly targeted by the media, which defames them, and the legal system, which persecutes them. It has been particularly galling when Church leaders tried to shift the blame to the victims of sexual abuse for "complicity" in the sexual relationship with the priest, or to parents of survivors for "neglecting" their offspring (Doyle, 2003, pp. 223–224). Devaluation occurred when the motivations of well-meaning critics were questioned or, even worse, when ad hominem attacks were used to divert attention from a challenging message to the character of the person speaking.

While clericalism and clerical narcissism may reside within the clerical world, it could not function so powerfully for centuries were it not supported by a synergistic lay clericalism.

LAY CLERICALISM

Russell Shaw, in his 1993 study of Catholic clericalism, says that the laity are in some ways more clericalized than the clergy (Shaw, 1993, p. 9). Prior to the 1980s when sexual abuse by priests began to capture public attention, the bishops handled clergy sex abuse cases in a highly secretive manner, effectively preventing media coverage, criminal prosecution, and civil suits. This would not have been possible without the acquiescence of the laity who often believed that cooperation with the bishops in such cover-ups was helping the Church.

Lay clericalism is grounded in an immature dependence on clergy to mediate the believer's spirituality and relationship with God. In Catholicism, priests control the faithful's access to the sacraments, and sacraments are the source of spiritual nourishment and security for the laity. In essence, threats to the hierarchical power cartel are threats to the personal spiritual security of individuals. Lay clericalism enables the privileges and arrogance of the priesthood, trading adult negotiation of spirituality for ongoing clerical patronage/patronization.

The clericalist mythology about the immense power of the priesthood, a mythology readily believed by Catholics with a need for spiritual security, has enabled clerics to carry on unchallenged for some time. An account of the famous Mount Cashel (Newfoundland, Canada) sexual abuse case, one involving orphans abused by Catholic priests and brothers for decades under the nose of police and social workers, contains a statement that aptly portrays the destructive power of lay clericalism:

The most eloquent insight into how men of the cloth had been able to perpetrate such monstrous crimes against their parishioners' children and get away with it for so long came from a woman whose cultural eyesight was 20/20. She laid the blame for the tragedy on the traditional role of the priest in Outport, Newfoundland, which she said was as close to God as you could get without playing a harp. Expressing a feeling shared by many of Newfoundland's 205,000 Catholics, she told the meeting, "If a child was born without an arm, people said it was because the mother said something against a priest. That was nonsense, but a priest with that kind of shield could get away with anything. We are victims of our heritage." [Harris, 1990]

The present scandal provided abundant evidence of lay clericalism and even tragically influenced child victims views of the men violating them. Catholic victims, conditioned by their religious indoctrination, looked on the priest-abuser with a mixture of awe and fear. The cleric's attitude of superiority and power elicited emotional security and trust in his victim. These strong feelings of security and awe often impeded victims from recognizing the seductive patterns the abuser was using to court them. The awe, fear, and wonder experienced by the victim are best described as religious duress. In many ways, religious duress is similar to the notion of reverential fear, a well-established concept in Catholic canon law. This is a fear that is induced from the respect, awe, or reverence one has for an authority figure. The victim fears the displeasure of the authority figure to such a degree that free will dissipates. Child or young adult victims were especially vulnerable to a priest-abuser. He was an adult with that status power over the victim, but also was a priest, a figure carrying vast spiritual authority over the child, his family, and his faith community.

As the current crisis unfolded, some lay individuals and groups could not grow beyond a clericalist mind and blamed the scandal on the disobedience to the pope and the hierarchy of individual priests and even victims and their families. Here, the idealization of the ecclesiastical caste is preserved, thus maintaining the laity's sense of spiritual security.

Other members of the laity blamed the crisis on a spirit of dissent they say arose after the close of the Vatican Council II in 1965 (Weigel, 2002, pp. 57–86). The focus here was on departures from traditional Catholic teachings about sex, especially contraception, that coincided with the so-called sexual revolution of the 1960s and 1970s. These folks claim that dissent inside the church and liberalized sexual mores in the wider culture worked together to corrupt the ideals of the priesthood and to create an environment that enabled clergy sexual abuse.

Still other laypeople maintained that clergy sexual abuse is grounded in a lack of fidelity to the clergy celibate promises. These individuals are especially critical of the apparent broad-based acceptance of homosexuality in the priesthood, which they insist is linked with same-sex abuse by members of the clergy.

Attempts to explain the scandal solely in terms of rejection of traditional moral norms, disobedience to papal authority, infidelity to vows of celibacy, and homosexuality are symptomatic of a laity that ardently wants to preserve an idealization of their Church, embodied in the hierarchy and the priesthood. Many lay clericalists, therefore, have been more devoted to protecting their fantasies of a perfect institutional church populated by an honorable clerical caste than they have been to extending themselves to victims. Sadly, too many of those victims, their families, and supporters have been ostracized rather than embraced by their lay brethren.

THE FUTURE

The present era of scandal has been a painful catalyst to the most substantial upheaval Catholicism has seen since the 16th century Reformation. The revelation that thousands of sexually abusive clerics roamed free in Catholic communities over the past several decades prompted a powerful response from segments of the lay population that, growing beyond clericalism, are no longer passively subservient to whatever the Church leadership instructs them to think, feel, do, and say about their church and their own spirituality. For these members of the laity and for some progressive and honorable clergy, the sexual abuse scandal exposed clericalism for the bane that it really is. Ironically, some of the harshest critics of clericalism are clerics themselves; men and women whose membership in the Catholic or Protestant clerical elite is far secondary to their commitment to the Christian message and mission. In a remarkable book, one of these priests, Fr. Donald Cozzens, writes,

Clericalism ... is always dysfunctional and haughty, crippling the spiritual and emotional maturity of the priest, bishop, or deacon caught in its web. Clericalism may command a superficial deference, but it blocks honest human communication and ultimately leaves the cleric practicing it isolated. [Cozzens, 2002, p. 117]

At no time in the past millennium have the teachings of Jesus of Nazareth been more sorely needed by the very institutions that carry on in His name. The institutional Catholic Church, identified by many with the papacy and the bishops, will continue to founder as long as its response to the sexual abuse of its young people by its priests hinges on the preservation of the status quo, including the culture of clerical narcissism. That is an approach bespeaking only spiritual and moral bankruptcy. The institutional Church—not just individual priests and bishops but the collective People of God who constitute the Church—must reclaim its origins in Jesus by proclaiming that the welfare and spiritual healing of countless clergy sexual abuse victims is its first priority. Only then will the Catholic Church begin to emerge from the dark shadows of destructiveness fueled by clericalism into the hope-giving and transparent light of Christianity.

REFERENCES

American Psychiatric Association (2000), *Diagnostic and Statistical Manual of Mental Disorders. IV-TR.* Washington, DC: American Psychiatric Association.

Associated Press (2002), Text of Bishop Gregory's remarks. *Newsday Online.*

Baars, C. (1971), The role of the church in the causation, treatment, and prevention of the crisis in the priesthood. Unpublished report.

Cozzens, D. (2000), *The Changing Face of the Priesthood.* Collegeville, MN: Liturgical Press.

——— (2002), *Sacred Silence.* Collegeville, MN: Liturgical Press.

Cullinane, P. (1997), Clericalism: Avoidable Damage to the Church. *Australasian Catholic Record,* pp. 181–191.

DeGiulio, K. (2002), Interview with Dr. Leslie Lothstein. *National Catholic Reporter Website,* August 9, 2002.

Doyle, T. (2003), Roman Catholic clericalism, religious duress, and clergy sexual abuse. *Pastoral Psychol.,* 51:189–231.

Dulles, A. (2002), *Models of the Church.* Exp. ed. New York: Image Books.

Frawley-O'Dea, M. (2004), The history and consequences of the sexual abuse crisis in the Catholic Church. *Studies in Gender and Sexual.,* 5:11.

Harris, M. (1990), *Unholy Orders: Tragedy at Mount Cashel.* Markham, Ontario, Can: Penguin Books.

Hoge, D. (2002), *The First Five Years of Priesthood.* Collegeville, MN: The Liturgical Press.

Kennedy, E. & Heckler, V. (1972), *The Catholic Priest in the United States: Psychological Investigations.* Washington, DC: U.S. Catholic Conference.

Kung, H. (2001), *The Catholic Church: A Short History,* trans. J. Bowden. New York: The Modern Library.

McHugh, J. & Callan, J., eds. (1923), *Catechism of the Council of Trent.* New York: Joseph A. Wagner, Inc.

Pope John Paul II (1993), Letter to the United States Bishops. *Origins, 23.*

———— (1999), Address to the Bishops of Ireland on their 'Ad Limina' Visit. June 26. *Vatican website, http://www.vatican.va/holy_father/johnpaul_ii/speeches/1999/june/documents/hf_jp-ii_spe_19990626-ad-limina-irlanda_en.html*

———— (2002), Address of John Paul II to the Cardinal of the United States, April 23, 2002. *Vatican website, http://www.vatican.va/holy_father/john_paul_ii/speeches/2002/april/documents/hf_jp-ii_spe_20020423_usa-cardinals_en.html*

Pope Pius X (1906), Encyclical letter, Vehementer Nos. *Vatican website, http://www.vatican/va/holy_father/pius_x/encyclicals/documents/hf_p-x_enc_11021906_vehementer-nos_en.html*

Rich, E. & Hamilton, E. (2002), Doctors used us. *The Hartford Courant,* March 24.

Sanchez, J. (1972), *Anti-Clericalism: A Brief History.* Notre Dame, IN: University of Notre Dame Press.

Shaw, R. (1993), *To Hunt, To Shoot, To Entertain.* San Francisco: Ignatius Press.

Silver, Beth (2003), Associated Press. Media unfair to priests, bishop says. *The New Tribune,* Seattle, WA, September 6, 2003.

Sipe, A. (1990), *A Secret World: Sexuality and the Search for Celibacy.* New York: Brunner-Mazel.

———— (1995), *Sex, Priests, and Power.* New York: Brunner Mazel.

———— (2003), *Celibacy in Crisis: A Secret World Revisited.* New York: Brunner-Routledge.

Sullivan J. & Convey, E. (2002), Pope takes action: Cardinals ordered to Vatican. *Boston Herald,* April 16.

Weigel, G. (2002), *The Courage to be Catholic.* New York: Basic Books.

12

Clergy Sexual Misconduct: Episcopal and Roman Catholic Clergy

The Reverend Anne Richards

"If the shepherd is not fed, he will eat the sheep."

—*Anonymous*

From 1995 until 2001, I served as a member of the senior staff of the Episcopal Bishop of New York. As Canon for Ministry Development, my responsibilities fell into a few main areas: I administered the ordination selection process, and mentored seminarians and newly ordained clergy; led the "clergy wholeness" initiatives sponsored by the diocese for its ordained clergy; and coordinated misconduct cases involving clergy of the diocese. These roles afforded me an interesting vantage point from which to reflect on the possible causes and meaning of sexual misconduct by ordained persons.

What follows are some thoughts about the current sexual misconduct crisis in the Roman Catholic Church, a crisis that is not limited
to that branch of Christianity. It is important to bear in mind that my
experience is limited, that I bring my own (largely positive) history as
a former Roman Catholic to it, and—most importantly—that gener-
alizations in this area are almost always misleading. Despite outward
appearances, every misconduct case is unique, and close examination of the people involved yields unique circumstances, unique motives, unique truths.

I have been ordained for 15 years, and have been involved in the
ordination selection process for 13 of those years. Persons are selected for ordination in the Episcopal Church in a very different way
than they are in the Roman Catholic Church, where a man can offer
himself for ordination largely "under his own steam"—that is, motivated solely by his own sense of "call" to the ordained ministry. Although particular Roman Catholic dioceses may have more or less
rigorous screening processes, once a man has put himself forward,
the initial impulse for ordination rests, ordinarily, with the individual
who wishes to be ordained.

It has been observed that now, as in the past, it is not unusual for a
Roman priest to "recruit" a young (or not so young) man for the
priesthood based on his perception of that person's potential and
gifts. Although this kind of mentoring approach to attracting candidates to the priesthood has merits, it should be kept in mind that
clergy rarely recruit candidates for ordination who espouse different
(or new) theological views, different views about the church, and so
forth. Rather, it has long been acknowledged that clergy who recruit
a person for ordination are usually putting forth some aspect of their
own character and personal history, in the "apple doesn't fall far
from the tree" sense. There is a powerful dynamic within any church
(as in any institution) to maintain the status quo. Even with the best
of intentions, when a priest—on his own—recruits a man for ordination, he is saying, "This person could be like me." If the recruitment
of new clergy were left solely to already ordained clergy, this would
result in a homogeneous body of clergy in terms of its ability to challenge a closed hierarchical system that is at least partly corrupted.

This notion of individual "call" as the basis for priesthood has a
long history in the church, and its misuse may be one of the reasons

that the Roman Catholic Church finds itself in trouble. In the early Church (that is, the Church of the first several centuries of the Common Era), there was no operative sense of vocational "call" in regard to ordination. (Bear in mind, also, that in the first 10 centuries of the Church's history, there was no celibacy requirement attached to priesthood.) In fact, men had to be recruited for ordination. They were recruited on the basis of the fact that they had emerged as leaders of their congregations, and were thus seen by the lay community as a whole as "naturals" for ordination. Apparently, not many were anxious to be ordained, ordination not being an especially coveted role.

In the monastic orders in the early Church, however, the situation was different. Being a monk or a friar has always meant being celibate—that is, refraining for life from genital sexual expression with anyone. (Celibacy is distinguished from "chastity," which is sexual wholesomeness or virtue broadly conceived and which is required of all, including married persons.) In order to live a celibate life successfully, one has to have a true "call" to celibacy; one has to have the sense that celibacy fulfills one as a human being and allows for a full expression of one's gifts and relationship with God; otherwise, the life will be only misery and struggle. The call must be there for the life to be lived well.

In the 11th century, when the Roman Catholic Church determined that its institutional life would be best consolidated by having its priests' loyalties tied solely to the Church, it imposed the celibacy requirement on its clergy. No longer would a priest's family and property exert influence on him; he would be "married to the Church." From the 11th century onward, then, the sense of "call" from monasticism was artificially imposed on the understanding of priesthood in the Roman Catholic Church.

It is impossible to underestimate how profoundly this shift in the understanding of a priest's sexuality and his relationship to God and the Church has affected the character of the priesthood in the Roman Catholic Church. At the very least, it has resulted in a body of priests whose aptitude for priesthood has been evaluated not solely on gifts for priesthood, but on willingness to attempt the celibate life, most often as individual heroic "sacrifice" of sexual expression rather than true call to celibacy. This elimination of the possibility of marriage or committed relationship for Roman Catholic priests, a decision made often in adolescence or very early in adulthood, can essentially isolate, put aside, or shut down a man's emotional life in ways that eventually prove unhealthy for him and for the institution.

Thus, in the context of the current crisis in the Roman Church, the first question that must be asked is not, "Why have these men become abusers?" but rather, "Why have these men been ordained?" It cannot be underscored too strongly that if a man enters the priesthood as a narcissist, he will remain a narcissist. He will be a narcissistic priest, and he will behave as such. There is nothing in the institution of the priesthood, or of the Church, that is by its nature designed to change that, just as there is not in any other profession.

A true call to celibacy is no guarantee that the vow of celibacy will be kept. Some (not all) members of monastic orders are also ordained—that is, they have taken both monastic vows and priestly vows. These "order priests" are responsible only to the head of their monastic order, and they are to be distinguished from "diocesan priests," who are responsible to the diocesan bishop and who minister, generally, in parishes, hospitals, and other diocesan jurisdictions. (It is diocesan priests who have captured the headlines recently.)

Many of these monks and "order priests" find the vow of celibacy to which they thought they were called impossible to maintain. There is no way to determine with complete certainty if there is any difference in the rates of their sexual transgression, because the judicatories deal only with the transgressions that are reported, not the transgressions that actually occur. The rates of reporting, however, are comparable, especially when one considers that there are far fewer order priests than diocesan priests in both the Roman Catholic and Episcopal Churches. The public impression that there is a lower incidence of sexual transgression among order priests is probably because monks and order priests generally (not always) lead a more circumscribed life than diocesan priests, with less access to people outside the community, which also means that their sexual relationships are often with each other and thus sometimes remain secret. That the public hears less about their transgressions is also probably a result of the extra layer of institutional protection afforded by the structure of their order and the fact that the bishop is not overseeing their internal affairs closely.

Religious literature from the Middle Ages onward contains strong innuendos about the sexual lives of monastics, including a stream of "spiritual friendship" literature that speaks fairly explicitly of sexual or sexualized relationships among monks living together in community. These relationships become especially problematical when the men involved are in an unequal power relationship—for example, a novice master and a novice. Such a relationship can not only jeopardize the order legally; it will also destroy the possibility of (say) a novice being able truly to discern his call.

Compounding this is the fact that, generally speaking, the monastic orders have no more thorough screening processes than the larger Church itself. Sometimes their screening process consists of simply the Minnesota Multiphasic Personality Inventory and an interview with an "in-house" psychologist (often another monk). This is sufficient for only the rare candidate, especially given the highly romanticized image of the monk. A "flight from the world" may cover a highly repressed and unexamined sexuality that will not permanently be restrained by the bonds of a religious vow. In my experience, the above comments hold for both Roman Catholic and Episcopal monastic orders.

What follows are some comments about how the priesthood is seen in the Episcopal Church. I offer these comments not to draw comparisons that are unflattering to the Roman Catholic Church, but to point out some measures that may serve to minimize the likelihood of misconduct (or, more properly, the breakdown of healthy functioning, of which misconduct is but a symptom) among Episcopal clergy. In the Episcopal Church, which ordains both men and women to the priesthood, an individual cannot be put forward for ordination on his or her own. He or she must be officially sponsored by their parish leadership (clergy and the lay) as having demonstrated, over time, within the give-and-take of parish life, the kind of character and personal attributes necessary for ordination: an interest in the spiritual life that manifests itself in the desire to help people grow and develop as Christians, stability of life, moral wholesomeness, leadership ability, the willingness to serve, and other desirable qualities. Though not foolproof (especially in regard to the more subtle character disorders and other factors that would speak against the advisability of ordination), this initial "screen" significantly affects the number of those who come forth for vocational scrutiny at the diocesan level.

It is impossible to underestimate the "correcting" influence of having many different people—clergy and lay, those who know him or her and those who do not—interview and scrutinize a candidate for ordination at every stage of the selection process, especially at the initial stage, within the life of the parish of which the candidate is a member. This puts the process on an entirely different footing than the "individual call" or "mentor" systems since it contextualizes the individualistic aspects of a person's desire for ordination, shifting it from "this is what I want" or "this is what I think God wants for me to do" (the "personal completion" model of vocation) to "this is what I and the community of faith think I should do so as to best use my gifts to serve the community."

The emphasis on community continues throughout the selection process, as interviewers and others responsible for screening ask the same question in ever-broadening arenas: "Are this person's gifts needed for the life of the diocese? For the larger church? For the work of religious endeavor generally speaking—the work of spiritual awareness and practice, the furtherance of peace and social justice?" This emphasis on community is theologically sound because it locates the action and purpose of God within the whole Church, not simply within an individual.

In the Episcopal Church as in other Protestant denominations, there is no celibacy requirement for clergy, which sprang forth from the Reformation, when imposed clerical celibacy was abolished in the churches that grew out of that movement. A very small number of Episcopal priests take a vow of celibacy, but only privately and by their own choice. However, the lack of a celibacy requirement does not mean that a priest is free to conduct his or her sexual life simply as he or she wishes. When an Episcopal priest is ordained, he or she takes a vow to be "a wholesome example" to the people he or she will serve. He or she also promises to obey the discipline of the Church as articulated in the national canons, or Church law, which explicitly state that sexual activity is to be confined to the marital relationship.

Most dioceses have further guidelines about what is and is not permissible, sexually speaking, for priests, including guidance about "honorable courtship" (a single priest dating a single parishioner in such a way that the parishioner's rights are respected and pastoral care is provided for), and about seeking the bishop's guidance when there are difficulties in a priest's marriage. Since each priest is under the pastoral direction of his or her bishop, if a priest is contemplating divorce (or marriage, for that matter), he or she is expected to let the bishop know what is transpiring. There is a general "no surprises" expectation for clergy in the Episcopal Church which helps keeps a priest's private life "in the light" and also builds in support and pastoral input.

How these canons and guidelines are applied varies from diocese to diocese. Certainly there is no active effort to invade priests' privacy or to investigate their private lives unless there is compelling reason to do so (as in the event of a serious transgression). Most bishops are extremely loathe to interfere in their clergy's romantic/sexual lives and will do so only if a priest's behavior is impacting the life of their congregation. (An exception is a conservative bishop who may make explicit his expectations for celibacy, and secrecy, for their gay clergy, since the Episcopal Church has not yet officially allowed the ordination of sexually active homosexual persons.) There is a trust built into the bishop/priest relationship that works, much of the time. "I don't do bedrooms," said the bishop for whom I worked.

It works—except when it doesn't. A priest—male or female, married or single, straight or gay—attracts sexual energy and generates sexual energy in a unique way. This is rarely discussed in the formation process or in the seminaries. The priest is a numinous figure, representing God and all the energies associated with God in the religious tradition: creativity, openness, vulnerability, self-transcendence, desire, and union. Our culture is not proficient at helping people understand and integrate those energies, and thus when they are experienced by a layperson who is on a spiritual search or in a personal crisis or growing in his or her faith, they tend to get directed at and focused on the person of the priest.

This is not ordinarily an intentional or deliberate decision on anyone's part. It is simply a fact that the concept of priest holds great psychic power. He or she stands on the threshold between the human and the divine, representing God. The writings of the mystics in every religious tradition testify that spiritual energy and sexual energy are the same energy, and thus the priest is—by virtue of his or her vocation—a sexual icon. The priestly garb, the black clothing and white clerical collar, intensify this sexual mystique. Like the "uniform" of the firefighter or police officer, the collar invests the priest with an allure that has nothing to do with who he or she is as an individual. Although for most priests, the collar represents the most "spiritual" aspect of his vocation, for laypersons the collar represents a glamour that for some is extremely enticing. "What's under there?" I recall a man once asking me, seemingly innocently. Intensifying this aura of charged sexuality is the fact that priests do not simply draw sexual energy toward them; rather, sexual energy flows between laypersons and priests in a way that may never reach awareness.

I am not speaking here of flirtation or provocative relationships; I speak rather of a basically healthy freeing up of life energy that, if handled respectfully, reflected upon, and integrated, can be life-giving for both layperson and priest. If not handled respectfully, reflected upon, and integrated, it can degenerate into sexual transgression. When sexual energy is handled wrongly, when the priest is not equipped or willing to respect a layperson as "off limits" for him personally, he no longer functions so as to represent God. He acts as God. He, and his victim, may never know the difference, which is why so many relationships resulting from boundary violations are so soundly defended by those in them as special, unique love relationships. They carry the scent of the divine, or a simulation thereof. Thus there is a particular form of denial built right into sexual transgressions involving clergy.

This denial spreads in ever-widening circles, affecting (at least temporarily) the victim, and the parish. I have worked with a number of female victims, and almost without exception was struck by what intelligent, committed, sensible people they were. They should have "known better." But they did not "wake up" to the reality of their situations until they had suffered egregiously in the relationship, realized it was a dead-end, and wanted to protect other women from the same fate. One female victim I worked with whose priest-lover deserted her when she got bone cancer still wrote him a thank-you note "for all the good times." Another woman wrote regular letters to her former priest-lover, many years after the sexual relationship was over and after she had become a therapist specializing in sexual abuse.

The widest circle of denial is the parish itself. Part of my job, after a priest was accused of sexual misconduct and the investigation had proceeded far enough to indicate with certainty that a transgression had occurred, was to go to the priest's parish to meet with parishioners to explain what was going on and how it was being addressed. Without exception, and even in the most dramatic cases of prolonged, egregious misconduct, the parishioners refused to believe that their priest had transgressed, reacted with great rage, and steadfastly tried to find alibis or excuses for him.

One priest who had dealt drugs, frequented prostitutes, compromised parish finances, and engaged in sadomasochistic sexual activity with retarded young men (and photographed it), was ardently defended by his middle-class, elderly parishioners who knew him as "Father Mike" (not his real name), the volunteer chaplain to the local volunteer fire department who could be found, most nights, down at the local bar throwing back a few with the local guys. Another priest, married with children, who had had numerous sexual liaisons with male teenagers and young adult parishioners throughout his career, was staunchly defended by his priest colleagues, who believed that as a bisexual he should be "left alone."

Another parish, whose extremely charming priest had completely falsified his identity and drawn them into colluding with him in INS fraud to secure him religious worker status in this country (status he was not qualified to receive), reacted with rage when told of his actions. "All priests lie!" said a parish leader. "Why should he be punished for it?"

During the time I was in the job, we had no reported cases of pedophilic priests, though there were numerous such cases in the Church at large during that time. One case had been resolved shortly before I took the position, however; it involved a married priest who served a small parish in the rural part of the diocese. He had numerous victims, and as a result of his transgressions he was "deposed," or formally removed from the ministry (the popular term for this is "defrocked"). He defended himself throughout, insisting that he had not done anything really wrong, and he continued to use the title "the Reverend" after he was no longer a priest. When the bishop warned him not to use this title, he responded with a vulgar letter. It took his parish many years to begin to recover from what had happened.

It has been observed that there are fewer reported cases of pedophilic priests in the Episcopal Church than there are in the Roman Catholic Church. I have no access to those statistics, but my experience suggests that it is an accurate observation. This may be because the Roman Catholic priesthood is a natural magnet for men with undeveloped sexuality.

Most new priests are fairly ignorant of the psychic import of their role. They are also not fully cognizant of how the Christian tradition itself reinforces some of the role's sexual mystique. St. Augustine declared that sexual desire was a tremor of the Fall, and that set sexuality on a downhill course for centuries. Once there were no more martyrs for the faith, then virgins became the most highly esteemed Christians. A one-dimensional understanding of the virginity of Mary also added to the Church's misunderstanding of sexuality. The imposition of clerical celibacy in the 11th century was the last stroke, implying that abstaining from sexual activity conferred holiness and made priests a "higher" class of people. The understanding that holiness means "wholeness" never completely disappeared, but it has not been the controlling belief. Most clergy learn of this intellectual inheritance in seminary, but they are not taught how that inheritance will affect them concretely.

Ironically, because many Episcopal clergy are married, their parishioners are aware (on some level) that they are sexually active. For some potential victims, this only increases the priests' allure, the unknown "private" areas of the priest's life serving as unspoken evidence of a broken taboo.

During the course of my work on the Bishop's staff, I met monthly for half a day with all the newly ordained priests of the diocese—that is, all priests ordained two years or less. We spent time debriefing, reflecting intentionally on their ministries, and giving each other feedback. Early on in these sessions, I would always offer to help the new priests reflect on how being ordained had affected their sense of themselves as people, their intimate relationships, and their sexuality. Many of the women were eager to do so, the men not always so willing.

In my experience, the first five years of priestly functioning are stressful for marriages, with the marital relationship having to go through reassessment and redefinition. For women priests, this often involved incorporating a new sense of their own authority and effectiveness into the marital relationship; for men, it had more to do with time management and the toll of many hours away from family, with the (usually female) spouse having to adjust to being a "clergy wife," an extremely difficult role to manage.

Martin Luther, of Reformation fame, was an Augustinian monk. He left the Augustinians, married a former nun, and had a family. His strong belief in the healthiness and importance of marriage and family in the Christian life still has a tremendous influence on the way Protestant clergy are formed. In the Episcopal Church, candidates for ordination are advised that they should not pursue ordination if their spouses are opposed to it, as the marriage vow comes first. This extends into their priestly career. Priests are frequently reminded that the marriage vow comes first, that no matter how compelling the demands of their parish, their first responsibility is to the well being of their wife/husband and children. This is more difficult to negotiate in practice than it is in theory, but it remains a useful flag for Episcopal clergy, especially since a clinical study done by the Episcopal Church of the wives of Episcopal priests about five years ago found the wives' physical and emotional health to be precarious.

In the Episcopal Church, once an individual has been put forth for ordination by his or her parish, that person goes through a process which (in New York) ordinarily takes a year or more to complete. It includes a full psychiatric evaluation (cognitive, personality, and projective testing, with a number of interviews with a psychiatrist and psychologist); a physical examination; a background check; a very detailed questionnaire that explores the candidate's family and sexual history, including sexual abuse, relationship history, history of drug use (including alcohol), involvement with the law, and other potentially problematic areas, including any sexual contact with minors and involvement with pornography; and reference checks. The purpose of such a thorough "preprocess" at this point is to pinpoint the candidates who are most whole in terms of life functioning. If no contraindications are found, the person goes on to a series of interviews with clergy and laypersons of the diocese appointed by the bishop for this purpose. Great weight, too, is put on the evaluations that come out of these interviews, especially as they pertain to the candidate's ability to thrive, not simply survive, in the priesthood.

Since we live in a "professionalized" culture, it is easy to conceive of priests as the "professional Christians," those persons who by dint of their commitment to God and the Church have decided to be a "full-time Christian." This individualistic approach to ordination (which greatly informs the selection process in the Roman Catholic Church) is potentially disastrous. Implicitly it puts forth medieval notions of personal piety as the foundation for priesthood, not the more realistic criteria of aptitude for ordained leadership. This misunderstanding of the priestly role was further emphasized in the 1960s and 1970s, when important principles from the therapeutic world began profoundly to influence the culture at large, including the religious culture. Roman Catholic priest Henri Nouwen's best-selling book, *The Wounded Healer*, put forth a model of the priest as a "wounded" person who ministers to others out of his own wounds, rather than out of his strengths. (Henri Nouwen, now deceased, was a homosexual who made that part of himself public only in the final years of his ministry.) This "wounded healer" model continues to have great influence. This way of seeing the priesthood has a certain partial theological value, since Christians believe that in the weakness of the cross God showed forth His power and love. However, as a model for priesthood, the "wounded healer" encourages a kind of displayed vulnerability and a disincentive to growth that does not serve the priest or the church well.

It also underlines the tendency to see the priest as the primary resource for spiritual nourishment. He is the "real" Christian, the "really spiritual" person, the one "ordained" and thus possessed of a "special" relationship with God. The highly sacramentalized spirituality of Roman Catholicism contributes to this also, making the priest an otherworldly figure who emanates mystery and spiritual power. This focus on priest as "holiest one" is both a setup for burnout, putting the priest in the impossible position of bottomless spiritual well, the one who must have an answer to a layperson's spiritual dilemma even when he does not have an answer. In addition, it subtly molds a priest's self-understanding and nudges it away from community faith leader toward therapist/helper for individuals, a role which he or she is clearly not qualified (or ordained) to fill. It also contributes to the aura of charged sexuality surrounding the sacralized figure of priest.

The education and training of Roman Catholic priests is oriented around theology and the institution of the Church, both essential areas. The area that is neglected, however, is people. This reflects the orientation of the institution itself. A typical Roman Catholic priest is highly motivated to serve the institution of the Church and to bring people to faith. Many of them are less motivated or prepared to accomplish these tasks primarily by serving people.

This is not simply a matter of emphasis. It is a matter of starting point and professional stance. Properly speaking, the priest is a servant leader. He or she gets to know a community of people, listening to and reflecting with them on who they are and what their identity and mission are. He or she teaches and preaches the spiritual tradition to the community; this tradition functions as both nourishment and direction for the parish. He or she organizes the parish so that it becomes a community; this is done through administration as well as pastoral care. The institution of the church is a container for the community, the priest guiding and leading it with the knowledge that (in the words of St. John) God's house "has many mansions" and that the truth is very broad and very deep.

In my experience, it is the rare Roman Catholic priest who approaches his work from this stance. Rather, he has been trained to begin with the institution, with whom his primary loyalty lies, and to labor to bring people into line with that institution and its beliefs, for their own good. He is the theologically educated one; he is the one who has made the "sacrifice" of his sexuality. People "owe" him deference and obedience. He is called "Father," a title that carries a huge psychic load.

The Roman Catholic church has in its priesthood created a separate class of people, clergy whose priesthood is the holiest element in the Church besides the Body and Blood of Christ. This is what accounts for the hierarchy's attempt, in even egregious cases of misconduct, to protect the priest from long-term consequences of his behavior. Preserving a man's priesthood is a very high value, as if somehow his priesthood is separable from his behavior.

Roman Catholic priests have an impossible job. Vatican II made it even more difficult. Pope John XXIII made bold moves for the empowerment of laypersons, moves that were quickly reversed after his death. The Church (at least in this country) has become more conservative, while laypeople (many of them more highly educated than priests) have become more convinced of their own dignity and competence as Christians and are not content to be treated as lesser. The crisis in the Roman Catholic Church now is a crisis of control, with sexuality as the presenting issue.

Although, at least in the past, Roman Catholic priests may have been protected from the consequences of their behavior by the institution, nothing can protect them from the consequences of trying to do the job the way they have been trained to: as an idealized figure, an idol, who is "above" the realm of ordinary folk and who must continue to "sublimate" (read "deny") his humanity in order to be who his superiors expect him to be. Friends who are Roman Catholic priests tell me of the alcohol abuse, the loneliness, and the anger that are so prevalent among their colleagues. One made his decision to leave the priesthood after he did a stint serving as chaplain in a church-run retirement home for priests. "I looked at all those alcoholic, bitter old men, and I knew I had to get out," he said.

Sexual misbehavior is a logical consequence of the frustration and rigor of this style of priesthood. Straight men who may have been willing to take a vow of celibacy when they were training for ordination as young men learn, after years of ministry, that celibacy (when not freely chosen) confers no special authority or wisdom. They function within an institution that esteems them highly—mostly on principle. They may be able to form healthy relationships with parishioners, but frequent assignments to new parishes can prevent long-term ties with people. One middle-aged priest who left the Roman Catholic Church to pursue priesthood in the Episcopal church said to me, "Not one of my superiors ever said thank you to me. Not one, ever." This makes me believe that the pedestal on which the Roman Catholic Church puts its priests can be a pedestal for public viewing only. Privately, as a human being, a Roman Catholic priest may be valued little by the church he serves.

When Episcopal priests are ordained (the word means "ordered"), they make certain vows. The vows are very specific and they reflect the job description, so to speak. There is a vow of obedience to the bishop and to the doctrine, discipline, and worship of the Church. There is a vow to continue to read the Scriptures always, to take intentional steps to grow in knowledge and strength, to work collegially, to pattern one's life so as to be a "wholesome example" to the people one serves, to persevere in prayer. To take the vows means to put oneself under a certain discipline. In the course of the ordination liturgy, the bishop points out that the role of the ordained person is to be pastor, priest, and teacher. It is a servant leadership role. Contrary to common perception, the priest has no real spiritual authority that is self-derived. He or she functions as a priest only within the jurisdiction of the bishop (from the Greek "episcopos"). Priestly authority is derived from episcopal authority.

In addition, priestly authority is an enabling authority in that its purpose is to foster growth in the Christian community. Despite widespread misunderstanding to the contrary, evidenced by possessive language such as "my ministry" on the part of some priests, priestly ministry properly exercised is not the possession of the priest, not part of his or her "equipment." A priest does not have "his or her ministry" in the same way that, for example, an opera singer has "her voice." Although it is to be hoped that everything a priest does, whether part of his or her public ministry or not, is marked by a certain priestly character, a priest has no authoritative ministry apart from the sphere of functioning to which he or she has been licensed by the bishop. To understand otherwise is to attribute to the priest a power that he or she cannot claim. I point this out now because the traditional image of the Roman Catholic priest as a figure of great spiritual power, the "alter Christus" (the "other Christ") stems in part from this misunderstanding.

In other words, the role of a priest is not to be a sacred figure from whom emanates spiritual power and who ministers to anyone who "needs help" or is "looking for God." Although the priest will of course sometimes do those things, essentially the priest is to be the leader of a community of faith, most often in the form of a parish. His or her job is to minister to the people he or she serves so that they can minister to the world. This is a very specific task that requires specific gifts: the ability to teach, preach, communicate, and give the kind of spiritual counsel that builds up a community of faith; and the ability to administer an institution financially, structurally, and pastorally. This task demands both a willingness to serve an extremely imperfect institution, which requires a kind of self-denial that is profoundly countercultural and the personal strength to thrive as an individual within that climate. In my limited experience, I have found that this is a relatively rare combination of gifts.

My colleagues in the psychiatric and psychotherapeutic professions have told me that in the last 10 years they have noted an increased number of very sick people seeking treatment. In the 1950s and 1960s, one colleague commented, he saw mostly neurotics in his practice, people with "problems in daily living." Now, he sees many more character-disordered people, many more narcissistic people, many more borderlines, many more people suffering from the consequences of abuse and addiction. Thus, the population that applies for ordination now includes persons with these problems. Indeed, given the common (though incorrect) assumption that the priesthood somehow confers wholeness on the priest, these very wounded people may be more drawn to the priesthood than are others, unconsciously seeking some kind of healing that is invisibly and sacramentally "conferred" by ordination rather than painfully and intentionally worked for in treatment.

Accepting these people for ordination results in a corps of priests who have a need to be ordained rather than a corps of priests whom the Church needs to be ordained. Dioceses that have a rigorous psychological screening process are able, much of the time, to disqualify these inappropriate but usually highly driven candidates. Dioceses that have less rigorous processes are not so able, and the extremely intelligent, well-spoken, charming narcissist often seems an attractive candidate for priesthood, especially to a bishop or interviewer who cannot see beyond a compensating self-presentation.

I mentioned before that the goal of our ordination process was, in part, to select people who would thrive, not simply survive, in the priesthood. It needs to be pointed out that even for healthy individuals, this is no easy task. The priesthood is a strenuous way of life. It demands emotional strength; the maturity that comes from an intentional, ongoing engagement with one's own history; tolerance of great ambiguity; relative comfort with a wide range of emotions; patience; the ability to withstand conflict and use it creatively; the ability to lead; and self-acceptance.

Most importantly in terms of the present topic, perhaps, is the ability to take upon oneself a largely public role while sustaining an interior life that is integrated with the public self while at the same time not shared publicly—in other words, the ability to learn to consciously hold boundaries. This is a constant and lifelong challenge for any priest. Undertaken consciously, it can be very fulfilling and freeing. Blundered into, it can lead to great grief and emotional hurt to others, because the emotional strains of the job are usually great enough to threaten the maintenance of appropriate boundaries, at least occasionally.

The Roman Catholic Church has traditionally ordained very young men to the priesthood, with the ordination process beginning, at least informally, as early as high school and sometimes earlier. In contrast, it has been widely observed that in the Episcopal Church in the past 25 years, most vocations to ordination have been felt by persons who are in their mid-30s or older. For many years, men and women right out of college were turned away from ordination on the basis of their age, and were told to "get some life experience" for awhile. While there are obvious benefits to postponing ordination, it seems clear now that the risks of ordaining people at midlife can in some cases outweigh those benefits. The Church is now encouraging younger people to come forth for ordination, understanding that a person in his 20s has more flexibility and openness to growth than an older person.

While people in their 30s or 40s often have much to offer the Episcopal Church, including a first career in the arts or law or medicine or the helping professions that can helpfully inform their second career, accepting these people is not uncomplicated. Sometimes these candidates bring a sense of restlessness and unfulfillment with them, speculating (not always correctly) that the priesthood is their "true" vocation. These candidates typically are articulate, well educated, conversant with the workings of the Church, and have a track record of lay ministry and an intentional spiritual discipline. They also bring their problems with them. "In the middle of the journey of our life," they may be in marriages made at an early age that have been ill-tended and are stalled, with the Church assuming the role of unconscious "lover."

A deep involvement in parish life may be more a manifestation of a need for control and order than potential for leadership. Such a candidate may not yet have struggled with family-of-origin issues. His intentional spiritual discipline may mask a relatively immature understanding of things religious. There is sometimes a low-level chronic depression or an alcohol dependence problem. Again, these are often "subclinical" issues, with the person presenting as highly motivated and highly credentialed.

Similarly, I am told that in the Roman Catholic Church the average age of ordination has risen from 26 to 34 over the past decade or so. This may bring some benefits. However, my psychiatrist and psychologist colleagues who assisted us in the selection process continually warned us to beware of older priesthood candidates who never succeeded in any professional or vocational path. In my limited experience teaching seminary students of all denominations in hospital chaplaincy internships recommended by some Roman Catholic seminaries (and required by most Protestant seminaries), these older Roman Catholic candidates for ordination are men who fall into this category. They are men entering early middle age who are at sea about who they are and what their place in the world is. While they may be highly motivated spiritually, and dedicated church volunteers, they are often immature, naïve, rigid theologically, and lacking in self-awareness. Unsuccessful in the world of people, they want to start over in a world they think is controlled by God. The Roman Catholic Church needs to figure out why it no longer attracts young men to the priesthood.

While older priesthood candidates may have the life skills that enhance ordained functioning, they are simply less open to growth and change by virtue of their age. The three-year seminary experience is designed to be transformative of the whole person, not simply a spiritualized graduate education. A very young person usually comes out of seminary a very different person than when he entered, encountering numerous crises (both spiritual and emotional) along the way. An older person usually experiences seminary in a very different way. It is more difficult for older candidates to surrender completely to the experience of a transformative educational/vocational process. Sometimes they view the requirement of a seminary education as a "necessary evil," occasioning family dislocation, increasing debt, and presenting the annoyances of being students again. Their theological perspective and way of understanding the world is already formed, and seminary is only the frosting on the cake, the "ticket" they need to begin to work as a priest.

This attitude can lead to a subtly adversarial relationship with the institution of the Church that begins to operate in the person even before he or she is ordained. In the course of my misconduct work, I have sometimes wondered whether this adversarial attitude can contribute to misconduct, with the priest (whether ordained at midlife or at a young age) acting out his rage at the institution by abusing one of its members. This is just an intuition on my part.

Many ordained persons come from families in which they were never truly "heard" and valued as the individuals they were, making them into people who lack a sense of self-worth and self-acceptance, who continually seek approval outside themselves to feel real. There is no way to underestimate the unsure footing on which such an emotional history puts an ordained person. It is initially experienced by a candidate for ordination as idealism, a strong relational pull toward other people, a pull that seems to lend credence to his or her vocation. Indeed, it is a convincing facsimile of the other-directedness that is required of an ordained person. But it is not "the real thing." Sexual misconduct can be one of the eventual outcomes of this dangerous emotional scenario.

The problems that eventually lead to sexual misconduct in midcareer can sometimes be seen early in priesthood. During the first few years of ordained work, typically the work itself (the sustained close contact with people, the rigorous work schedule, the demands of being a spiritual leader) will flush out in the new priest the issues that he or she needs to work on in order for the ordination that has been conferred sacramentally on him or her to begin to become real. Although it is true that the drama and energy of becoming ordained can provide the emotional and spiritual "steam" to keep a person relatively happy functionally for about five years, after that a crisis occurs. The crisis can be resisted, or accepted. If it is resisted, a breakdown in healthy functioning that may include misconduct can begin, a breakdown that I would call self-loss. In my experience, this self-loss happens invisibly and insidiously, with misconduct being but one of the ways that it finally erupts into the visible realm as a kind of desperate assertion of self.

The following are characteristics of the early-career crisis, seen from the perspective of my own work with newly ordained priests:

First of all, idealism gives way to fatigue. The new priest discovers that there is no way he can do all the work, all the time, and still feel human. The work of a parish priest is cyclical (Christmas comes every year, and no matter how "well" you did it last year, it will come again this year). The work is never done and in some sense you are always starting from a blank slate. Priests who have not established a routine of rest and self-care will deal with their fatigue by working harder. Eventually the fatigue and stress become habitual and oddly sustaining.

Secondly, the new priest discovers that people are only human. They are wonderful, but they will do what they will do. They will think what they will think. They will not always listen to the priest. They will not accept all he learned in seminary. They will reject the most convincing methods of church growth. They will resist his charm and his intelligence. The new priest discovers that being a pastor is more like herding cats than shepherding sheep. This is an extremely disarming experience. It can make the priest feel misunderstood, not seen, and ineffective. Most new priests react to this reality by working harder. At the start of the movie *Tootsie,* Dustin Hoffman tells young actors to take roles that "fit" them as actors, and when they do, to take on the role gently. "Don't attack the role," he advises. Many new priests would do well to heed that advice. Instead of drawing back a bit to observe and reflect and just let things happen, they pounce on their responsibilities in an effort to be "a good priest." If they have a family history of not being "seen," this attacking of role is more likely to occur.

A priest is rarely "seen" as the person he or she is. This is counterintuitive, and comes as a disappointment to the new priest who places a high value on being seen. The duties of the job would seem to make "being seen" relatively easy—after all, a priest is often preaching, giving spiritual counsel, sharing experiences at a deep level, teaching, being with people at moments of crisis and joy. But functioning effectively as a priest involves a delicate negotiation with one's self about "being seen." The priesthood involves self-offering, not self-immolation. Constant sharing of self is a sure road to burnout. More importantly, the priest needs to remember always that even if self-disclosure were appropriate to the role, it always backfires because the priest is rarely seen as the person he or she is. Each person who encounters the priest projects onto him or her a number of things: their experience of God; their history with the Church, and sometimes with their parents; and their understanding (or lack thereof) of what the word "religion" means.

This is a heavy load for a priest to bear. The clerical collar is an identifying mark, but it is also an obliterating mark. When I put a collar on each morning, I am no longer "Anne Richards," but "the Reverend Anne Richards." There is a difference—but only for me. There is no difference for my parishioners, even though they may think there is. The very nature of the role creates a boundary between public and personal, a boundary that must be observed for me to do my job.

Part of the priest/parishioner relationship is the working out of that boundary insofar as it helps the parishioner understand that any process of growth, including spiritual growth, involves learning healthy boundaries, especially as it relates to the question at the heart of any spiritual path: "Who am I?" Thus, learning boundaries has not so much to do with "limits" or "beyond this point you shall not go," but rather as the delineation of the self as it stands among other selves and with God. In the early years of her career, a priest begins to live within this delicate area, hopefully consciously.

It is also at this point that a new priest may experience anger in a way that surprises him. Religion is highly idealistic in the abstract. Practicing religion results in the collision of idealism with realism. The psychological profile of most candidates for ordination shows a marked discomfort with the expression of anger, and a need to avoid conflict. If the new priest does not confront his anger early in his career, he will act it out anyway, by "throwing his collar around," so to speak (asserting his authority, invoking policies, laying down the law), or by directing it at his superiors, most often at his supervising priest or his bishop, or the unfortunate parishioner who either challenges him or does not conform to his idea of what a good parishioner should be.

It has been said that when a priest gets into the pulpit for the first five years of his ministry, he is preaching to his parents. There is, it seems to me, a profound truth in this quip. For the child who has not been cherished, the priesthood seems to offer a sure path to be seen and heard as the individual one really is, with its very public role and its opportunities to talk about truth and goodness and love. The problem is, the priesthood is not meant to be for that. Although it is hoped that a priest will find, within his vocation, who he is "really" meant to be, the exercise of his true personhood, in day-to-day reality, is a profoundly other-directed profession. It requires a setting aside (not a denial) of the self that creates room for other people to become who they are really meant to be.

That happens within the other person, and it is often invisible to the priest. Thus the priest must learn, often painfully, the limits of his effectiveness, even as the person he really is. He cannot keep insisting that other people (his parents, his parishioners) validate him. Only in setting his parishioners free from that implicit demand can the priest be really free to be a priest. This is a task that should begin in the early years of the priesthood.

In a sense, these are all authority issues: personal authority, priestly authority, and institutional authority. Most priests are surprised by how ministerial work inevitably brings to the fore their "authority problems." When their parishioners do not respond to them as they would like, issues about personal authority (what it is and how it is exercised) emerge. When one's work seems ineffective and when one's internalized image of the ideal priest (an image every new priest holds within him, often unconsciously) begins to falter, issues about priestly authority (what is this job really about?) come forth. And when the new priest begins to experience the limits of living under a vowed discipline that does not allow him to live as a free agent, issues of institutional authority erupt (Is the Church worth working for?). Thus, finding one's place in the Church, broadly speaking, is also a process that must begin early on. In this way, the transition from the highly individualistic "call" part of the priest's vocation to a more corporate, less self-regarding understanding of one's life work can begin.

Priests are God-bearers. They are meant to be channels for the Divine. Human, fallible, imperfect, deeply flawed—they are still vessels for God to work through. This quality is not "bestowed" ready-made upon the person when he or she is ordained. The grace and strength are given sacramentally, but it remains the task of the ordained person to grow into the vow to be an instrument of God's grace. The profound challenges of the early years of priesthood include, then, the challenge of understanding that even one's most deeply held understanding about who God is must change. There are many people sitting in the pews of churches every Sunday morning who are highly accomplished, but whose understanding of God is essentially their childhood understanding.

A priest can help people mature in faith only if he understands that the God of his childhood is dead, because it was only an image. The only God that is real is the God who is always elusive, the God of change and life as it is lived, the real God who stands beyond experience while shining through it. This means that his parishioners themselves will teach the priest about who God is. If the new priest does not take up this challenge, he or she will function ministerially in the realm of the "should," trying to recreate the past and stifle creativity. Many priests fight this challenge their entire careers.

As mentioned earlier, the loss of self that can lead to professional misconduct happens invisibly and insidiously, usually over many years. If the priest suffers from a character disorder, it can manifest more quickly, because priesthood will never satisfy the emotional needs of such a person. In my limited experience, this loss of self has as its background the failure to engage the formational issues described above: the frustration that grows from long-term fatigue; anger at people because they resist one's authority and insist on being free human beings; anger at the institution for not being perfect and a wish that the institution of the Church be the "perfect family" one never had; an immature need for approval and affirmation from the outside; and a failure to grow in one's understanding of God.

No matter how much the priest or the people around him idealize it, this loss of self leads to an acute sense of deprivation that has any number of consequences. The incidence of untreated clinical depression among clergy is high, as is (as mentioned above) alcohol abuse or misuse. There is a great deal of marital unhappiness, and it bears repeating that the physical and emotional health of clergy wives in the Episcopal Church is at an all-time low. Many priests, and their spouses, talk often of great loneliness and spiritual emptiness.

I do not think sexual misconduct is any higher among clergy than it is among other parts of the professional population, but its consequences are different, affecting both the public sphere of the parish and the private sphere of the people involved. But perhaps it can be said that sexual misconduct is an "occupational hazard" of the priesthood, especially for the priest who has not engaged with its inherent challenges. "If the shepherd is not fed, he will eat the sheep." That aphorism has a certain internal logic, and in a sense, sexual misconduct does also. When a man (and there were no cases of sexual misconduct on the part of a female cleric while I was on the job) finds himself 15 or 20 years into a strenuous ministry, with his sense of purpose or accomplishment largely unchanged since ordination, his marriage having suffered as a result of the time demands of his job, there is at least a chance that he is going to reach out for the nearest thing available to make him feel "real" again: another human being.

The great majority of cases I considered involved married heterosexual male priests who had inappropriate sexual involvements with adult women. I am not sure that male priests realize how much sexual energy they attract simply by virtue of their role. Personal attractiveness and pastoral skills only increase this allure. Understanding this and monitoring oneself is part of learning to handle the projections you receive as a priest, knowing for sure that they will come your way. When a male priest begins to feel an attraction toward a female parishioner, he often feels "ambushed" by his feelings, but can be quickly overtaken by them. Often this connection with a female parishioner is invested with the same energy and idealism as the original "call" to ordination. The priest admits that he knows that technically it is "wrong," but claims that essentially it is "right." His ability to hold comfortably to this contradiction is a measure of the split within himself, between the person he believes he "really" is and the person he is in the real world. In other words, that original need remains operative, having never been successfully engaged, and it is powered by his implicit refusal to accept the public, essentially self-denying role of priest because that too has never been successfully negotiated. Many sexual abusers remain idealistic about the abuse they have inflicted.

I mentioned that there were no reported incidences of sexual abuse by female clerics during the time I served on the bishop's staff. I believe it is because male priests tend to "act out" their problems, whereas female priests tend to "act in" their unhappiness by overeating, drinking too much, social withdrawal, and deciding to remain in jobs in which their full potential is not realized. The fact that so many female clerics are obese deserves further study.

I am sometimes asked what it was like handling misconduct cases as a woman. The answer is that I was hated and feared, and as a result of doing it I'm sure I couldn't get elected dogcatcher in Hoboken. Many of my clergy friends misunderstood what I was doing (they called me "the sex cop"). My life was threatened. On one occasion I had to move out of my home for a few days to elude an offending priest who was supposedly going to "make me pay." I had to rent a metal detector for my office in order to interview one abuser who was known to carry a gun strapped to his ankle.

I am not at all sure, however, that the job is any easier for the men who do it. It is tough work, but it is worth doing. Over time, I realized that I found it rewarding because I was doing it, at least in part, for all the faithful priests who have the courage to deal—over a life-time—with the issues and problems that come with the priesthood and who labor, often anonymously, in minor positions, doing good work. It was also worth doing for the offending priests, which I realized when a priest who had gone through a lengthy disciplinary process for misconduct with women called me after he had been rehabilitated and restored to parish ministry. "I just want to tell you you did a good job," he said. "Thanks," I replied. "No problem." I realized then, and continue to realize, what a great gift that telephone call was.

13

A Protestant Approach to Clergy
Sexual Abuse

The Reverend Laurie J. Ferguson

Most public conversation about sexually abusive clergy has focused on the Roman Catholic Church. My perspective on abusive
clergy is different. I come from a Protestant, specifically a Presbyterian, background. My perspective is also a clerical one. The Reformed tradition is dyed into my DNA, as I am a fourth-generation
Presbyterian pastor. This chapter addresses sexual abuse from a
Presbyterian viewpoint and examines our tradition's approach to
clergy sexual misconduct. It suggests ways that we might collabo-
rate, regardless of our denomination or tradition, to confront and
end sexual abuse by clergy.

Presbyterians put as much emphasis on our polity, the way we govern the church, as we do on our theology, what we believe. It is our
polity, our Church administration, that defines us. Our church structure was created in resistance—or protest—to the Church that was,
the Roman Catholic Church. The hallmark of this protest is that we

refused to have a hierarchical leadership. We insisted on parity between lay leaders and clergy and a system of governing that ordains laypeople to leadership, gives them equal power to clergy, and requires decisions to be made by groups, not by individuals. Our theology states that the Spirit is free to speak more fully through a group's wisdom than through one flawed human being. I believe in this structure. I even believed it was superior to any other church structure—until I began to deal with clergy sexual abuse.

Contrary to myth, Protestants also struggle with the trauma of clergy sexual abuse. The myths assume that we don't have the same problems because we have different requirements for our clergy. One myth is that sexual abuse stems from celibacy. Our clergy are not required to be celibate—in fact they are encouraged to marry. Yet we have sexual abuse. Another myth is that if women are allowed into the clergy so it is not such a "male club," there won't be sexual abuse. Again, sadly, the inclusion of women into positions of power has not altered the reality that our clergy also perpetuate sexual abuse. There is even the myth, believed for a long time by many Presbyterian clergy, that our polity, the equality of sharing power, and the checks and balances of decision making would eliminate the dynamic of clergy sexual abuse. However, even our church government does not protect us from the human dynamic of abuse of power and office.

When an allegation of abuse is made in our church—and there have been many—the allegation goes to the regional administrative body, composed of elected clergy and lay leaders. They either refer it to a committee or form a committee to investigate and deal with it. In 22 years in my presbytery, which covers Westchester, Rockland, Dutchess, and Orange counties in New York State, I have been asked to serve on six subcommittees that have investigated six pastors in our local Presbyterian jurisdiction, though I have not been asked to serve on all the investigative committees. Several of these cases involved male and female minors. In each situation we encountered the same dynamic—a reaction from the laity that was new and baffling to me. Trying to understand this dynamic ultimately led me to graduate school to study psychology. I needed tools to understand what I was seeing and hearing.

When an abuse allegation comes to our regional body, we are obligated to go to the local congregation where the pastor serves. In order to investigate, and potentially remove a pastor, a congregation must be informed that an allegation has been received. The congregation holds some of the power to fire or even require a leave of absence. There is no external hierarchy that can just demand it. Rather, my committees had to work with the congregational leaders.

When lay church leaders heard there was an allegation of sexual misconduct against their pastor, the most typical collective responses were a refusal to listen, hostility, dismissal of evidence, and then, if the identity of the victim became known, ostracizing the victim, the victim's family, and at times anyone who stood with them.

The response of the laity was total—complete—denial.

This primitive defense was rigidly overused, not just by individuals, but also by congregational collectives. The defensiveness led to splitting, scapegoating, selective amnesia, and repetitive retraumatization. Congregations "refused to know," and in this sense, often functioned much as the Roman Catholic hierarchy when confronted with sexually abusive priests. A telling irony is that we Presbyterians often wished we had bishops and the hierarchy that comes with them. Instead of dealing with endless layers of committees, one person would have the power simply to pull a pastor out.

It seems we all have fantasies about what would make dealing with clergy sexual abuse easier. But there is no one way or easy way to deal with the power of denial. It simply moves among the players. It was the profound depth and power of denial that stunned and then frustrated me as we began to deal with sexual abuse.

The Indigo Girls have a song that begins, "It's one perfect world if you learn to look the other way." Denial is always in service to something. What it supported in these instances was the idealization of the perfect pastor and the projection of a congregation's religious and spiritual authority onto that pastor. Congregations learned to "look the other way" in order to preserve the illusion of that perfection.

In the congregation's unconscious, the pastor was operating as the one who spoke for God, who held grace and forgiveness, knowledge and power, and who was the conduit for salvation. This may not sound revolutionary or surprising to a Catholic audience, but our polity and our theology were supposed to guard against this. Sharing power, checks and balances—these were built into the system so abuses of any kind wouldn't happen. Much of our theology is based on the "priesthood of all believers."

We *say* that we are each responsible for our own salvation; we each have a connection with God irrespective of ordained clergy. Yet, the unconscious desire for an authoritative figure that would carry our aspirations and projections of God and be responsible for our salvation is stronger than any humanly designed theological paradigm.

What was revealed in these investigations was the way congregations gave up their responsibility to do their own spiritual work. In an unconscious bargain, they traded their internal and independent spiritual power for a dependent relationship on a pastor's faith and charisma. They idealized him as the one who really knew and spoke for God and in consequence they lived out an immature faith that refused to recognize any wrongdoing that privileged an idea of perfection over true goodness, and ignored the reality of sin. Their reliance on the idea of his perfection was more compelling than the suffering of any one individual, particularly someone viewed as powerless, a minor or a woman.

We share in our different religious worlds two very similar dynamics: the powerful defense of denial, no matter what the cost, and the practice of idealization and projection. In the Roman Catholic tradition, the bishops idealize the Church, which must be protected at all costs. In my denomination, the idealization of a particular pastor takes precedence. For both traditions, the idealization contains a projection that the laity strives to maintain: that someone else will do our spiritual work for us, someone else holds our spiritual lives in their hands.

Perhaps what the Catholic scandal asks of each of us is to be willing to mature beyond dependence in our faith, dependence on an institution or on a particular leader, into a more personally owned spirituality.

In one of his letters, the Apostle Paul wrote to his congregation, "When I was a child I thought like a child, I acted like a child. But now that I am an adult I have given up my childish ways." In another letter he exhorts his congregation to "grow up together into full maturity in Christ."

Immersion in clergy sexual abuse is a painful way to grow up, and it is happening on the backs of the most vulnerable, those who have been most hurt by clergy abuse. Yet the witness of survivors and those who stand with them, based on powerful truth telling, is providing a cascading river of courage and opportunity for so many others beyond the bounds of the Catholic Church.

I know firsthand that in my denomination some women and men have found the strength to speak about their abuse by Presbyterian pastors because they have watched Catholic women and men speak out and they have seen them be believed.

The work Catholics are doing, messy and difficult as it is, has issued a call, a command, to other denominations and faiths to join in the work for restorative justice. The example of the Catholic struggle compels all of us to be willing to struggle to hear the truth and respond.

Still, there is more to do if this is to be a kind of *kairos* moment. *Kairos* is a Greek word that signifies a moment when time offers transformation and change. It is pivotal and full of possibility. Yet time only becomes *kairos* if such a moment is recognized and if there is a response to the opportunities presented.

We live in a culture that is fascinated by a Hollywood notion of evil. Almost every genre of film has its depiction of what is "evil." There is rarely nuance; our imaginations are filed with pictures like the ones from the Lord of the Rings, where evil is ugly, dark, easily identifiable, and most of all "other" and "out there."

In reality, as we know only too well, evil looks ordinary. Evil is not other. It is often entwined with the good and we sometimes excuse it because of that.

Hannah Arendt, a German philosopher, explained this to us several decades ago. After interviewing Eichmann, she was astounded to discover that this man who had done horrific and unspeakable things was an ordinary man. His monstrosity was not easily identifiable. She said he had learned obedience but had never learned goodness. That is what left a place for evil to grow.

The task for all of us—people of all faiths and no faiths, psychoanalysts and analysands, priests, pastors, survivors, congregants—is to stand together, supporting one another. We must reach across the aisles and across the barriers and claim a common work of telling the truth and hearing the truth, even when denial wields its power. We continue together the complicated work of recognizing and naming evil where we have seen and experienced it in order to experience healing. This is the way we begin to grow up into full maturity, and help our churches and our culture mature.

I conclude with the words of Sister Joan Chittister (2004), a Benedictine nun:

> If the banality of evil in this time is to be confronted, you and I must come to understand that what the world is really missing is us. The banality of evil rests on our bland unawareness that we are the only thing between it and success. The fact is that every holocaust begins or ends with me and you. The good in evil is not an argument that evil is good. The good in evil is only the good we bring to it, the good we do in the face of it.

This *kairos* moment demands me and you. We are given the challenge of embracing the task together.

REFERENCE

Chittister, J. (2004), Be the light. *Spiritual. & Health*, 48:48.

14

Women Priests and Clergy Sexual Misconduct

The Reverend L. Murdock Smith

Clergy sexual misconduct is not limited by religious denomination. Nor is it limited by national origin, ethnicity, or culture. It is not limited by marital status, age, or sexual orientation. Perhaps more surprisingly, it is not limited by gender. To assume that sexual misconduct is confined to males endangers vulnerable individuals and faith communities. The language of mental health states that sexual misconduct is a form of psychopathology while the Church declares it to be a sin. In any language, it connotes a breakdown of appropriate boundaries for an individual, among individuals, and within the community of faith in which it occurs.

Throughout society, there is a tendency to deny that women can be sexual transgressors. We have learned, however, that women—including mothers and clergy—are capable of violating fiduciary boundaries by sexually abusing children or engaging in inappropriate relationships with adults. One well-known secular case involved Mary Kay LeTourneau, a 34-year-old married mother of four, who had sexual relations with one of her middle school students, a

13-year-old male. There have been similar cases in Louisiana and Tennessee.

On two occasions, I have become rector of a parish in which there has been clergy sexual misconduct by my predecessor, a female priest. Two different parishes, two different dioceses, and two different areas of the country were involved. Both parishes were between 125 and 150 years old, with about the same membership, and located in urban, albeit quite different, settings.

Parish I was established prior to the American Civil War to serve Episcopalians in its small New England city. The closest other Episcopal parishes are in towns 30 to 45 minutes away. This parish has been a strong presence in the community for a number of generations and holds a substantive physical presence just off the town square. It is a multigenerational congregation with members from across the economic and vocational continuums. After a successful pastorate spanning about 25 years, there were two short pastorates each marked by troublesome dynamics so that, within seven years, Parish I had two rectors and three priests-in-charge.

Into this unsettled situation came the new rector of Parish I, a woman who brought gifts as a teacher and scholar but who had limited experience in leading a congregation. This rector had been divorced for some time and had a teenaged son. She was pursuing an academic doctorate in Old Testament Studies. Her previous experience as a priest had been on staff at a large Manhattan parish known for its ministry to the gay, lesbian, bisexual, and transgendered community. Her gifts as a teacher had been most apparent in this urban parish.

Parish I's female rector was active in diocesan affairs, including the development of policy guidelines regarding personal relationships between priests and parishioners. All diocesan clergy were required to sign a document that stated that they would comply with these directives.

Although some parishioners in Parish I resisted a woman priest, she generally was received with a willingness to support, or at least not actively oppose, her new ministry. She brought a liberal theology to a fairly theologically traditional parish. Some members of the congregation welcomed this change, but there was a reasonably large contingent that preferred the parish to remains "as we always have been." More problematic perhaps was an increasing perception among the congregation that the new rector was not accessible to them. In reality, however, the situation in Parish I was not much different than with many new ministries in which some parishioners are happy, some are unhappy, and most just want to move along. And, as with every parish priest, the new rector brought both gifts and deficits to ministry.

At some point, a relationship developed between the rector and a woman who regularly attended services and participated in the life of the parish. This person had come to Parish I from another parish in the diocese where, it was reported, she had been involved with the female priest there.

Eventually, the relationship between the rector and her parishioner came into the open in the life of Parish I, as well as within the broader community. Initially, the priest denied the relationship but, soon after, acknowledged its existence.

There are as many descriptions of what subsequently transpired as there are participants in the story. Some components are clear: there was clergy conduct contrary to diocesan policy; a letter of resignation from the rector was accepted; she made an effort to withdraw the resignation; the lay leadership of Parish I called in the bishop to help mediate the conflict; the bishop and his canons sought to be pastorally responsive to all parties involved while maintaining the integrity of diocesan standards for clergy conduct; and there were threats of legal action for unlawful termination of employment. Most important, both the parish and the priest were injured, with many parishioners feeling betrayed by their priest's behavior.

There was an effort by some bystanders to cast this incidence of clergy sexual misconduct as a matter of sexual orientation. In fact, however, the situation in Parish I was incidental to the priest's sexual orientation. In other circumstances, this parish could have adjusted well to a gay or lesbian rector. Much more important here was that a positive relationship between pastor and parishioner was never forged. In part, that was a function of the brevity of tenure between the priest's arrival in the parish and her misconduct. Even more central was that a large segment of the congregation found the priest to be emotionally, spiritually, and personally inaccessible. She did not often use her office at the church, and staff members and congregants were not always sure how to locate her. Some described her as judgmental and distant, although others, including me, did not find her so.

In Parish I's situation, the bishop was proactive and transparent. The priest was placed under inhibition, with specific actions she had to complete before she could be restored to full sacerdotal functioning. She and her partner relocated to another diocese where they followed the bishop's recommendations. The bishop's response was pastoral rather than punitive. He recognized that this priest needed counseling to better understand her identity and the demands of her priestly role. She, in turn, not only complied with the bishop's requirements but also completed her doctorate. At last report, she was teaching in a seminary and was ministering in a parish. She appears to be a welcome member of the diocese to which she moved.

The bishop applied a comparably proactive and pastoral response to Parish I. Based on his suggestion, the lay leadership did not start an immediate search for a new rector. Rather, they agreed that the bishop would find a priest to work with the parish to help rebuild it after multiple years of dysfunction, including the most recent clergy misconduct. I was called to be long-term Interim Rector. Although there was much conflict and pain from this encounter with clergy sexual misconduct, Parish I worked toward a positive resolution. It was a good ministry for me with the parish eventually restoring its ministries, revitalizing its buildings with a successful capital campaign, and ultimately calling a new priest who continues to serve as rector of Parish I. Key to the restoration of this parish was the bishop's active facilitation of healing for both priest and faith community. Instead of abandoning the Church's wounded, which is too often the case, the bishop made room for the light of day, openness of thought and speech, and the action of the Holy Spirit to bring healing.

Parish II is in a large, commercial, Southeast banking city. Established in 1877 as a mission to foundry and mill workers, it became a parish in 1904, and moved to its present location in 1912. From 1914 through the mid-1980s, there were only four rectors, three of whom became bishops. The parish has a long history of involvement in Christian social ministry, the first Boy Scout troop in the city was started at the parish, and the principal founders of a number of city-wide ministries (such as Hospice, Friendship Trays, and Crisis Assistance Ministries) were congregants. This is an intentional parish with members traveling distances and passing other Episcopal churches on their way to Parish II. The parish is welcoming, hospitable, and multigenerational, with lively Anglican worship and superior Christian formation for children, youth, and adults. Parish II has always been on the liberal end of the theological spectrum but also embraces members who are more traditional.

The bishops of the diocese had long been supportive of the ordination of women and they promoted women clergy into leadership positions. Most parishioners of Parish II were excited when a woman was called to be a rector. She was from within the diocese and had a successful ministry at a large parish in another city in the state.

The new rector's ministry started off well but soon there were some concerns about her. Parish II had long been welcoming to gays and lesbians but the new rector reflected a conservative Episcopal perspective that was inhospitable to homosexuals. Many gay and lesbian parishioners felt that they could no longer be part of the parish when the rector so clearly rejected their identities.

In addition, the rector's interactions with the parish's staff deteriorated rapidly. As in Parish I, parishioners in Parish II experienced their rector as inaccessible. Staff reported that there were often times when she could not be found. In an active and extroverted parish environment, this quickly became problematic. Although the priest was a good preacher and a good pastor to some families, there was an unevenness to her ministry.

At some point, the priest developed strong feelings for a married female parishioner. This woman's marriage was in a difficult time and the parishioner clearly was in an emotionally and spiritually vulnerable state. Her husband told the bishop about the relationship between his wife and the rector. The priest went on medical leave and was instructed to have no further contact with her parishioner. She also was instructed to seek counseling but she did not. Furthermore, neither she nor the bishop fully disclosed the rector's experiences at Parish II to at least one subsequent faith community she was called to serve. The parishioner's marriage ended in divorce, the woman transferred to another parish, and the husband left the Church. In this case of sexual misconduct, a marriage was destroyed and a member of the Church was lost.

Unfortunately at that time, the diocesan process regarding clergy misconduct maintained a commitment to secrecy. It was not appropriately open or proactively pastoral for either priest or parish. Rather, the departure of the rector was blanketed within a narrative of medical leave and depression, and the parish community felt that they were not adequately informed about the rector's situation. Despite the official silence, her sexual misconduct quickly became part of the congregational conversation. Misinformation, partial information, lack of information, and bias dominated the discourse. The diocese did send a team to talk with parishioners but that dialogue did not sufficiently meet parish needs. When I was in final discussions with the diocese about becoming rector at Parish II, I asked one official to tell me what could be shared with Parish II. I was told that he could not tell me much because the rector's "separation agreement" contained non-disclosure provisions. Once in the parish, I was able to piece together most of the story. As is usually the case, therefore, the non-disclosure agreement proved both useless and undermining of healing within the parish.

It has taken several years for this parish to move beyond the negative impact of its former rector's problematic ministry and sexual misconduct. The bishop's approach in this situation unfortunately intersected with the Southern tendency to mask unresolved conflict with hospitality and good manners, at least to another's face. Fortunately, this "dialect" is part of my mother tongue and I am familiar with both its charming and more insidious characteristics. One of the changes I initiated at Parish II was an intentional effort to be as open as possible while still honoring the etiquette many of us learned at our parents' knees. Today, the parish once again is working together to accomplish common ministry goals.

My experience in these two situations of clergy sexual misconduct convinced me that the more open and direct the process is subsequent to misconduct, the better the prognosis for healing of all parties. It is essential that both diocesan and parochial leadership take proactive and pastoral roles in guiding both the priest and the parish. The Church's proven tools and gifts for healing are prayer, pastoring, and clarity of thought combined with a willingness to be open to the Spirit. Intentional use of these gifts in diocesan and parish life enhances prevention of clergy sexual misconduct and promotes redemption when it does occur.

A diocese is like an extended family and it is the bishop that sets to tone and character of the family. Episcopal bishops do not have the absolute power of a Roman *pater familias,* but there still is immense authority conferred by ordination and accorded in part through transferential processes. As symbolic uber father of the faith community, the "parent bishop" provides the "rules" necessary for healthy family structure, clarity about acceptable behavior within the family, but also the freedom to encourage maturation and independence.

The styles of the two bishops involved in these cases were quite different. Some of the differences reflected culturally mediated approaches to conflict management representative of the Northeast and the Southeast. The effectiveness of the bishop in Parish I represented a leadership style that was open, direct, and focused on healing and reconciliation for individuals and communities. Because Bishop I was accountable for his own boundary preservation, and since he was comfortable with his own authority, he was able both to advise about and model appropriate interpersonal boundaries and judicious exercise of authority. To that extent, he enacted the role of a father who was secure enough to combine discipline and generosity in ways that promoted growth for both parish and priest.

The bishop for Parish II also wanted to facilitate a positive outcome for his priest and her parishioners. However, he was unable to combine authority and compassion effectively. Rather, he enacted, to some extent, the role of an ineffectual father whose authority is compromised by that ineffectiveness. In this case, the lack of transparency with parish members, in particular, left them feeling excluded from family matters that directly impacted them.

It is also important to state clearly that I do not perceive either of these cases of sexual misconduct by clerical "mothers" to be significantly correlated with the priest's sexual orientation. They were first and foremost about the misuse and abuse of the pastoral relationship and related therefore to power more than to sex.

Both priests were consciously or unconsciously working on consolidating their identities as people and as priests. To some extent, they became "parents" to their parishes before knowing deeply who they were as individuals. As in nuclear families, parish families function best when their "parent"/priest is secure enough as a human being and as an authority figure to relate to parishioners with both openness and appropriate boundaries. These two priests, psychologically and spiritually struggling to define themselves, were vulnerable to violating boundaries and to allowing others to transgress the priest–parishioner parameters. Emotionally confused or needy mothers in nuclear families sometimes use their children to shore up their identities. Similar dynamics were at work in these parishes.

As noted earlier, little has been written about the specific dynamics of sexual misconduct by women clergy and how or if it differs measurably from that of men. One dynamic I noticed in these two cases is that parishioners seemed more surprised and perhaps felt more betrayed by their female priest's sexual misbehavior than they would have been by a man's. As in the wider society, women are held to a higher standard in terms of interpersonal and family relationships. While we are disturbed, but not surprised when men transgress against those who are vulnerable and dependent on them, we are horrified when women cross the line with dependents or subordinates.

Many of us unconsciously still want perfect and perfectly nurturing mothers and are shocked when maternal figures turn out to have feet of clay. Both priests discussed here already had disappointed their parish families with their perceived unavailability. When they were then found also to have violated personal and sexual boundaries, the intensity of the laity's anger and distress was perhaps even stronger than it would have been toward a male priest.

The greatest lesson I have learned in replacing these clergy in their parish ministries is that clergy must have a clear sense of identity—as a human being, as a man or a woman, as a priest, and as a member of a spiritual community. This in turn means that the Church must be as judicious as possible in its selection processes, training programs, and ongoing support of clergy in ministry. The health of any congregation is mediated always by the health status of the wider Church.

15

The Priestly Phallus: A Study in Iconography

Mary Gordon

Where do I stand so that my voice will be well heard? What is the optimum place of audibility in a whirlwind?

My head has ached and spun with the words, words, words, spoken and written about pedophile priests. Why should I add to them? What could I say that would be either truthful or helpful? I have no special training. No expertise. I can present neither data nor theory. Only perhaps this: the observations of a novelist, a woman brought up in an environment where priests were a strong and pervasive presence, someone who at one point in her life left the Catholic Church in outrage and disgust, then after 25 years, came back to it in a search for the combination of historical and formal beauty and a lived commitment to social justice whose source is the heated regions of the heart rather than the cooler zones of reason. It is not easy to continue a relationship with an institution that more often disgusts and outrages than supports me. As Flannery O'Connor said, turning on their heads the traditional terms of martyrdom, Catholics must suffer much more from the Church than for it.

I speak, then, as a woman, a feminist, an artist, a critical left-wing Catholic, someone whose inner life was formed and enriched and vexed by priests, someone infuriated by the current hypocrisy of the hierarchy in relation to the recent cases of pedophilia, but as a novelist and former analysand, someone curious and concerned about the inner landscape inhabited by these priests, known as predators, but who must also be something else, some things else, than that. This is not to say that I share the Vatican's or the bishop's protectionism: only that both by biographical accident and professional habit, I am interested in the caves dug out behind the battle scarred terrain.

I would like to begin by suggesting that the question of pedophile priests is a question that is centered around a particular species of maleness. Priestly maleness. A maleness rarefied, attenuated, isolated, set apart, and therefore in its singularity, a useful object for understanding maleness in its more ordinarily imbedded manifestations. The two requirements for the priesthood are baptism and maleness: one a visible sign, one an invisible one. The most important sign of maleness is the phallus, and what is the nature of the priestly phallus? If we understand that, apart from urination, the function of the phallus is sexual activity, what is the nature of a phallus in a male who must vow to suppress his sexual nature, to act out a maleness in which sexual arousal is only a problem to be overcome, and penetration forbidden? One of the paradoxes in the lore of the priesthood is that a candidate had to be physically examined to insure that he was genitally whole: a castrato would not be eligible for ordination, nor would a hermaphrodite. Nor, it goes without saying, would a woman. It is required that genital expression in the potential priest must be something to be given up rather than something never within reach. For a priest then, maleness has to be legible; the conundrum is this: male sexual identity is the *sine qua non* for the priesthood, but his sexual identity must remain symbolic, abstract, potential. But there is the symbolic phallus and the literal penis between the literal legs. And these two are not, as priests have learned to their anguish, the same.

If the phallus is the hidden sign of the priesthood, his hands are the visible one. In the ceremony of ordination, the seminarian, about to be allowed, through ritual, into the priesthood, has his hands bound, then anointed. The hands must be intact and whole in order for the priest to perform the consecration of bread and wine into the Body and blood of Christ. In the lore, if a priest undergoes an accident and his middle finger or thumb are missing or amputated, he is no longer allowed to consecrate the host. A bishop had to give the mutilated priest a dispensation—that is to say, special permission, in order for him to be allowed to say Mass. When I was growing up, if there was a priest visiting in a house, a white linen towel had to be left for him in the bathroom so that he could dry his hands on it. He was not supposed to dry his hands on an ordinary towel, or on a towel a non-priest had used. His hands were fetishized. The official word for it was consecrated. Made sacred. His hands, and by metonymic extension his whole being, was made sacred, and in turn he could make sacred. He, and he alone, could turn ordinary bread and wine into the body and blood of Christ. The doctrine of Transubstantiation requires that Catholics believe that this transformation is not symbolic, but actual, that the substance of bread and wine becomes the substance of Christ. So the priest was in possession of extraordinary power, a power that belonged only to him as a priest, not only the power to transform but also the power to forgive sin or to refuse to forgive it. This kind of sacred power was invested in him only by ordination. What is the nature of this power? What do we mean by sacred? We mean, of course, set apart, placed out of the ordinary, in the category of the divine. A priest's hands were God's; his penis was nobody's. Not even his own. This combination of the divine and the denied, the super-valued and the delusional marked the image of the priest, the ideal by which he was supposed to live and to which we, as the faithful, were meant to respond.

How did this ideal, this image, this icon, differ from the female sacred beings available to the Catholic imagination: nuns? For one thing, no single part of the female body was fetishized, consecrated, anointed, blessed, as the priest's hands were. This is because women have always been denied the supernatural agency given to men: they cannot say Mass, they cannot make bread and wine into flesh, they can not raise their hands in blessing and forgive sin. A nun is a special kind of lay person: a priest is considered, by the very virtue of his consecration, an order apart. A nun, therefore has more in common with other women than she does with priests. Although there were, in the past, strict limits placed on the friendships that nuns could have with one another, they always lived in community, and their identity as nuns was importantly formed by their relationship to other nuns. Priests lived semi-autonomously in rectories with other priests; each of them came and went as he pleased; most priests had cars; they could eat in the rectory or not, they could eat and drink in public, as nuns could not—they could travel: there are no jokes about priests having to travel in pairs, as there are about nuns. Priests, then, were encouraged in a life of hyper-individuality; nuns were nuns by virtue of a relationship to other nuns. The body of a nun was entirely covered up; her garments were never ornamental, unlike the priest's whose highly embellished vestments, worn when he said Mass, were a sign of the community's regard. Even in the 1950s, priests could wear shorts and bathing suits; they often did when they were chaperoning or supervising groups of boys; no nun was ever seen in anything except full habit: no possibility of peekaboo here, no ironized now you see it now you don't performances that so marked the priestly presentation—no double message about a sexy nun. Think of the movies: In The Bells of St. Mary's, even Ingrid Bergman in her habit is off limits to the erotic imagination: she belongs to God alone. Bing Crosby in his straw boater hat, with his connections to the world of show business and sports, is a man of the world.

It is not irrelevant to be thinking of movies. The love Catholics had for priests was something like the love we had for movie stars and something like the love we had for God. It only narrowly skirted idolatry. Let's think for a moment of the most successful movie priest: Bing Crosby's Father O'Malley in two immensely successful, even Oscar nominated, films: *Going My Way* and *The Bells of St. Mary's*.

Father O'Malley, Bing Crosby's movie priest, was endlessly giving to everyone and intimate with no one. He seemed to have no needs. In *The Bells of St. Mary's*, one thinks for a moment that he and Ingrid Bergman will fly into each other's arms, but they never do: he's saying goodbye, sending her off for treatment of her TB. There is no problem Father O'Malley can't solve—just dial O for O'Malley he tells everyone, a 24/7 spiritual 911. But there is no number he would ever call, no one available for him. But then he is entirely emotionally self-sufficient.

This was the ideal that priests, particularly American priests, were meant to live up to. This ideal was inculcated in the imaginations of Catholics at a very early stage of childhood; most men who are priests now made the decision to become a priest; that is to say, the decision to be greater than an ordinary man but to claim less of his birthright when they were barely out of childhood themselves. There were preparatory seminaries that accepted boys at 13 years of age; most candidates entered at 18, directly after high school. For many years, this boy would inhabit a world in which he had almost no contact with women—even access to his biological family was strictly limited and supervised. In being cut off even from a bond with even a mother or a sister, the priest was entirely and radically removed from the sphere of female regard. No female judgment touched him, and female standards were considered so low as to be absolutely irrelevant. Is it possible to conjecture that this kind of hyper-maleness, connected inevitably to idealization, denial and isolation put the priest in the position of the lonely child, and therefore made the vulnerable child a tempting focus of sexual desire?

A priest was meant to be connected only to God. The connection of the non-priest with the priest was a connection of strangers; the priest was observed, mostly at a distance; until the mid-1960s he said Mass with his back to the congregation. This combination of the idealized and the denied, a combination that skirts cleanly over issues of ordinary adult identity formation, marks the biographies of most men who are priests in the Catholic Church today. It was, and is, a crazy making combination for the priests and the people they served.

There were, for priests of course, great compensations for what they had given up, both sexually and as relational beings. The community bestowed on them a place of honor that had enormous libidinal rewards. Every Catholic mother prayed for the blessing of having at least one son become a priest. But with the reforms of the Second Vatican Council, which tried to humanize many aspects of the church including the formation of priests and nuns occurring at the same historical moment as the steady erosion of the authority and prestige of the Catholic Church, an erosion linked directly to its unrealistic and intransigent position on birth control, this honor was tarnished and diminished. Priests were removed from their pedestal, told that they were creatures who required intimacy (a good thing so long as it was never, never sexual), and yet required to maintain their unique positions of both power and authority: only they could perform the sacred ritual, only they could forgive sin. There was a hemorrhaging of men from the priesthood in the 1960s and 1970s and a crisis of lowering numbers of boys entering the priesthood. The drowning shame of leaving the priesthood to marry was diminished as more and more men did it; the unspeakable stigma attached to homosexuality became less pronounced in the world at large—there were fewer reasons to enter the priesthood and fewer reasons to stay. Who, then, was left? Why did they stay?

I fear that I am approaching dangerously near a territory I do not wish to enter: the territory that suggests that the only reasons for entering the priesthood and staying in it are pathological. I know many priests whom I respect deeply, and although I am not privy to the details of their sexual lives in all cases, I know that some make the kind of compromises that many of us who have taken vows have made at one point or another in their lives. The difference is that when married people pretend to be monogamous, they don't have to pretend to be above and beyond the lure of sex. Priests do. And I would like to suggest that there may be a few, a very few natural celibates (I have met several, some men, some women, who have described themselves this way) for whom the lure of genital sexual contact is not irresistible. The structural error of the church is insisting that this rare occurrence, natural or hard won celibacy, must be the norm for someone who will take on a position of authority and ritual power.

Many Catholic priests are gay, discreetly sexually active. The demographics of the priesthood mean that many priests are past middle age, and have made some sort of peace with their sexual histories. But this is not the aspect of the current situation that I am mean to discuss. If there is, and has been, an epidemic of pedophilia in the Catholic priesthood, what does it say about the special kind of maleness that is an inextricable part of being a Catholic priest?

I think it cannot be denied that pedophiles are much more commonly male than female. This is a mystery that I cannot even to pretend to be able to explore. When nuns abuse children, the libidinal flavor is psychological humiliation rather than genital violation.

I will digress for a moment now to speculate on the similarities of the case of the therapist who violates the trust of his patient and the

priest who violates the trust of his parishioner. There are iconic similarities between the priest and the traditional analyst that were an issue in my own analysis, an issue that I believed the literature had not
touched on because most psychoanalytic writers and thinkers were
not Catholic. In both cases, the priest or analyst is anointed and apart
from the patient/parishioner. In both cases, the lived life of the
anointed one is not accessible to the non-anointed. In both cases,
this inaccessibility is said to be for the benefit of the patient/parishio-
ner: in the case of the analyst, the blankness allows for greater range
of transference, in the case of the priest, the empty biography makes
space for the pure or unaccented word of God. Both the priest and
the analyst serve as points of refuge and safety; in addition they are
sources of wisdom, or at least of some sort of help in the task of living
a good life, however that life may be defined. In the case of the priest,
the goodness that is being pointed toward has a moral cast, and it has
been tragically the case of the modern church that this goodness has
been disproportionately defined in sexual terms, so the hypocrisy of
the sexual transgression, on the part of the priest who has laid down
the sexual law, is particularly embittering. But the sense of betrayal
when boundaries are breached by either the priest or analyst is at
least as much ontological as it is ethical: the promised creature has
been replaced by a different animal, an animal whose desire is now
part of the conversation, a creature whose needs were said to be non-
existent or irrelevant, and that are now exigent: at the center of the
lens. In both cases, the aura of anointing is so powerful as to suggest
that in being chosen as desirable, one is honored. The sense of
honor and the sense of outrage—added to by an anxiety about in-
gratitude—how can I say no to one who has given so much, who has
helped me so much—makes notions of consent specially vexed in
the case of both the priest and the analyst. But in the case of the
priest, the unwanted sexual advance may seem to come not just from
the mouth of the anointed, but from the mouth of God. Questions of
salvation may hang in the balance and not only the parishioner's
sexual future but her or his eternal spiritual life are in jeopardy.

It is possible to say that there is an institution called psychoanalysis, but it is a shaky proposition at best. No one, however, would
question the notion that there is an institution called the Catholic
Church. And so the identity of the priest takes its shape from the in-

stitution; the breaching of the boundaries of this identity is therefore an institutional question. And it is on this level that the scandal of pedophile priests is most egregious. It is possible to say—and I don't think we yet have the data to support or to deny such an assertion—that pedophilia is no more common among priests than it is among other populations that have access to children. But this is beside the point. The particular kind of access that priests are given is a product of their institutional identity; the kind of safety that their roles suggest comes to them from the authority of the institution. Therefore, the institution must examine itself to see what its structure and history has contributed to the problem. And this is precisely what the Catholic Church refuses to do. Both the historical cover-ups and the new zero toleration policies are tactics for avoiding deep structural examination. Even the words "zero toleration policy" suggest that a considered look at individual cases means that one "tolerates" the sexual abuse of children in some cases. (When did you stop beating your wife?) This new policy combines the worst aspects of American and church culture: it can be seen as a preemptive strike against American litigiousness, and it partakes of the Roman appetite for *fiat*. What it does not do is dismantle the structure of idealization. What it does do is place the emphasis on punishment rather than on healing, a habit of mind that the Catholic Church finds all to familiar, a habit of mind that ensures the calcification and then replication of the status quo. A status quo that insists on the transcendent value of the icon of superhuman or perhaps semidivine male: desirable, untouchable, untouched, his father's son, in whom, to quote God the Father at the moment of Jesus' baptism in the Jordan, He is always well pleased.

The events of September 11th, 2001, might have been an opportunity for Americans to examine ourselves: without entering into craven self-abasement, we could have taken the step of questioning what it is that makes people hate us so that our annihilation would seem a larger good? The Catholic Church could use the moment of the scandal of pedophile priests to examine the problems of its attitudes toward sex. But retreating to the bunkers, waving the flag or the cross are easier gestures than the long, slow process of self-understanding. The Church is made up of humans, so its reluctance to change is understandable. This position could be more sympathetic if they understood that in their humanity, clergy are subject to at least as high a level of scrutiny, responsible for at least as good faith an effort at truth telling, as the others of their kind. The human kind, that is to say.

16

Celibacy and Misogyny

Gillian Walker

The sexual transgressions of Catholic clergy are not necessarily worse than those in other religious or secular institutions, but they fascinate the laity and non-Catholic observers because they violate the Catholic clergy's public commitment to celibacy and to the promulgation of a restrictive sexual moral code.

The contemporary sexual abuse scandal in the Church exposes the failure of mandatory celibacy and throws into question the complex body of traditional Catholic teaching about sexuality and gender upon which mandatory celibacy is based and upon which misogyny is institutionalized. This chapter looks at the interconnection between the church's sexual teachings and its abusive power transactions which have provided the scaffolding for a hierarchical system that feminist theologian Elisabeth Schussler-Fiorenza (1999) has termed "kyriarchy," or "the rule of the emperor/master/lord/father/husband over his subordinates (p. 114). Stressors generated by this sexually repressive and "kyriarchical" system have resulted in the eruption of sexual abuse of Catholic minors by the priestly caste just as the system's will to maintain power has resulted in the massive cover-up of abuse.

MANDATORY CELIBACY

Upon reading the Gospels, free of the influence of later Church teachings which celebrated the virtues of celibacy, one might be startled to find that there is no textual reference to Jesus as a celibate, nor evidence that Jesus was not or had not been married. In fact, given the Jewish belief in the importance of procreation, Jewish religious teachers customarily were married and had children. Had there been a contemporary tradition from which Jesus had departed in order to embrace celibacy, it surely would have been worthy of Gospel comment.

While the Gospels were written many decades after Jesus' death, by men who most probably did not know him directly, Paul was indisputably a contemporary of Jesus' immediate disciples, and had access to information about Jesus' actual life. In fact Paul, who was once married but preferred celibacy, admits he has no teaching from Jesus on the matter and perhaps even more tellingly fails to cite Jesus' "celibate" life as an example for others.

Nevertheless, Catholic doctrine gives celibacy a scriptural pedigree, maintaining that Jesus, Mary, Joseph, and the apostles were all celibate after their calling. Because the canonical scriptures do not provide direct evidence for the celibate status of the Holy Family and the Apostles, from the second century onward the Church was forced to use imaginative scriptural exegesis (conveniently overlooking contradictory evidence) to advertise their stalwart celibacy as a model of Christian virtue.

Genesis, the Gospels, and the Pauline texts are spuriously invoked to legitimatize a "kyriarchical" church (and world) that controls sexuality, maintains women's inferior position, and insists on heteronormativity. Initially as a colonized sect operating within the ruthless and powerful Roman Empire, the early Christian movement, beginning with Paul (who prized his Roman citizenship), came to admire and eventually to mimic oppressive Roman administrative structures. As the embryonic church developed its rituals, structures of belief, and administration, it internalized both the sexual pessimism and the misogyny of late antique Greco-Roman philosophy, along with the empire's abusive love of power, as it gradually submerged evidence of Jesus' original radical, reformist, and anti-imperialist mission.

CATHOLIC TEACHINGS ON CELIBACY

The earliest strains of the celibacy tradition reflect the Christian embrace of Stoic ideals, which appealed to the potential convert market of a Hellenistic middle class increasingly disillusioned with the libertine excesses of the empire. Ironically, the teachings of ideals of chastity and continence, which later evolved into an ideology used to oppress women, were seen by early Christian women as a means of liberating themselves from the dominance of fathers and husbands. In the early years of the Christian church, pagan women converts assumed leadership roles in the network of house churches, and for a short time even had the power of bishops. They wanted their leader Jesus to seem no less virtuous than pagan holy men who customarily took vows of virginity, and as a virgin he became for these women an idealized and available spiritual lover. By the fourth century, Christian obsession with celibacy had grown, perhaps as an outgrowth of an ascetic movement which had swept the eastern empire.

Idealization of sexual continence was elaborated in the foundational teachings of the early Church Fathers from Tertullian to Origen (ca. 183–254), Jerome (340–420), Ambrose (340–397), and above all, Augustine (354–430), all of whom believed that sensuality or "voluptas" was associated with, if not the cause of, man's fall from paradise in original sin.

For Tertullian and Jerome, sexuality could be controlled by will. The most desirable course of action for the Christian was to rectify man's fallen state by embracing continence, a state of purity, refraining from any sexual activity. Origen took drastic steps to quell his desire for real sex with real women. Taking literally Matthew 19:12 in which Jesus challenges his followers to "become eunuchs" for the heavenly kingdom (i.e., practice continence if they divorce rather than remarry or fornicate), Origen castrated himself.

Ambrose, Augustine's teacher, believed that sexuality represented a deeply polluting mixing of soul and body, male seed and female blood, that did not exist before the fall and which the Christian must remedy by sexual abstinence and fasting. For Ambrose, as for his successor Augustine, women should be virgins or continent and clergy should be celibate, because Christian perfection was measured by the "degree of a person's withdrawal from sexual activity" (Brown, 1988, p. 359).

For Augustine, it was not the sexual act itself that occasioned the fall; for himself, Adam and Eve would have enjoyed a sexual relationship in the Garden. Rather, it was their act of disobedience that led to a distortion of the workings of human will, one in which sexual drives escaped conscious control.

While most councils encouraged clerical celibacy, it was only in the 12th century that the Second Lateran Council settled the issue. From that time onward the rule of clerical celibacy in the Latin rite was absolute.

The pernicious consequences of these teachings and rulings have been discussed by the contemporary Trappist monk, Thomas Merton, who toward the end of his life came to believe that the human capacity for joyful erotic love of the other is central to the knowledge of Divine love. Merton believed that the ancient traditions of Neo-Platonism and Stoicism were responsible for the Catholic separation of flesh and spirit, for "degrading matter, stimulating self-hatred and a loathing for the flesh … that degrades and perverts the sexual instinct leading it into forms of expression which, in their sadomasochism and hypocritical selfishness are far more dangerous, much more radically impure than the normal expression of erotic love" (Merton, 1985, pp. 114–115).

THEORIES: FOUCAULT AND DOUGLAS

Two bodies of contemporary theory are important for understanding what Richard Sipe (1995) has called ecclesial "celibate sexual/power structures" as they evolved over time: Foucault's concept that the uses of sexuality are bound to mechanisms of power and control, and anthropologist Mary Douglas's exploration of how purity rules operate to construct and enforce the boundaries of socioreligious systems that are then perceived as special and holy.

Ironically, as Foucault (1978, p. 45) suggests, Western thought has been permeated by the Augustinian view "that endowed sex with an inexhaustible and polymorphous causal power" and understood the nocturnal emission as representing an unconscious desire that always escaped the control of conscious will. As Foucault (1977, p. 111) noted, "In Christian societies, sex has been the central object of examination, surveillance, avowal, and transformation into discourse.... Since Christianity, the Western World has never ceased saying: 'To know who you are, know what your sexuality is.'"

The Catholic Church's elaborate codes of sexual regulation, together with its rigid hierarchical structure, illustrates Foucault's (1978) argument that the regulation of the body's most intimate and secret aspects is intertwined with operations of power and control. The more central sexuality became in Catholic teaching, the more power a sexually pure clergy had over the economy of sin and salvation.

Foucault, in his late essay, Sexuality and Power (1978), argued that as Christianity became a more elaborated administrative system, a merger occurred between its sexual values, largely influenced by Stoicism, and the idea of

> 'pastoral' control of both the individual believer and the stateless roving flock inherited from Judaism. The metaphor of a benevolent but autocratic pastor leading cows and sheep is apt here because the believer, like the cow or the sheep, must be blindly obedient to the pastor's rule, and in return for obedience, the pastor uniquely guides him to salvation. [p. 122]

Foucault believed that Christianity inaugurated a new form of power. Instead of punishment for infractions by the State, Christianity offered the new belief that the pastor could demand of an individual "total, absolute and unconditional obedience." Through an elaborated system of sexual prohibitions and penalties, the sexual body of the believer could be rendered disciplined, docile, obedient, and easy to govern. Christian humility represents the internalization of obedience to this code (Foucault 1978, p 124).[1]

---

[1] Papal Encyclicals *Casti Connubii* (1930), *Humane Vitae* (1966), *Familiaris Consortio* (1981), *Veritatis Splendor* (1993); all reaffirm the Church's position on sex, contraception, and homosexuality. *Inter Insignores* (1976) is on the exclusion of women from the priesthood. *Sacerdotalis Caelibatus* (1967) reaffirms mandatory celibacy of an all-male priesthood.

Christians were expected to turn for discipline to the pastor, and then upward through the chain of authority to the ultimate pastor, Il Papa. Here, obedience to pastoral laws supersedes civic law. A contemporary example is the initial action of the Vatican/Papa in the current sexual abuse scandals, where bishops were discouraged from submitting the names of priests suspected of abuse to the civil authorities for disciplinary action.

Foucault (1978) writes that the Christian pastor knows not only the deeds of his flock but also the internal life, the secret thoughts, emotions, fantasies, desires of each individual soul, which is revealed to him through the process of "exhaustive and permanent confession." Ecclesiastical surveillance of the individual believer increasingly took the form of mandatory confession, enforced by the threat of severe penalties in the afterlife for noncompliance.

For Foucault, confession always takes place within a power relationship where the one who confesses is in a subordinate position to the unspeaking

> authority who requires the confession, prescribes and appreciates it, and intervenes in order to judge, punish, forgive, console, and reconcile ... The technique of interiorization, the technique of taking conscience and the technique of alerting oneself to oneself, with respect to one's weaknesses, with respect to one's body, with respect to one's sexuality, with respect to one's flesh is the essential contribution of Christianity to the history of sexuality. [Foucault, 1978, p. 126]

The historic regulation of sexuality also became associated with Christianity's growing sense of itself as better—that is, of higher moral standing than competing groups. In this sense, early Christianity sought to shore up its authority in the face of increasing Jewish rejection and Roman skepticism by presenting itself, in Mary Douglas's (1982) term, as a purity society. Douglas's thesis is that social groups can be "likened to the human body; the orifices are to be carefully guarded to prevent unlawful intrusions (p. viii).... The symbolism of the body, which gets its power from social life, governs the fundamental attitudes to spirit and matter (p. xiii)" (or one might add vice versa).

Purity societies are obsessed with protecting the integrity and purity of the body from penetration/pollution from outside the society, that is, from the penetration of foreign words or teachings. They also focus on the development of sexual regulations and cleansing rituals that either prevent pollution or restore a polluted body to purity. Historically, orthodox belief systems that defined themselves against heretical teachings emerged in the second century simultaneously with teachings regulating sexuality and favoring *enkratia*. Hence orthodoxy and purity became linked in the minds of Christians.

Early Christian obsession with chastity also coincided with early persecutions of Christians, supporting Douglas's (1982) thesis that a group under social pressure from the outside will insist on adherence to strict norms of physical self-control as a sign of the conformity of its members. If pagan persecution constituted pressure from without, for some "orthodox" Church Fathers, the proliferation of Christian sects initiated an internal battle to establish the one true and literal interpretation of what they held to be sacred, God inspired, and historically true accounts of Jesus' life and teachings.

The fundamentalism associated with this early evolution of heresiology is today embodied in the Congregation for the Doctrine of the Faith (the Office of the Inquisition), until recently headed by Josef Cardinal Ratzinger, who now is Pope Benedict XVI. Ratzinger's obsessions include a rigidly authoritarian demand for unquestioning adherence to "legitimatized" Church teachings, which are used to validate an obsession with the regulation of sexuality, a homophobic purge of homosexual religious, a misogyny that prohibits any consideration of the ordination of women and an unwillingness to open the Church to an appreciation of the salvific powers of other religions.

SEXUAL REPRESSION AND THE RETURN
OF THE REPRESSED

In order to shore up belief, contradictory historical evidence must be repressed as heretical and therefore of no standing. Because celibacy has been mandatory for priests since the 12th century, most Catholics never considered that priests once were permitted to have married sex lives, much less that the majority of 21st-century priests still have sex lives. And of course we Catholics also believed that Jesus was a celibate. Each Sunday, and often at home, we stared at a naked, crucified Jesus, sporting a filmy piece of almost, but not quite, transparent cloth over his genitals. Despite the rawness of that depiction, Jesus' sexuality was a place of absence. We were taught he was a virgin, celibate, so pure that he had no sexual desire (although we were encouraged to have a romantic desire for him) and, as such, he provided a model of celibacy for his successor priesthood.

Leo Steinberg's (1983) startling essay on Renaissance painters' handling of Jesus' sex organs brought to consciousness what we had been trained not to see:

> Normative Christian culture—excepting only this Renaissance interlude—disallows direct reference to the sexual member. The object itself is taboo, incompatible with common decency not to say reverence. In this respect, Christian culture lies at the furthest remove from cultures whose ritual imagery not only acknowledged the phallus, but empowered it to symbolize something beyond itself. [p. 45]

Yet, the sexual tensions of Catholicism arise precisely from this mandatory display of the absent/present sexuality of Jesus. For the Christian, the absence of the represented organ, suggesting Christ as "eunuch for the kingdom of heaven" (Matthew 19:12), or at least as perfectly continent, became central to belief about Jesus' role. Here, Christ is not just a Savior in a general sense, but one who specifically, through his own sexual continence, provides a model of a man perfectly in control of his will. Jesus becomes the contrast to Adam, whose will was bent away from God by his desire for Eve who, in turn, drew him into disobedience and toward lustful sex. For Catholics, original sin is causally linked to a will distorted by sexual desire and weakened by male vulnerability in combination with a mouthy woman's seductive disobedience.

The injunction not to see or value male or female sexuality is reinforced by an elaborate penitential code that emphasizes the repression of normal sexual desire. In Sipe's (1995) terse summary of Catholic sexual doctrine, "Every sexual thought, word, desire, and action outside of marriage is mortally sinful. Every sexual act within marriage not open to conception is mortally sinful. Sexual misbehavior constitutes grave matter in every instance" (p. 7).

Prohibited erotic desire inevitably reemerges, albeit often taking strange forms. It may be sublimated in the highly eroticized, mystical experiences of Jesus cast in the role of Divine Lover as recorded in religious texts or paintings. Erotic strivings also can be detected in the counterpleasures of the extreme asceticism of saints, or in the zeal for torture of martyrs who frequently died to preserve their chastity (MacKendrick, 1999). At the most extreme, repressed erotic strivings may emerge in sadomasochistic fantasies, saturated with religious imagery, as in the writings of Jean Genet or of the Marquis de Sade.

MANDATORY CELIBACY:
FACTS AND CONSEQUENCES

Much of what we know of the sexual struggles of American priests has been learned from psychologist and ex-priest Richard Sipe, who since 1960, has interviewed over 1,500 of active and resigned American Catholic priests in a massive research project on clerical celibacy. Sipe describes mandatory celibacy as a devil's pact in which priests trade their promise of celibacy for a

> brotherhood of guaranteed employment, respectability, prestige, and power ... All of the benefits accrue automatically as long as the semblance of celibacy is publicly or officially espoused ... Power is conferred and maintained unless public exposure threatens scandal. [Sipe, 1995, p. 85]

Sipe's studies show that while 40% of priests are intentionally celibate, only a small percentage of priests actually can be said to have arrived at a state of absolute achieved celibacy. The rest show varying degrees of celibate practice, ranging from priests who lapse periodically or chronically (brief sexual encounters), to priests who engage in long-term sexual relationships with men (10%) and women (20%) (Sipe, 1990, p. 265; Sipe, 1995, p. 78) If one includes masturbation in a consideration of priestly celibacy, then 80% of American clergy are in violation of church teaching on sexuality at any one time.

Both Sipe (1990, 1995) and Mark Jordan (2000) have written eloquently about the complicity of the hierarchy both in the cover-up of abuse and other clerical violations of the celibacy code. Jordan's main focus has been on the conflict between official Church teaching on homosexuality and its actual practice in the Church. Both writers agree that, in the past, many young men were encouraged to enter seminaries in their teens and thus were far too young and sexually inexperienced to understand their own sexuality or to know the discipline required to honor a vow of celibacy. Furthermore, as Jordon notes, seminary admissions actually encouraged a lack of sexual experience as a "predictor and safeguard of celibacy. What they didn't know couldn't tempt them" (Jordan, 2000, p. 149). In fact, many men Sipe interviewed sought the refuge of seminary as a way of repressing conflictual homoerotic feelings.

Yet many young men had their first sexual experiences or serious love affairs in seminary where distinctions were often blurred between abuse by a superior and initiation into an expression of a denied and desired homosexuality. Sipe found, in fact, that some superiors condoned homosexual activity as being less dangerous to celibacy than heterosexual experience. As one superior put it, "Once they get the taste of that, [heterosexual sex] it is very tough to keep the discipline" (Sipe, 1990, p. 105).

As the majority of Catholics implicitly challenge the Curia's power to regulate their intimate lives by ignoring the Church's sexual teachings, the Curia becomes more intransigent and repressive, even going so far as not only to ban the distribution of condoms for Africans at risk for the AIDS pandemic, but also to lie about their usefulness. In the defense of power, the AIDS murder of dispensable and defenseless women and their offspring seems preferable to bending the teachings on sex. When challenged by a new generation of Biblical scholars on the historical origins of its sexual teachings, the Curia responds by either producing further textual "proofs" grafted onto already shaky exegetical foundations, or summarily mandating belief. This distortion of facts on behalf of preserving Church authority and limiting exposure to scandal has been an enduring pattern of ecclesial behavior, which has emerged in full force during the recent sexual scandal.

The underlying fear of the hierarchy is that opening an honest discourse on celibacy, and on the Church's teachings on sexuality, would reveal and undermine the present system of power relations that undergird the institution and are precariously balanced on problematic reading of scripture and history. Such discourse also necessarily would turn to reconsideration of the role of women in the Catholic Church, a topic equally shrouded in biased interpretations of scripture intended to maintain "kyriarchy."

FOREVER EVE AND EVIL:
INSTITUTIONALIZED MISOGYNY

My Catholic education about sex and gender began when I was six. I was in England to visit my Scottish grandmother, an austere Catholic with piercing blue eyes and white hair drawn in a bun. Her first and perhaps only present to me was *A Book Of English Martyrs,* a red, leather-bound volume with black and white woodcuts of martyrs shown in various states of ecstatic prayer, with heads bowed in humble submission to whatever their torturers had in store for them, or at the moment before their execution. The text, however, would have put De Sade to shame, and there was always that faint perfume of sexuality wafting through the stories. My grandmother wanted me to know that some of these ravaged folk were my ancestors and by implication, should the time come, I would be expected to follow in their footsteps.

I read my little red volume passionately again and again and, despite the many times I have moved houses, it faithfully shows up among my books. I soon added to my list of English martyrs those edifying Italian figures of determined virgins who, resisting sex, lost breasts, were tortured on wheels, and submitted to an assortment of gruesome ends.

When I went back to America, Grandma gave me the talisman of a small, framed, black-and-white picture of Teresa of Lisieux. Dressed as a bride bearing a bouquet of roses, she appeared to be in ecstasy before a depiction of the bridegroom Jesus, the familiar sad-eyed Jesus of Veronica's veil. At night, I would crawl out of bed to imagine myself as a kind of amalgam of Teresa meeting her lover Jesus, and one of my assorted female martyrs being slowly tortured as I resisted the dangerous desires of earthly males so that I could give myself utterly to the Divine Lover.

As a daughter of Eve, I had been taught that the essence of sin was failure to keep a tight rein on my desire for sexual pleasure. I was encouraged to catalogue sexual sins for their severity (mine were always of the hellfire sort), and I had been taught to hate my female body for its passionate, unruly ways. Church doctrine is infused with the message that women are transgressive, that feminine beauty is a tool of seduction, not a manifestation of interiority—that we must be kept in check and subordinated to men's rule.

In a Catholic family, there were always visits with intellectual priests and monks who were friends of the family. It is hard to capture the air of eroticism suffusing those "fatherly" visits, the eroticism inherent in the presence of the oedipal power of the father, with his privileged access to the Divine.

Even after years committed to outgrowing paternal authority, I can still feel its frisson when I meet a priest whose sermon I admire. To paraphrase Jessica Benjamin (1988), I am still in love with the ideal of power that has been denied me. I may run out of the Church in revulsion, but I still long for communion's surrender to the Divine in its most sublime sense. I still feel the erotic excitement when the ordinary falls away and the sacramental becomes inextricably mixed with the glorious male ceremonial exercise of liturgical power.

FEMALE SEXUALITY: FROM EVE TO MARY

After a short-lived bright beginning, when early Christian women served as apostles, priests, and bishops, misogyny set in; the Church's historical relationship with women has been increasingly to theologize and legislate mouthy, unruly Eve out, replacing her with an increasingly submissive Mary the Virgin Mother. Benjamin writes (1988),

> Though the image of woman is associated with motherhood and fertility, the mother is not articulated as a sexual subject, one who actively desires something for her self ... Just as the mother's power is not her own, but is intended to serve her child, so, in a larger sense, woman does not have the freedom to do as she wills; she is not the subject of her own desire. [p. 88]

Reading Benjamin, I saw Mary, the archetype of the Christian mother goddess, a pale trace of the fertile, sexual, archetypal mother goddess of the ancient and eastern religions. Mary is almost always bundled up to conceal her sexuality, and her power is not her own but lies in her ability to plead our case to the ruling Divine male hierarchy. Catholic teaching also erases Mary's sexuality. She is spared the pains of childbirth that are visited on Eve's daughters, and some traditions describe her son Jesus passing through her vagina as a ray of light without disturbing its sealed perfection. Jesus' brothers and sisters who crowd through the gospels must be demoted to cousin-hood so that Mary can remain chaste and Joseph, her husband, can model devoted celibacy.

Catholic beliefs about sex/gender relationships are inscribed in a series of images of a rather weird Divine family—images that greet Catholics in every Church and that have influenced Western constructions of gender, sexuality, and family power arrangements. The father God is notable by his absence, but the crucified son is raised high above the congregation, an almost-naked, wounded, subtly effeminate, desexualized, implicitly castrated image of male suffering. Below him a woman's body, bundled in demure blue and white robes, hair often veiled, raises hands in prayer and supplication—a maternal female body robbed of sexuality and exuding virginal submission to both the son/God and the absent father. Because the male God's suffering constitutes expiation for Eve's sin, and because mother Mary's unique purity reverses Eve's legacy, the mother-son pair constitutes a subtle but omnipresent reminder of the murderous destructiveness of women's sexuality.

Mary's chastity also does the work of expiating Adam's choice of lustful sex with Eve over loyalty to a jealous, lonely God. Mary chooses to go to bed only with God and thus refuses the pleasures of an earthly partner. Her devotion to her son (who is also God) is so profound that in this Divine and curiously incestuous family, Jesus is frequently shown as his mother's heavenly bridegroom.

The moral of Christian sex/gender discourse? Men are wounded and suffer because they fall prey to women's sexual powers with the ultimate result the death of the God/man. Virginity and submission to the male are idealized as feminine expiation, just as male celibacy is constituted as a sign of superior power and godlikeness. Going to bed with God is better than sex. Human sexual love only gets you into trouble and has no good role to play in a Christian narrative of restoration and rebirth.

The longing for the erased mother/woman is manifest in a theology which associates Jesus' bleeding with his salvific feeding of humankind. In the Middle Ages, blood and milk were thought to be of the same origin, and ascetics had fantasies of drinking Jesus' blood as they would mother's milk (Bynum, 1987). In fact, in late medieval portraits, Christ feeds humanity with blood that streams from his nipple (Reineke, 1997.) Paradoxically, however, the blood offered at the Crucifixion and in the Eucharistic sacrifice, which women are banned from performing, is the blood of the mother that has become the body and blood of the son. In his death, then, Jesus becomes/displaces the mother, appropriating a rather gruesome version of her nutritive role. Similarly, the male priest displaces the nurturing mother at the Eucharistic table.

Perhaps not surprisingly, in many early Christian texts, for a woman to enter the kingdom of Heaven, she must become "male." Holy ascetic women fasted so vigorously that their menstrual bleeding ceased, their breasts shriveled, and their withered bodies, no longer recognizably female, were thought to be dazzlingly pure (Shaw, 1998). The tradition of female mutilation of the body in order to destroy all traces of its unruly outpouring of sexual attractions permeates Christian hagiography. Holy women starved themselves, enclosed themselves in tombs until they died, and delighted in mutilating their faces and bodies until they become repulsive. A holy woman believed that since her fleshly difference from Jesus excluded her from the altar, she could at least be like Jesus in the extremity of her physical suffering (Bynum, 1982, 1987).

In the early Church, male hostility to and fear of woman's body was sublimated in the often gruesome, sadomasochistic, eroticized tales of the lives and deaths of female martyrs, like those portrayed in my red book. For early Christians, if a good Christian woman was a virgin, a better Christian woman was a virgin who died in a particularly horrible way for her faith, better still if on the way to death she resisted gruesome tortures designed to force her to break her vow to her Heavenly Bridegroom that she would remain chaste.

Even today, seminarians are trained to repress their attraction to women's bodies, to despise their own sexuality, and to fix their adoring eyes only on the wounded, glamorized, seminaked Divine male body. Homoerotic feelings are bound to be elicited by the monotheistic God, yet they pale compared to those stirred up by women. Male celibate clergy, strong enough to stand up to the Devil, are still water before women's wiles. As a result, even today, when a priest disobeys his vow of celibacy with a woman, tradition tells him that it is *he* who is only human, but that the woman is his seductress. *She* is an Eve leading him to betray his promise to God.

EUNUCHS FOR THE KINGDOM OF HEAVEN

While pious femininity requires martyrdom and masochism in the Catholic tradition, gender and sexual submission of another sort is required of men who would be priests. Modern representations of Jesus attempt to desexualize him by endowing him with a feminine, pretty-boy demeanor, which, paradoxically, only serves to increase his homoerotic appeal. In addition, the central Christian religious symbol is a crucified Jesus whose actual male crucified body would have been naked. Jesus' penis has to be modestly hidden under a thin veil that sometimes reveals/suggests its outline (Steinberg, 1983). As we know from female erotica, that which is veiled and thus "forbidden" becomes erotically charged. Although "seeing" the divine phallus is forbidden, its transgressive subliminal presence is homoerotically charged to male celibates who see themselves as "married" to Jesus.

The complex homoerotic relationship of the worshipper to the Divine Phallus has been explored by Howard Eilberg-Schwartz (1994). Eilberg-Schwartz deconstructs the Hebrew representations of the male Deity that Christians inherited and elaborated. He notes that, for Christians, when Saint Paul says that a man stands in the same relationship to Christ as a woman to a man, Paul is imposing a heterosexual metaphor of desire on what is, in fact, a homoerotic association. In order to be married to Christ, the holy male renounces sexuality, becoming a "eunuch for the kingdom of Heaven."

In this sense, the celibate priest is feminized. Indeed, as Jordon (2000) writes, he even camps it up in liturgical lace. Yet, in the context and structure of Church patriarchy, he loses none of the prerogatives of male power. By appropriating a female persona, he implicitly enacts the homoerotic aspects of his relationship with a male father/God, thus attempting to displace Mary, whose claim to heaven is her unique virginal experience of sleeping with God. As a male "virginal bride" in relation to a male God bridegroom, celibates celebrate their divine marriage in texts that are as fulsomely erotic as any in secular love poetry.

Eilberg-Schwartz points out that the erotic romance is intensified and made more complex because the male God is also the all-powerful Divine father who is frequently envisioned as instigating murderous rivalries because he has only one blessing to give. Such a God is the object of male ambivalence about the father's power, about the subject's desire for the father, his wish to be desired by the father, to be like him, and his failure to attain the ideal the father represents.

The Christian narrative hypercharges this homoerotic/father-son relationship in that, unlike the celibate Yahweh, the Christian father/God also is engaged in a primary heterosexual romance with the Virgin. His opening of her womb, his fathering of his Divine son through her body, leaves the male worshipper on the sidelines, displaced by the Divine romance, and by the father's primary attention to a woman whose sexual powers must be carefully erased by her (secretly invidious) rivals for his Divine attention. By the 16th century, not only has Mary's sexuality disappeared, but the male rivals have vanished Mary as nutritive mother with the "drying up" of the long tradition of her breast-feeding her Son.

THE NEED FOR CHANGE

Both Wills (2000, 2002) and Carroll (2002a) have addressed the refusal of the Church to examine "the institutional, theological, or dogmatic aspects of Catholicism" (Carroll, 2002a, p. 12) when modern scholarship reveals them to have been in error, or when history shows them to have caused actual harm. The Church believes that both its teachings about sexuality and its right to dictate belief are firmly based in scripture. Ecclesiastical reform requires an examination of how scripture has been read to legitimize the control of sexuality (which is linked both to misogyny and homophobia) and to secure structures of male power (and vast wealth).

In antiquity, a Church that was founded on belief in the Incarnation, an act of Divine love, the unity of spirit and flesh, and the immanence of God in creation became the proponent both of a profound dualism between the sexual body and the pure spirit, and of a hierarchical God who controls from above. The foundational scriptures themselves were, and continue to be, subjected to interpretations that conform to the needs of a sex-fearing, authoritarian, patriarchal, hierarchical, rigid, faith-based system.

These authorized readings pushed aside Jesus' original reformist vision of an egalitarian, communal group of believers (which in-

cluded marginalized peoples—women, the poor, the mad, the out-
cast), who protested the oppressive practices of wealth and imperial
and ecclesial power, and centered its teachings on love, compassion,
and the immanence of God's action on earth.
The underlying fear of the Church hierarchy is that opening an
honest dialogue on celibacy and sexuality would reveal and undermine the present system of power relations that undergird the institution and are precariously balanced on dubious readings of
scripture and history. Carroll (2002) has proposed that real reform
demands that the church face the difficult task of acknowledging that
it is a human institution, which like its mythical founding father, Pe-
ter, can err, acknowledge its errors, and repair wrongs. This will require "fundamental changes in the way history has been written,
theology has been taught, and Scripture has been interpreted"
(Carroll, 2002a, p. 32).

REFERENCES

Benjamin, J. (1988), *The Bonds of Love: Psychoanalysis, Feminism, and the Problem of Domination*. New York: Pantheon.
Brown, P. (1988), *The Body and Society: Men, Women, and Sexual Renunciation in Early Christianity*. New York: Columbia University Press.
Bynum, C. (1982), *Jesus as Mother: Studies in the Spirituality of the High Middle Ages*. Berkeley: University of California Press.
——— (1987), *Holy Feast Holy Fast: The Religious Significance of Food for Medieval Women*. Berkeley: University of California Press.
Carroll J. (2002a), *Towards a New Catholic Church: The Promise of Reform*. Boston: Houghton Mifflin.
——— (2002b), The Sadness of a Catholic. *The Boston Globe*, December 17.
Douglas, M. (1982), *Natural Symbols: Explorations in Cosmology*. New York: Pantheon Books.
Eilberg-Schwartz, H. (1994), *God's Phallus and Other Problems for Men and Monotheism*. Boston: Beacon Press.
Foucault, M. (1976), *The History of Sexuality, Vol. 1: An Introduction*, trans. R. Hurley. New York: Random House, 1980.
——— (1978/1999), Sexuality and power. In: *Religion and Culture*, ed. J. Carrette. New York: Routledge, 1999.
——— (1977), Power and Sex. In: *Michel Foucault: Politics Philosophy Culture Interviews and other Writings 1977–1984*, ed. L. Kritzman. New York: Routledge, 1988.
Jordan, M. D. (2000), *The Silence of Sodom: Homosexuality in Modern Catholicism*. Chicago: University of Chicago Press.

MacKendrick, K. (1999), *Counterpleasures*. Albany: State University of New York Press.

Merton, T. (1985), *Love and Living*. San Diego: Harvest Book.

Reineke, M. (1997), *Sacrificed Lives: Kristeva on Women and Violence*. Bloomington, IN: Indiana University Press.

Schussler-Fiorenza, E. (1988), *In Memory of Her: A Feminist Theological Reconstruction of Christian Origins*. New York: Crossroad.

——— (1999), *Jesus—Miriam's Child, Sophia's Prophet: Critical Issues in Feminist Theology*. New York: Continuum.

Shaw, T. M. (1998), *The Burden of the Flesh*. Minneapolis: Fortress Press.

Sipe, A. W. R. (1990), *A Secret World: Sexuality and the Search for Celibacy*. New York: Brunner Mazel.

——— (1995), *Sex, Priests and Power: Anatomy of a Crisis*. New York: Brunner Mazel.

Steinberg, L. (1983), *The Sexuality of Christ in Renaissance Art and in Modern Oblivion*. New York: Pantheon October Book.

Wills, G. (2000), *Papal Sin: Structures of Deceit*. New York: Doubleday.

——— (2002), *Why I Am a Catholic*. Boston: Houghton Mifflin.

17

The Confusion of Priestly Secrets

Mark D. Jordan

WHAT KIND OF SECRET WAS CLERICAL ABUSE?

You can take the question as asking whether the abuse really was a secret. It looks, in fact, like a perfect example of the open secret—evident truth refused. In January 2002, when the *Boston Globe* broke stories about Cardinal Law's repeated transfers of accused priests, it was hardly a revelation. Well-publicized American cases stretch back at least to 1985, when the national media picked up the story of Gilbert Gauthe from Louisiana (*Boston Globe*, 2002, p. 38). Since then we have received a steady flow of reports: Mount Cashel in Newfoundland and Covenant House in New York, diocesan priests in Chicago and the friars of Santa Barbara, James Porter from Fall River, MA, and Rudy Kos from Dallas. So what was the revelation? The number of crimes alleged against Fr. John Geoghan was high, but about the same as the estimates for Porter. Geoghan had been transferred repeatedly and then (it turned out) recommended to another diocese, but other cases also included transfers and commendations.

Indeed, for a reader of the history of the Catholic priesthood and male religious orders, the news from Boston sounded like one more chapter in a chronicle that began in the Middle Ages. From court records to popular satires, priests and monks have been accused for centuries of abusing the minors entrusted to them. Sometimes the minors are parishioners or prostitutes; at other times, seminarians or novices. Sometimes the minors have not yet entered puberty, but most often they are pubescent teenagers. Sometimes those we would label "minors" were not considered minors under the law, since the age of majority has varied considerably by time and place in Christendom. Despite efforts at secrecy and the general hazards for historical records, cases of an enormous variety have left their traces in the archives (Jordan, 2000, pp. 120–130).

The journalistic disclosures of 2002 add more entries, another chapter or two to the long chronicle, with its brutal facts, and banal stereotypes. If many cases concern men and boys, the chronicle is not about "pedophilia" in the prevailing clinical sense, much less "ephebophilia" (if there is such a clinical entity). Nor is the villain in this chronicle same-sex attraction, however much church officials in many centuries have wanted to turn clerical abuse scandals into another occasion for burning sodomites. The extended chronicle recounts how officially celibate religious authorities abuse the young and vulnerable—not only boys but girls, not only altar boys or students or novices, but servants and penitents and patients. The only fixed characters in this particular chronicle are clerical privilege and the dreadful or silly tactics it deploys to maintain silence.

Churchly stratagems begin by wanting to deny abuse, one way or another. Cardinal Law or his deputies transferred Geoghan not just because any large organization likes to remove its terrible mistakes. The Boston chancery was following precedents already well established in the Middle Ages. Sodomitic priests caught with boys or young men were exiled from the city or diocese. Stricter sentences ordered that they be sent to remote monasteries for a lifetime of fasting and prayer. In the 20th century, rural American monasteries were still used to hide delinquent priests—alcoholics, fathers in the biological sense, "molesters." With the American Church's turn to psychology as management, penitential exile got reconceived as mandated therapy. Penance was supplemented or replaced by

12-step programs and counseling. Successful therapy led to reassignment. Unsuccessful therapy led to more counseling. More often than not, at least until recently, ways were found to issue a clean enough bill of mental health to get the priest back into service.

The imperative was not so much to cure—or to protect—as to confine trouble and its news within its walls. Pious Catholics are conscious of living under two jurisdictions: a local or national secular authority and a universal religious law. Catholic religious law prefers to prosecute and punish Church officers on its own. So bishops, who once asserted benefit of clergy to shield their priests from the king's bailiffs, still tend to divert ugly cases from the police. Settlements are offered to victims or their families in exchange for a promise to keep quiet. If these inducements do not work, stronger pressure can be applied: vigorous rebuttal, charges of disloyalty, counteraccusation, perhaps even exclusion from the parish. If the local bishop falters, or a national conference of bishops affirms too absolutely that it will cooperate with civil authorities in prosecuting pedophiles, the Vatican is ready to remind all concerned of some old principles. Half a year before the scandal broke in the *Boston Globe,* as priests were being prosecuted in American criminal courts, both the Pope and his chief doctrinal officer reaffirmed Roman jurisdiction over clerical abuse of minors and invoked traditional rules of secrecy (John Paul II, 2001; Congregation for the Doctrine of the Faith, 2001).

Stratagems for keeping silence often employ loud denunciations of male–male desire, protestations of priestly purity, and pulpit thunder against the horror of sexual abuse. This is not simple hypocrisy—if hypocrisy can be simple in religious institutions. Denunciations, protestations, and thunder help to distance "the Church" from internal crime more effectively than implausible claims that a bishop did not know what he was reading or writing. Once a case is reported widely enough, church officers agree quickly that its perpetrator must be a sort of monster. Monstrous crimes cannot arise from within "the Church" by definition. Priests abusing boys—that is utterly alien to Catholic life. So the cause must be some external influence, Satan or the degeneracy of the surrounding culture. Bishops and cardinals join the chorus to distract attention from these frequent events and the inherited forms of clerical power that surround them.

Networks of clerical power are systems for enforcing specific silences. They try at first to keep silence in ordinary ways: they hide acts and offenders, they hush observers, and they deny allegations. If those tactics fail, then clerical voices begin speaking loudly. They are eager to dissociate themselves from the particular crime, but they want further to prevent any particular case from becoming the occasion for asking broader questions. They aim not only to distance the church from a scandal, but to use scandal in order to prevent further speech (Jordan, 2003, pp. 10–33).

Alongside clerical systems of silence, there are systems for denouncing priestly secrets. The sexual irregularity of Catholic priests was one of the staples of Protestant polemic, as it was earlier of popular or learned satire. If there are regular ways for trying to keep secrets inside church walls, there are also fixed genres for broadcasting secrets on the outside. The phrase "Catholic secrets" has often meant, especially since the Reformation, the alleged sexual crimes of Catholic priests. So the cascade of reports and bulletins during the spring of 2002 fit neatly into American stereotypes. More than 150 years ago, the invented classic of American anti-Catholicism, *Awful Disclosures of the Hotel Dieu Nunnery of Montreal* ("Maria Monk," 1836), offered as its choicest disclosure the nighttime baptism and burial of strangled infants born to nuns prostituted by priests. The clerical crimes disclosed in the last few years were hardly invented, but their telling fit all too neatly into the genre of "Catholic" secrets hysterically disclosed.

I use "hysterical" deliberately. The most familiar American genres for revealing priestly secrets are overwritten melodramas that gesture frantically at something hidden without bringing it to light. The sensational formulas of journalism, all too constant from Maria Monk to CNN, attest to a secret without being able to speak it—no matter how much talking goes on. In their frantic reactions, they act it out, but cannot analyze it. The secret remains—because behind the scandalous secret there is something more obscure, a secret about secrets. In 2002, the best reporters kept saying that the scandal was not so much about the abuse as the cover-up. The final horror came not in the crimes of Geoghan or others like him, priests deformed by their own abusive upbringings, as children and seminarians. The coldest crime was in the system of secrecy, the arrogance of power, and the bureaucracy of intimidation and denial. The secret that had to be kept concerned a well-practiced routine for keeping horrible secrets.

What kind of secret was clerical abuse? The question should be: *Where* exactly was the secret about sexual abuse among the Catholic clergy?

SUSPENDED VOCATIONS

The Roman Catholic Church is united as one in name only—except in the eyes of the faithful or the fantasies of a central bureaucracy. Its imaginary space is more a feudal fiefdom than a Cartesian grid. In this space, secrets are not an aberration. They are the fabric of space. They mark off provinces, cities, neighborhoods for different dialects of secrets. Journalists and civil lawyers have found it difficult to map churchly secrets, whose variety ought to be counted prerequisites for having a hierarchy or clerical caste. For different reasons, official apologists or theologians simplify Catholic space and its capacities for keeping secrets. Here, as in so many religious cases, novelists are more accurate.

The last novel by the unclassifiable Pierre Klossowski—novelist, artist, philosopher–theologian, psychoanalytic exponent—tries to break or reframe genres for revealing priestly secrets about sex. His novel, *The Baphomet*, assumes the old charges against the Knights Templar, one of the medieval military orders. When he wanted to suppress the order, the king of France found it useful to prefer charges of sodomy—because they were indefinite and easily believed, because they carried such serious punishment. The charges were mostly false, but they have persisted in cultural imagination. Klossowski retrieved them into a visionary theater of pleasure, deception, violence, repetition, and simulacra of salvation. In the novel's "historical" prologue, with its references to *Ivanhoe* and royal trials, a noblewoman prostitutes her adolescent nephew to the local Templars in hopes of gaining their land. Lust for the "young Ogier" moves the plot of the prologue, then carries the novel forward into a heaven of souls, a dreamscape that joins epochs, only to end in an epilogue of our haunted present.

Klossowski published a completed text of *The Baphomet* in 1965. He continued to depict its central figures for another two decades. He sketched and colored graphic images of young men, religious authorities, and Christian symbols. The young Ogier, clad as a medieval page, is assaulted by one Templar (Klossowski et al., 2002, p. 62). Naked, he is fondled by several more (p. 73). The Grand Master admires the young man's incorrupt body in spinning eternity (p. 76). Once again in page's livery, Ogier—or Ogier's simulacrum—haunts the unlucky narrator who wakes to find him in some present Paris (Klossowski, 1988, cover and plates 3–4). Klossowski's illustrations elicit and exorcise the old clerical demons, but they bring them forward into our time—a time when "sexual" crime passes too quickly as the only priestly sin and the only ecclesiastical secret. If Klossowski's drawings risk eliciting the pederasty they analyze, they also remind us to be puzzled by our reactions to this old story about monks and boys, which we recognize and refuse, which we allow to be repeated so that we can savor our surprise.

Thirty years earlier, Klossowski's (1950) first novel offered a more condensed and vivid portrayal of the persistence of priestly secrets into modern times. *La vocation suspendue, The Suspended Vocation,* rehearses many things, but the plot is immediately concerned with the parodic possibilities in the rivalry of imagined (or satirized) Catholic groups and their regions of secrecy. Since its publication, the novel has been read reductively as a barely concealed and rather provocative autobiography. Beginning in 1939, when he was 34, Klossowski experimented with several religious orders. He even began a canonical novitiate with the Dominicans but left after only three months. He then joined a lay community attached to the Dominican house of Saint-Maximin and undertook theological study. Klossowski left that community to try again in Jesuit seminaries and with the Franciscans (Arnaud, 1990, pp. 186–187). At the end of four years, he returned to Paris and took up Luther. Two years after that he abjured Lutheranism. Still it would be silly to read the complicated parody in his novel as if it were no more than a settling of old scores or an attempt to sell yet another clerical scandal—especially when autobiography is mocked on the novel's first page.[1]

---

[1]A more complex argument is needed to deal with another part of Klossowski's biography: he lived through Nazism as the son of a Jewish mother. In writing about Klossowski's younger brother, the painter Balthus, Nicholas Fox Weber (1999) has insisted on the mother's inheritance and on the brother's continued denial of it. Still Balthus is not Klossowski. For Klossowski, it is especially important to question the relation of biography to writing—or to performed identity—in such a dangerous and terrifying situation. Where the revelation of an inherited secret could bring death, the secret would make our lives simulacra—were they not already simulacra for Klossowski.

Klossowski's fiction has the form of a literary essay on another book. Indeed, *The Suspended Vocation* is the name, not of the essay we read, but of an anonymous, third-person narrative printed in only a hundred copies during an unspecified year of the 1940s at Bethaven, then discovered by our essayist in a single copy at Lausanne (Klossowski, 1950, p. 11). An opening parody of the academic love of bibliographic detail, this detail also introduces the central themes of copy and concealment. We never get to read the discovered book. Indeed, as far as *The Suspended Vocation* is the title of the essay about the book, it lacks a pair of quotation marks: The essay should properly be entitled *"The Suspended Vocation,"* as if it meant "Concerning *The Suspended Vocation.*" We only read about the book, in the order and under the topics chosen by our essayist. Printed in a limited run and found by chance, the book is already a secret. By refusing to reproduce it, the essayist helps to keep it while acting out some parts of it.

The essay opens with a meditation upon writing as masking. The meditation is an excursus on the genres of religious (or antireligious) narrative in France after the Middle Ages. The excursus concludes that a Christian writer fully conscious of the limits of art in communicating the supernatural is like the "false prophet of Bethel," who seduces Judah with lies—and so accomplishes the will of God (p. 21). The means available for the work of Christian writing "consist rather more of contradicting the unknowable ways of God than of imagining them" (p. 22). But we do not know, as the essayist confesses, whether this subtle self-understanding was shared by the anonymous author of the discovered book. Indeed, as later confessions show, we do not know anything about the relation of the anonymous author to the narrative's protagonist (though it is likely to be one of hatred, pp. 32–33); whether the anonymous author is a sodomite concealed among the persecuting clergy (though that too is likely, pp. 32, 62, 64); whether the Anonymous is an unbeliever (p. 23); or when and where exactly the events unfold (though it may all be an allegory of Nazi-occupied France, pp. 53–54 and pp. 24–25). We are equally ignorant of our essayist, who also remains nameless and without evident religious affiliation. The frame constructed around this little book is a series of concealments through which conjecture, an evidently dissatisfied form of fiction, attempts to pierce (compare with the essayist's projection, p. 22).

The story inside the frame is roughly this: There is a war within the Catholic church between two principal parties. The one, the Black Party, has temporarily gained sole control of the Inquisition. Its clerical legionnaires are supported by lay adherents more than willing to use coercion. It deploys its power through police and bureaucracies, but also though "medical clinics" that are really detention camps. The other party is known as the Devotion. Lacking the armed organization of its adversary, it spreads underground, as it were, by preaching a particular form for venerating Mary, the cult of Our Lady of the White Marriage. (A "white marriage" is one in which the partners agree to abstain from sexual intercourse for reasons of piety.) Each of the principal parties controls certain "zones," certain seminaries or religious houses, in which they vie for recruits and punish prisoners. Each is constantly spying on the other and on itself. Anyone may already be a double agent, and anyone may go over to the other side. Heresy is betrayal, infidelity, and perversion (e.g., p. 48). Other parties are also on the battlefield. There is an order of nuns, for example, that works to make peace between the Black Party and the Devotion. In so doing, of course, it also aspires to take over the Inquisition (p. 58). Charity is exercised as a form of institutional combat—when it is not commanded as a pedagogical debasement.

The narrative's protagonist, a seminarian, Jerome, wanders the divided landscape. His is a late vocation: he has returned to the sacraments after a Bohemian existence and, indeed, after both homosexual and heterosexual relations (pp. 36, 64). He begins as a novice in a religious house loosely affiliated with the Black Party, but one that protects those whom the Inquisition would persecute—out of a sense that the methods of the Black Party violate the teaching of Thomas Aquinas and especially the distinction between natural and supernatural. Jerome objects that the distinction only aids heresy because the "natural" is a demonic invention. So Jerome leaves to begin another novitiate elsewhere. In the second house, he errs by making certain suggestions about an enigmatic fresco in the church—suggestions that enrage the local lay brothers attached to the Devotion while endearing him to a visiting bishop. The bishop "adopts" him into his diocese, but places him as a spy in a house of those charitable nuns. Suspended between the parties, Jerome finds himself the pawn in double- and triple-crosses. In the end, he leaves the religious life altogether, but perhaps not his vocation. What becomes of him is not clear although the anonymous narrator pretends to have encountered him some time later, healed of his spiritual uncertainties and happily married—if the marriage is itself not based on concealed identities and mysterious callings. Jerome's vocation is suspended, not abolished. It is suspended as much by the endless interpretive possibilities as by any decision to leave priestly formation and return to secular life. Every vocation hangs in suspense, because there can be no certainty about whether it is what it seems.

The anonymous narrative, as you can see already in clumsy outline, is as full of concealments and deferrals as the frame built around it. Concealments produce secrets, and secrets require lies or silences. To keep secrets is to give occasion for the reports of spies and the conjectures of secret police. Concealment also sets the stage (theatrical metaphors are frequent here) for discoveries and revelations, which are the main engines of the narrative's movement. The range of secrets is astonishing: they include doctrinal beliefs, devotional practices, and political motives, of course, but also one's identity or religious state. There is the invisible seal of the sodomitic identity, but also of priestly ordination (pp. 61, 103). A demon may masquerade as a beautiful young man (p. 72), a famous inquisitor as a debauched painter (p. 132).

In Klossowski's novel, the supernatural appears best through the absence of any supernatural phenomena (p. 37). The objects of faith are the pretexts and masks of dark forces—or they are divine realities, which, once enunciated, become distorted under demonic light (p. 77). If the Prince of Darkness may appear as an Angel of Light, must the Angel of Light appear only as Darkness (p. 134)? The great instance of the metaphysics of concealment is the Church itself. Its secrets are somehow older and deeper than the modern disciplines of secrecy, including psychoanalysis. The comparison condenses around the figure of Fr. Persienne, priest–analyst. Jerome is drawn to him at first by the taste for power—not so much the analyst's power as that of the priest transmuting bread and wine into body and blood. Or he is drawn to the monstrous hybrid of the natural and the supernatural, in which secular art dismisses the fictive agency of the devil from mental sufferings—in order to attribute them to the Holy Spirit (p. 93). But Persienne's gospel is revealed (or so it seems) as purely secular, as a destruction of faith in the name of faith. His arcana point to a two-faced divinity, death and desire (p. 96). Enraged by his apparent capitulation to the secular, Jerome attacks the priest for remaining within the Church. Persienne replies that only the Church has the power to teach hope before death. Jerome objects again: then those in power who know the secret, the analytic arcana, manipulate the rest, both the clergy and the faithful? Persienne laughs, "My child, if there is a secret, it is not consciously in the hearts of men. Today all believe as they say, and what they say, they believe. The secret is in the institution, in the phenomenon of the Church which escapes men and which leads them where they must be led" (p. 99).

In this string of references, and perhaps especially in the exchange between Persienne and Jerome, some elements are too familiar for those of us who have lived through the latest uncovering of Catholic secrets, where "secrets" means concealed sexual crimes. Klossowski's essayist and anonymous narrator know the genre too—and some of the facts on which it typically feeds. We are not surprised, then, to read of the conversion and ministry of La Montagne. His secular genius exercised itself in the education of delinquent youth—in establishing a network of schools, groups, and "youth cities" (p. 61). La Montagne was also, before his religious conversion, an "out" and outspoken defender of the "race" of sodomites, a reinterpreter of their role in history and in the advancement of spiritual causes (p. 62). He spent his fortune on youth work, but also on a collection of statues of "adolescent gods and ephebes" (p. 68). A juvenile court had placed in his care a boy or young man (*"enfant"*) of no more than 15, whom La Montagne planned perhaps to adopt (pp. 65–66). And so on. It is hard to read this now except as queasily prophetic, but then it is important to remember that this sort of story of clerical secrets goes back to France in the 1940s and then far beyond. It is an old story—of a kind much overdetermined by genre expectations.

Do not be blinded by the scandalous sense of clerical "secret." However much Klossowski's essayist and anonymous narrator eroticize religious personalities and institutions, they also remind us that sexual crimes are hardly the only Catholic secrets. They may not be the most dangerous or the most important. They also may not be the most indispensable, however long they have seemed a by-product of the peculiar institution of mandatory celibacy. Klossowski's essayist and anonymous narrator are both engaged, if differently, with the evocation and critique of more complex conditions of secrecy in theology, religious formation, spiritual experience, and liturgy or iconography. I can show this at a single point from Jerome's second, unsuccessful novitiate.

In the religious house he joins, the apse of the chapel contains a fresco meant to allude to the "arcana" of the Devotion to Our Lady of the White Marriage (p. 39). On instructions from a dead or vanished priest, a lay brother paints on it endlessly without being able to finish it (pp. 40–41). It is a triptych. In the left panel, angels crown the Virgin Mary as queen of heaven, while famous theologians dispute under her feet. In the center panel, Mary appears at Lourdes to Bernadette Soubirous, confirming the dogma of the Immaculate Conception.[2] To the right, in the third panel, there are most incomplete figures. Pope Pius IX, who promulgated the dogma, kneels in adoration of the vision. Beside him, below him, there is the ghostly figure of a young Carmelite nun who, on her deathbed, offered her life for the dogma's proclamation. The triptych is about Marian cults, but it is also about sexless relation: every one of the figures mentioned is, like those crowning angels, sexless. This applies most especially to the male/female couple of Pius IX and the dying Carmelite.

The images of the convent's fresco are difficult to see—indeed, the best light falls on them at solemn vespers, when the altar is unusually full of candles. They are decisively revealed only when an unused lamp was fitted with a new bulb. Then, before Jerome's arrival, the community discovered that among the theologians under Mary's feet were Bernard of Clairvaux and Thomas Aquinas, their backs turned on her crowning, their faces veiled. Veiled, the onlookers concluded, because they were famous for arguing against the Immaculate Conception. They forced the painter to repaint the figures so that they turned to face Mary without veils (p. 43). Later in the novel, we will be told that the panel was meant originally to show all

[2]In the last of Bernadette's visions, on March 25, 1858, Mary is reported to have said, "I am the Immaculate Conception." The dogma had been proclaimed a few years earlier, on December 8, 1854, in the papal bull, *Ineffabilis Deus*.

its theologians with veiled faces, so as to represent the triumph of faith over theology's rationalist speculations (p. 75). But we may also remember that Moses kept his face veiled after talking with God—and so we may wonder whether the theologians hide their faces rather to protect those who look at the mural.

Then there is the unfinished right panel: curiously, though the figures of Pius IX and the Carmelite nun are barely sketched in, the nun's face is the most finely finished part of the whole fresco—the image of a young woman's face in ecstasy (pp. 41–42). Jerome suggests to the painter that since the fresco already contains two images of Mary, and since the right-hand third is so empty, it ought to be completed instead with an image of "She who weeps" seated before two children, that is, with the iconography of the apparition of Mary at La Salette to the shepherd children, Maximin and Melanie.[3] Our Lady of La Salette entrusted each of them with a distinct secret—so secret that even the other could not overhear its communication. (These were originally passed on to Pope Pius IX, but then published in various versions. Even the published versions contain many obscurities.) We are told later that La Salette was indeed part of the original plan for the fresco, but that the prior of the religious house refused to permit the image.

The fresco is the basis for the whole novel, but let me use it simply as an icon of some kinds of secrecy. Consider the secrecy of divine mysteries which cannot be argued or explained; of unexpected vision, which cannot be grasped or deciphered; of prophecies about the future, which cannot be divulged; of human lives caught up into angelic existence; of heavenly tears and dying ecstasies. These are the arcana of the Devotion, but also the idioms of traditional Catholic theology. Clerical secrecy is not just an excuse for crimes. It is the origin and the condition of some of the most familiar forms of Christian teaching. More than Jerome's dilemma or the novel's irreducible play of meanings, the suspended vocation is the presence of the holy in a world of fallen bodies, of bodily simulacra. It is the persistence of an ancient Christianity among peoples, including "the faithful," who cannot accept its claims for absolute secrets—or who can translate such secrets only into the abuse of sexualized power.

---

[3]The apparition happened on September 19, 1846, 12 years before the visions of Lourdes.

SECRET GOSPELS

Klossowski's *Suspended Vocation* is obviously not a plea for recovering Christian tradition. Its relation to the churchly past is more ambivalent, more parodic. The book engages Nietzsche's doctrine of the mask. It develops notions of constructed similitudes or simulacra. Klossowski's is equally attentive to the unpredictable conversion or reversal, the peripety, as motive and limit of human identity. All of that, yes. Even so, the book poses powerful questions about our forgetfulness of the avowed secrets of Christian tradition. Secrets are not aberrations in Christianity. They are written at the heart of some of its oldest versions. Secrets are not only products of a priesthood or its hierarchy. Claims for secrecy are the seed crystal around which ritual hierarchies coalesce.

I do not mean administrative secrets, though there are plenty of those in Roman Catholicism and other Christian churches. The Roman Church, with its bristling law codes and labyrinth of courts, manufactures and then manages all sorts of administrative secrets. There are budgets and personnel matters, but also marriage cases or sensitive pastoral quandaries. The internal working documents of religious orders are sometimes marked with the classification, "For the Eyes of Ours Only." The label applies to hundreds of other kinds of paper. Administrative secrets extend quickly enough into the nominally or specifically religious. Extensive comments on the fitness of candidates for ordination or religious vows are often collected and evaluated secretly. So too are offers of appointment as a bishop—especially when they are rejected. Every Catholic diocese is still supposed to keep a "secret archive" with very limited access (*Code of Canon Law*, 1983, Nos. 489–490). The current scandal has raided a number of them for court exhibits or journalistic disclosures. One classified document was a 1962 directive from the Holy Office (as the chief doctrinal agency was then known) requiring secrecy in cases of sexual "solicitation" by clergy (Holy Office, 1962). In one official English translation, the document begins by stating that it should be "diligently stored in the secret archives of the Curia as strictly confidential. Nor is it to be published nor added to with any commentaries." In earlier decades, and sometime still today, the "secret of the Holy Office" was invoked to cover any number of persons or procedures. Judgments of heresy and their legal consequences—including prohibitions from teaching or publishing—were wrapped in enforced silence. In the Catholic Church, as in many religious institutions, "religious" secrets preserve the halo around authority or conceal the disedifying gap between teaching and practice.

Administrative secrets have figured importantly in cases of priestly abuse, but they are not the only or the most important secrets implicated in the recent scandal. Administrative secrets are an effect or inference from doctrinal and ritual secrets. The priest is figured as the keeper of secrets about God and souls. The priest performs secrets in the hidden causality of sacraments—and especially in the miraculous transformation of each Mass. Secret teachings and secret rites run back into the founding stories of many versions of Christianity, including Roman Catholicism. The classic Catholic doctrine of "tradition" as an alternate source of divine revelation amounts to the claim that decisive secrets have been passed down by word of mouth among initiates. Sometimes, and not least under John Paul II, these secrets have included messages from apparitions of Mary. More significantly, they include central dogmas of the faith, including the founding claim by church authorities to interpret scriptures and traditions. Roman authority is in part the claim of a secret teaching passed down through Roman authority.

The core secrets of Christianity can claim higher authorization. In the "Sermon on the Mount," Matthew's Jesus speaks this admonition: "Do not give dogs what is holy; and do not throw your pearls in front of pigs, or they may trample them and then turn on you and tear you to pieces" (7:6 New Jerusalem Bible). A few chapters later, the gospel's narrator says, "In all this Jesus spoke to the crowds in parables; indeed, he would never speak to them except in parables" (13:34 New Jerusalem Bible; cf. Mark 4:33–34). From these and similar verses, many Christian theologians have inferred that the most important revealed truths should not or could not be spoken plainly in public. They were confided only to "apostles"—that is, for modern Roman Catholicism, to the Pope, his bishops, and their delegates.

A similar secrecy has been practiced in some liturgical traditions. In Eastern Orthodox communion rites, the priest presents the consecrated bread and wine with the words, "Holy things for the holy."

He reminds his congregation of the moral and ritual demands on those who approach the table. He also echoes the imperative of secrecy from Matthew. After all, in many of those same liturgies, an earlier line, sung by the deacon, recalls for the congregation the time when the unbaptized or the lapsed were physically excluded from the celebration of the holy mysteries. Western church rites allude to that physical exclusion when they lead children or those preparing for reception into the church out of the sanctuary before the Eucharistic consecration. Holy things for the holy: Christian rites are secrets, mysteries, and the uninitiated cannot be present even as witness.

What justifies these deep secrets in Christian doctrine and ritual? Theologians derived justifications from Matthew's verses. Sharing communion or creed with the unworthy could "profane" them—pollute them or blaspheme against them. It might also bring danger to the unwary teacher or liturgical minister: "They will turn on you." Improper exposure could cheapen the secret truths in such a way that they could never be learned or taught afterward. Unreserved teaching, teaching without regard for proper preparation, will harm certain kinds of learners. Unreserved teaching may also betray or beget a lack of reverence in the teacher. Performing it, you harm yourself. Similar reasoning applies to liturgy. Premature exposure to the rites might produce contempt, which would prevent their ever being understood or joined.

Contrast these secrets with the forms of administrative secrecy discussed earlier, but then see that the two are institutionally confused. The secrecy of doctrine or rite is tangled with institutional regulations through the notion of sacred hierarchy. The fifth-century theological writer we receive under the pseudonym "Dionysus the Areopagite" shows the connection in the structure of his work. He is best known as the author of treatises on the unknowability of divine attributes and the flight into God through wordless darkness. But pseudo-Dionysius passes from his *Mystical Theology* to a treatise on *Ecclesiastical Hierarchies,* in which Christian priests, as teachers and ritual celebrants, open the way of ascent. They mediate divine illumination into our darkness. They tend to the most important secrets. The hierarchies of their offices and rituals form the indispensable veil around the invisible.

No institutional analysis of Catholic secrecy can forget the constitutive link between holy secrets and hierarchical power—for at least two reasons. First, theological claims about secret teachings and hidden sacramental effects are invoked to justify keeping other sorts of secrets, including administrative secrets. Second, and more importantly, the core priestly secrets can endow other sorts of secrets in church with a sense of rightness and inviolability. Priests confuse the secrets they are supposed to keep. They can be misled, not least by hierarchical cultures, into believing that what holds true of some of their secrets must hold true for all. If scandalous journalism makes the mistake of reading all Catholic secrets "down" into concealed sex, clericalism makes the mistake of reading all priestly secrets "up" into sacred mysteries.

Georg Simmel's famous treatment (1908) of the sociology of secrets can clarify the contrast. For Simmel, much of the social allure of the secret depends on the possibility that it might be told.

> Peculiarly enough, these attractions of secrecy are related to those of its logical opposite, betrayal—which, evidently, are no less sociological. The secret contains a tension that is dissolved in the moment of its revelation. This moment constitutes the acme in the development of the secret; all of its charms are once more gathered in it and brought to a climax .... [1908, p. 333]

By contrast, and on traditional understanding, the core priestly secrets of Christianity cannot be told. They can be profaned or cheapened, distorted or flattened, but they can never be revealed. The dogmas of the Trinity or the Incarnation are strictly incomprehensible. The Eucharistic transformation of bread and wine into body and blood cannot be discovered by the senses. Priestly secrets charm without the real prospect of betrayal.

There is nothing mysteriously holy in sexual crimes committed by priests. They evidently have been revealed—and will continue to be. Still the institutional subterfuges and personal doublings that now fill the public record can be understood as confusions or perversions of priestly secrets. Catholic priests trained in the 1950s and 1960s (many of the worst offenders went through seminary in those "golden" years) were led to believe that they carried secrets—administrative and group secrets, of course, but also divine ones. The former could be betrayed; the latter could not. The priest was a living secret, the agent or actor for an essential secret. Could there be any stronger container for hiding sexual crimes—especially from oneself? The priest is a sacred figure who is a vicar for the hiddenness and immunity of the divine. His ordination sacralizes not only his privilege, but his body. If that body should carry "disgusting" secrets, they can be sealed under the grandest secrecy. They can be locked up alongside the mystery of God—which no one can betray.

In Klossowski's *Suspended Vocation,* Catholic priests or members of religious orders keep secrets because they want to survive, to succeed, to avoid betrayal, capture, and punishment. They also keep secrets because they must, because they are themselves enigmas, because their encounters with the divine are always ambiguous. And then they keep secrets because they cannot not keep them—because the supernatural appears through its opposite, because erotic excess is indistinguishable from the vision of the Immaculate Conception. The ecstatic flush on the face of the dying Carmelite, the most finished part of the always unfinished fresco, is indistinguishable from erotic rapture—as we learn from the most famous representation of another Carmelite, Bernini's Saint Teresa. But the fresco is always unfinished, endlessly revised, violently disputed—and so the secret stays as safe as the secret of her visions.

The confusion of priestly secrets interchanges divine mysteries with sexual crimes. The exchange figures on many pages of the particular chronicle of sexual abuse by members of the Catholic clergy. It may be especially easy—or inevitable—in our modernity. Klossowski dedicated *The Baphomet* to Michel Foucault, who had written an essay on Klossowski that became the novel's preface. Elsewhere, in an essay on Klossowski's friend, Bataille, Foucault announces that the discourse of sexuality has now filled up the space once occupied by Christian theology.

> Sexuality is not decisive for our culture except as spoken and to the extent that it is spoken. Our language has been eroticized for the last two centuries: our sexuality, since Sade and the death of god, has been absorbed by the universe of language, denatured by it, placed by it in the void where it established its sovereignty and where it, as Law, endlessly poses limits that it transgresses. [Foucault, 1963, p. 248]

It trivializes this transformation to conclude that churches now have nothing to hide but sexual secrets—unless these secrets are to be understood, not as newspaper stories, but as distorted rites. Catholic priests in America have been led to imagine their forbidden and always masked sex with the logic of theological secrets—a logic redoubled now that sexuality has become our shared theology. The secret of the modern Catholic priest *must be* a secret of sexuality. How could there be any other kind?

REFERENCES

Arnaud, A. (1990), *Pierre Klossowski*. Paris: Eds. Du Seuil, 1990.
Investigative Staff, *Boston Globe* (2002), *Betrayal: The Crisis in the Catholic Church*. Boston: Little, Brown.
Code of Canon Law (1983), Washington, DC: Canon Law Society of America, 1998. Translated from the corrected Latin text of 1989.
Congregation for the Doctrine of the Faith (2001), Epistula de delictis gravioribus eidem congregationi pro doctrinae fidei reservatis [May 18, 2001]. *Acta Apostolicae Sedis, 113*:785–788.
Foucault, M. (1963), Préface à la transgression. In: Dits et écrits, 1954–1988, ed. D. Defert, F. Ewald, & J. Lagrange. Paris: NRF/Gallimard, 1994, pp. 233–250.
Holy Office (1962), Crimen solicitationis [Instruction on the Manner of Proceeding in Cases of Solicitation, March 16]. Over the signature of Cardinal Ottaviani, who cites the approval of Pope John XXIII.
John Paul II (2001), Sacramentum sanctitatis tutela [Apostolic Letter on Crimes Reserved to the Congregation for the Doctrine of the Faith, April 30]. *Acta Apostolicae Sedis, 113*:737–739.
Jordan, M. (2000), *The Silence of Sodom: Homosexuality in Modern Catholicism*. Chicago: University of Chicago Press.
Jordan, M. (2003), *Telling Truths in Church: Scandal, Flesh, and Christian Speech*. Boston: Beacon Press.
Klossowski, P. (1950), *La vocation suspendue*. Paris: Gallimard.
Klossowski, P. (1965), *The Baphomet*, trans. S. Hawkes & S. Sartarelli. Eridanos Library 9. Hygiene, CO: Eridanos Press, 1988.
Klossowski, P., Blanchot, M., Mahon, A., & Wilson, S. (2002), *Decadence of the Nude* (La décadence du Nu). London: Black Dog.
"Maria Monk" (1836), *Awful Disclosures of the Hotel Dieu Nunnery of Montreal*. New York: Kessinger Publishing Co., 2003.
Simmel, G. (1908), The Secret and the Secret Society. In: *The Sociology of Georg Simmel*, ed. and trans. K. H. Wolff. Glencoe, IL: Free Press, 1950, pp. 307–376.
Weber, N. F (1999), *Balthus: A Biography*. New York: Knopf.

About the Contributors

Andrea Celenza, Ph.D., is Faculty, Boston Psychoanalytic Society and Institute; Faculty and Supervising Analyst, Massachusetts Institute of Psychoanalysis; Assistant Clinical Professor, the Cambridge Hospital, Harvard Medical School; Private Practice, Lexington, Massachusetts.

Murray L. Cohen, Ph.D., is an Emeritus Professor of Psychology. From 1956 to 1985, he was consultant to the Division of Legal Medicine in Massachusetts, involved in directing research and treatment of the 'sexually dangerous person.' Between 1985 and 2004, in his practice as a psychoanalyst, he continued working with men and women with sexual perversions.

The Reverend Thomas P. Doyle, O.P., an ordained Dominican priest, is an expert in the canonical and pastoral dimensions of clergy sexual abuse and has served as a consultant and expert witness on several hundred clergy abuse cases. He has written several books and articles on a variety of subjects related to Church law and practice. He was awarded Voice of the Faithful's 2002 Priest of Integrity Award, the Cavallo Award for Moral Integrity in 1992, the Isaac Hecker Award from the Paulist Fathers in January 2003, and the Civil Justice Foundation of the Association of Trial Lawyers of America 2005 Community Champion Award. Doyle is a fully certified Alcohol, Drug, and Addictions therapist who resides outside Washington, D.C.

Kathleen M. Dwyer (Kathy) is a coordinator of STTOP (Speak Truth TO Power), Co-Director of the Truth and Recognition Coalition, Inc., and a member of the Legislative Reform Committee to eliminate the Statute of Limitations in sex crimes in Massachusetts. She has been an activist and artist for more than thirty years.

The Reverend Laurie J. Ferguson, Ph.D., is a Presbyterian minister and clinical psychologist who served on the Hudson Valley Presbytery's committee on clergy sexual misconduct. She lives and works outside New York City.

Mary Gail Frawley-O'Dea, Ph.D. was the only mental health professional to address the U.S. Conference of Catholic Bishops at their seminal 2002 Dallas meeting on the sexual abuse crisis. She is the former Executive Director of the Trauma Treatment Center at the Manhattan Institute of Psychoanalysis, serves on the Practice Committee of the Division of Trauma Psychology of the American Psychological Association, and is a member of the Advisory Board of the Leadership Council on Child Abuse and Interpersonal Violence. Frawley-O'Dea appeared in the 2006 award winning documentary film, Deliver Us From Evil, and is frequently quoted commenting on the Catholic abuse scandal in the print media. She is co-author of *Treating the Adult Survivor of Childhood Sexual Abuse* and author of *Perversion of Power: Sexual Abuse in the Catholic Church*. Dr. Frawley-O'Dea is in private clinical and supervisory practice in Matthews, North Carolina.

Richard B. Gartner, Ph.D., is Training and Supervising Analyst at the William Alanson White Institute and Founding Director of its Sexual Abuse Program. A past president of MaleSurvivor: The National Organization Against Male Sexual Victimization, he serves on the editorial boards of *Contemporary Psychoanalysis*, the *American Journal of Psychoanalysis*, and the *Journal of Trauma and Dissociation*. He is the author of *Betrayed as Boys: Psychodynamic Treatment of Sexually Abused Men* (Guilford, 1999) and *Beyond Betrayal: Taking Charge of Your Life after Boyhood Sexual Abuse* (Wiley, 2005), and the editor of *Memories of Sexual Betrayal: Truth, Fantasy, Repression, and Dissociation* (Aronson, 1997). He practices in New York City.

Virginia Goldner, Ph.D., is Founding Editor, *Studies in Gender and Sexuality*, and Clinical Professor of Psychology, Postdoctoral

Program in Psychotherapy and Psychoanalysis, Derner Center for Advanced Psychological Studies, Adelphi University.

Mary Gordon is the author of five novels: *Final Payments, The Company of Women, Men and Angels, The Other Side,* and *Spending*; a collection of short stories, *Temporary Shelter*; two collections of essays, *Good Boys and Dead Girls* and *Seeing Through Places*; a memoir, *The Shadow Man*; and a biography of Joan of Arc. She is McIntosh Professor of English at Barnard College.

Mark D. Jordan is Asa Griggs Candler Professor of Religion at Emory University. Before coming to Emory in 1999, he taught at the University of Notre Dame and other Catholic universities. Trained as an historian of Christian thought, he teaches a range of courses from introductory Catholicism to LGBT religious identities. His books include *The Invention of Sodomy in Christian Thought*, winner of the 1999 John Boswell Prize for lesbian and gay history, and *The Silence of Sodom: Homosexuality in Modern Catholicism*, a Lambda Literary Award finalist. His latest is *Blessing Same-Sex Unions: The Perils of Queer Romance and the Confusions of Christian Marriage*.

Gerald E. Kochansky, Ph.D. was an Assistant Clinical Professor of Psychology in the Department of Psychiatry at the Massachusetts Mental Health Center, Harvard Medical School, a Supervising Psychologist at MMHC, and was in private psychotherapy and forensic consultation practice in Brookline, Massachusetts. He has treated a wide range of individuals, including many Roman Catholic priests and seminarians, and was particularly interested in narcissism and its relevance to clergy, corporations, and civil and criminal law.

Tom Lewis has published two novels, was a speechwriter for two New York governors, and recently managed a successful political campaign in northern Connecticut where he lives.

Father M. is a Roman Catholic priest who has been a pastor in a large suburban parish and is now involved in urban ministry.

The Reverend James Martin, S.J., is a Jesuit priest and Associate Editor of *America*, a national Catholic magazine. He is author of numerous books on religion and spirituality, including most recently, *My Life With the Saints* (2006).

The Reverend Anne Richards was educated at Smith College (B.A.), New York University (M.A.), and the General Theological Seminary (M. Div.). She is a priest of the Episcopal Diocese of New

York, and has served as Chair of that diocese's Commission on Ministry, the interviewing/screening commission that assists the bishop in selecting candidates for ordination. She has worked as a hospital chaplain, as a parish priest, and as an assistant to the 14th Bishop of New York. She currently serves as Chaplain at Grace Church School in New York City.

The Reverend L. Murdock Smith, Ph.D., is an Episcopal priest and psychologist. He is a family and marital therapist and Clinical Member of the American Association of Marriage and Family Therapy. He has served parishes in North Carolina, Tennessee, and New Hampshire. He has worked as a therapist, principally with persons who are chemically dependent and/or are adult survivors of childhood sexual abuse.

Gillian Walker, M.S.W., is Assistant Clinical Professor at New York University Medical School, Senior Faculty at the Ackerman Institute. Age and impending mortality drew her to the study of religion and she is currently a doctoral candidate in Society and Religion at Drew University. Currently, her major scholarly interest is exploring the influence of massive cultural trauma in the writing of Biblical texts and on the formation of the early Christianities. She is also the author of books and articles in the areas of AIDS, learning disabilities, chronic illness, and single-parent families, and is in private practice in Manhattan.

Author Index

A, B

Arnaud, A., 236, *248*
Baars, C., 152, *161*
Bagby, R., 42, *56*
Benjamin, J., 224, *229*
Benn, A. F., 39, *57*
Berlin, F., 42, *55*
Berry, J., ix, *xv*
Bibring, E., 44, *55*
Blanchot, M., 236, *248*
Blaney, B., xiv, *xv*
Bollas, C., 4, *17*
Boucher, R., 40, *55*
Breckenridge, T., xiv, *xv*
Bridges, M., 41, *56*
Briggs, D., x, *xv*
Bromberg, P. M., 86, *100*
Brown, P., 216, *229*
Bruni, F., ix, x, *xv*
Bryant, C., 40, 42, *55*
Burge, K., xiii, *xv*
Burkett, E., ix, x, *xv*
Bynum, C., 225, 226, *229*

C

Callan, J., 149, *162*
Calmas, W., 48, *55*
Carroll, J., 228, 229, *229*
Carroll, M., xiii, *xvi*
Cebula, J., xiv, *xv*
Celenza, A., 39, 42, 46, *55*, 59, *69*

Chittister, J., 194, *194*
Christensen, G., 42, *56*
Cohen, M. L., 40, 48, 55, *56*, 70
Coleman, E., 42, *56*
Convey, E., xiv, *xvi*, 156, *162*
Cooperman, A., 27, *34*
Cozzens, D., x, *xvi*, 8, 152, 160, *161*
Cullinane, P., 148, *161*

D

Dahlby, Fr. C., 23, *34*
Das, S., 2, *17*
Davies, J. M., 3, *17*, 78, *83*
DeGiulio, K., *161*
DiGiulio, K., 23, *34*, 156
Dillon, S., xiv, *xvi*
Dolbee, S., xiv, *xvi*
Dorian, B., 42, *56*
Dostoevsky, F., 122, *136*
Douglas, M., 218, 219, *229*
Doyle, T., 157, *161*
Dulles, A., *161*

E, F

Eilberg-Schwartz, H., 227, *229*
Eisenberg, C., 23, *34*
Elias, M., 23, *34*
Exner, J., 39, *55*
Fagan, P., 42, *55*
Fallik, D., xiv, *xvi*
Faulkner, W., 123, *136*

Subject Index